BORDER CROSSINGS
Thomas King's Cultural Inversions

Arnold E. Davidson, Priscilla L. Walton,
and Jennifer Andrews

Border Crossings

Thomas King's
Cultural Inversions

UNIVERSITY OF TORONTO PRESS
Toronto Buffalo London

ISBN 0-8020-4134-5

Printed on acid-free paper

National Library of Canada Cataloguing in Publication

Davidson, Arnold E., 1936–
Border crossings : Thomas King's cultural inversions / Arnold E.
Davidson, Priscilla L. Walton and Jennifer Andrews.

Includes bibliographical references and index.
ISBN 0-8020-4134-5 (bound)

1. King, Thomas, 1943– – Criticism and interpretation. I. Walton,
Priscilla L.   II. Andrews, Jennifer Courtney Elizabeth, 1971–   III. Title.

PS8571.I5298Z62 2003   C813′54   C2002-903802-2
PR9199.3.K4422Z62 2003

Photographs on pages 100, 101, and 109 by
Thomas King © Dead Dog Café Productions Inc.

University of Toronto Press acknowledges the financial assistance to its
publishing program of the Canada Council for the Arts and the
Ontario Arts Council.

This book has been published with the help of a grant from the Humanities
and Social Sciences Federation of Canada, using funds provided by the
Social Sciences and Humanities Research Council of Canada.

University of Toronto Press acknowledges the financial support for its
publishing activities of the Government of Canada through the
Book Publishing Industry Development Program (BPIDP).

For Judy

Contents

Acknowledgments ix

Introduction: Whose Borders?   3

1 Comic Contexts   29

2 Comic Inversions   49

3 Genre Crossings   75

4 Comedy, Politics, and Audio and Visual Media   95

5 Humouring Race and Nationality   122

6 The Comic Dimensions of Gender, Race, and Nation:
King's Contestatory Narratives   157

7 Comic Intertextualities   197

Notes   205
Works Cited   211
Index   221

Acknowledgments

Books are always collaborative endeavours, reliant upon a much larger group of people than the individuals whose names appear on their covers; this book is no exception. We are especially grateful to the research assistance of several students at Carleton University and the University of New Brunswick who tirelessly searched for references, read drafts of the book, and offered their valuable suggestions: Shannon MacRae, Jonathan Dewar, and Kristel Thornell. Thomas King generously provided access to his photographs. The support of colleagues and friends has also made this project a pleasure. Warm thanks to Linda Hutcheon, John Ball, Brian Greenspan, Cheryl Dueck, Helen Hoy, Randall Martin, Parker Duchemin, Larry McDonald, and Winfried Siemerling.

At University of Toronto Press, Siobhan McMenemy, Jill McConkey, and Suzanne Rancourt showed great enthusiasm for the manuscript, from beginning to end. The generous responses of readers to various sections of the book kept us busy. The reports from ASPP readers, the University of Toronto editorial board, Jamie Barlowe, and Laura E. Donaldson proved to be especially helpful.

The Social Sciences and Humanities Research Council of Canada, Carleton University, and the University of New Brunswick have been particularly generous in supporting this book. The awarding of a Research Grant, a Postdoctoral Fellowship, and a New Faculty Grant paid for research assistants and enabled us to complete the manuscript in a timely fashion.

Finally, this book would not have come to fruition without the support of our partners, Michael Dorland and Christopher Butler. It is written in tribute to the intellectual vitality and immense generosity of Ted Davidson (1936–99).

BORDER CROSSINGS
Thomas King's Cultural Inversions

Introduction: Whose Borders?

Thomas King is one of the first Native writers to generate widespread interest in both Canada and the United States. He has twice been nominated for Governor General's Awards; his first novel, *Medicine River* (1990), has been transformed into a CBC movie; and his books are reviewed in a range of publications, from the *New York Times Book Review* and the *Globe and Mail*, to *Maclean's*, *Newsweek*, and *People* magazines. Moreover, he has authored and been part of the ensemble cast of a CBC radio show, *The Dead Dog Café Comedy Hour* (1995–2000), which gained immense popularity with listeners across Canada for its subversively humorous vision of Natives on both sides of the border. King's cultural position offers knowledgeable representation of both societies, even as it engenders the critical yet generous view of cultural relations that characterizes his fiction. It is not surprising, then, that King's texts have proved popular with both Native and non-Native readers, as well as with literary and popular audiences.

The author characterizes himself 'as a serious writer. Tragedy is my topic. Comedy is my strategy' ('Definitely' 60). Indeed, his comic strategy comprises a series of cultural reversals that throw into question traditional discursive constructions. The following study will examine how King's texts explore cross-cultural problems like Native rights and race relations, while incorporating critical Native issues within their narrative structure: the title of *Green Grass, Running Water*, for example, plays upon a clause frequently appended to Native treaties, treaties which are abrogated over the course of the novel.[1] Nevertheless, by situating these concerns within a comic framework, King avoids the polemics that often mark cultural critiques, and his writings, consequently, preserve the ability to engage, entertain – and educate. The ensuing pages are devoted to analysing how King's works maintain this delicate balancing act.

Biographical Border Crossings

For King, the acts of reading, mis-reading, and re-reading are central to his texts and the subject of much of his humour. As a mixed-blood man, born in the United States but now a Canadian citizen, King is especially sensitive to the power of borders. Yet he is also extremely interested in the spaces 'in-between' those borders, whether they are literal or figurative. Part-White[2] and part-Native,[3] King is neither simply one nor the other, and thus his perspective is both inside and outside of the borders under examination.

King's biography vividly illustrates how this situation of border-crossing 'in-betweenness' has shaped his life and work. Born in Sacramento, California, in 1943 to a Cherokee father and a German-Greek mother, Thomas King grew up in a female-dominated household. His father, an army man and an alcoholic, was absent for much of the time and abandoned the family permanently when King was five. Although his father decided to return to the family four years later, a decision supported by his wife, he never actually did and was eventually presumed dead. His mother, a hairdresser by trade, raised King and his brother on her own, in a warehouse that housed both her beauty shop and the family's living quarters. Though non-Native herself, it was the efforts of King's mother, including taking her sons on trips to Oklahoma to visit Native relations, that kept them aware of their Cherokee heritage. Thus King's childhood involved a continual movement between communities and across various racial and cultural boundaries.

After attending a Catholic boarding school and completing high school in his home town of Roseville, King attended Sacramento State for a year. He then took on a variety of odd jobs to support himself, becoming an actor, a casino dealer, and later an ambulance driver and a bank teller. He finally finished a diploma in business administration at a California junior college and set off in 1964 on a steamer, going, King thought, to New Guinea. The ship was, in fact, travelling to New Zealand, which led to several years of equally eclectic jobs and travel through both New Zealand and Australia, before King was hired as a photojournalist for a 'Sunday supplement magazine *Everybody's*' (Weaver 147). While working in this capacity, the author wrote his first (unpublished) novel, a story of American astronauts and Cold War Russians. In 1967, King again crossed the ocean and returned to California, where he soon resumed his education, taking courses in drafting at Seattle Free University and then finishing a bachelor's degree in English literature at Chico State.

King eventually settled into academic life permanently, earning both a master's degree and a PhD in English. He successfully defended his doctoral dissertation, titled 'Inventing the Indian: White Images, Native Oral Literature, and Contemporary Native Writers,' at the University of Utah in 1986, and then went on to serve as the coordinator of the American Indian Studies and History of the Americas programs at Utah and in California. Although rarely discussed in relation to King's creative work, a closer look at his doctoral dissertation proves enormously helpful because it provides another context for King's own literary border crossings – specifically his fusion of oral traditions with written text and his vast knowledge of canonical American literature (with its Native stereotypes), often invoked in his own fiction to subversive ends. The thesis begins by exploring non-Native constructions of the American Indian as symbolic of 'death and nobility' (29) from the first European contact onward, and then offers a detailed examination of how Natives are presented in three nineteenth-century American texts from different genres: poetry (Henry Longfellow's *The Song of Hiawatha*), novels (James Fenimore Cooper's *The Last of the Mohicans*), and drama (John Augustus Stone's *Metamora*). This historically focused analysis considers how the dual clichés of the 'dying Indian' and 'the Noble Savage' were cultivated and sustained through the literature of the period.

To counter these objectifying narratives, King's later chapters provide an alterna(rra)tive[4] to this dominant discourse of Eurocentric and Judeo-Christian righteousness. He surveys a range of Native oral creation stories, arguing that these narratives collectively offer another way to look at the world. King specifically contrasts the biblical account of the world's creation in Genesis with the multiplicity of origin stories that are part of Native North American tribal cultures. With this counter-foundation in place, King then examines how three recent Native American writers – N. Scott Momaday, James Welch, and Leslie Marmon Silko – draw on these myriad alternatives to portray their own versions of Indianness. As he explains:

... the main difficulty that confronted Indian writers was the well-defined, well-rooted images and assumptions that had, over the years, been constructed by non-Indians, authenticated by history and literature, and sanctified by the popular mind. These assumptions were literary phantasms which functioned effectively as 'masks' through which few writers were able to strike. (101)

In his study of Momaday, Welch, and Silko, King pays careful attention to the bridge between the written and the oral, specifically concentrating on how the borders between the two are broken down through the creation of a hybrid narrative structure. He argues that each of these authors creates texts that are both stories of alienation (e.g., *House Made of Dawn*, *Winter in the Blood*, and *Ceremony*) and oral creation narratives that order the world in a distinctively Native fashion. King argues that all three use repetition and ritual to structure their stories, avoid a standard Eurocentric plot-line that includes climax and catharsis, and favour a circular narrative formulation, elements that will become part of his own writings.

King's dissertation represents an attempt to create a space for Native literature that operates in-between the borders, borrowing from and employing traditional narrative structures and techniques, even as Native authors depict societies and characters that 'are managing to survive white encroachment,' whether on the reservation, in a rural setting, or in a large city (194). Similarly, King's own life and work over the last twenty years has involved the crossing of multiple borders, both figurative and literal, in his academic and creative endeavours. In 1980, King took up an academic post in Native studies at the University of Lethbridge, moving north of the forty-ninth parallel, where he began to gather the stories that would form his first novel, *Medicine River*. During his time in Alberta, he co-edited and wrote the introduction for a collection of essays, entitled *The Native in Literature* (1987), which explores depictions of Natives in Canadian texts. As King explains, '... the traditional assumption [has been] that a discussion of the Native in literature means simply an examination of how the presence of the Native has influenced white literature' (13). He inverts this notion, claiming

such an approach obscures the influence that white culture has had on Native oral and written literature and the influence that Native oral literature has had on contemporary Native writers. Unfortunately, the majority of critical studies which have considered the influence of the Indian on white writing have considered only the physical and in some instances the spiritual presence of the Native but have generally ignored the presence of Native literature. Likewise, studies interested in Native oral literature spend too little critical energy on contemporary Native literature, suggesting by omission that the two have nothing in common. (13)

The resulting collection addresses three different areas of inquiry: literary depictions of Natives by White explorers and settlers; the representation of Natives by specific non-Native Canadian writers; and the literature produced by Natives, in its written and oral forms. King, in his introduction, anticipates the ways in which these essays engender an examination of the spaces 'in-between' traditional White-authored portraits of Indians, ensuring a multiplicity of perspectives that create dialogue across borders rather than merely reasserting the solidity of the borders that typically divide Native and non-Native communities.

In an effort to increase access to the work of First Nations authors, King also edited a collection of recent Native prose, *All My Relations: An Anthology of Contemporary Canadian Native Fiction* (1990). That same year, he published a ground-breaking essay, 'Godzilla vs. Post-Colonial,' in which he argued that Native writing is not 'post-colonial writing' (12), but rather can and should be described on its own terms. In this essay, King cautions against reading Native literature as postcolonial precisely because such a designation focuses on the colonial moment, which has virtually nothing to do with the Native cultural traditions that preceded it. Instead, King proposes a series of definitions that displace postcolonialism altogether and acknowledge the wide range of Native narratives, from those written primarily in a Native language and intended for a single tribal audience (what he calls 'tribal' literature) to the body of literature he describes as 'associational,' which is 'created, for the most part, by contemporary Native authors' and depicts a Native community, but is accessible to a larger audience (12–14). This essay provides a crucial option for writers and scholars who want to avoid Eurocentric paradigms.

Likewise, King's anthology pays careful attention to the uniqueness of Native literature as well as its diversity. He explains in the introduction that the anthology is intended to show the richness of Native literature and offer a series of alternatives to portrayals of Indians that, though sympathetic, 'have also been limited in their variety of characters, themes, structures, and images' (xi). As he points out, 'most Canadians have only seen Natives through the eyes of non-Native writers' and yet 'Native literature – that is, written literature – has opened up new worlds of imagination for non-Native audiences' (xii). Because King and his work occupies that 'in-between' space within and without the borders, he is particularly aware of the usefulness of producing texts that examine those borders between the written and the oral, the Native and the non-Native. In this introduction, King not surprisingly emphasizes the importance of oral heritage shared across tribes, and struggles to find a working definition for what is a much-contested issue: how to define who is a Native writer. He suggests caution when trying to fix such a definition:

> And, when we talk about Native writers, we talk as if we have a process for determining who is a Native writer and who is not, when, in fact, we don't. What we do have is a collection of literary works by individual authors who are Native by ancestry, and our hope, as writers and critics, is that if we wait long enough, the sheer bulk of this collection, when it reaches some sort of critical mass, will present us with a matrix within which a variety of patterns can be discerned. This waiting is neither timidity nor laziness on our part. There are a great many difficulties in trying to squeeze definitions out of what we currently have ... Perhaps our simple definition that Native literature is literature produced by Natives will suffice for the while providing we resist the temptation of trying to define a Native. (xi)

Though perhaps unsatisfactory to some, especially those who perceive King's 'simple definition' as reductive and potentially debilitating to those who lack the appropriate blood quantum to claim a tribal identity, he employs the possibilities of 'in-betweenness' here to avoid excluding those who may not meet a single set of criteria, especially when based upon race. He is hesitant to assume that race automatically 'imparts to the Native writer a tribal understanding of the universe, access to a distinct culture, and a literary perspective that is unattainable by non-Natives' (x). As someone who was raised both inside and outside the Cherokee culture, he is acutely aware of the danger of imposing rigid distinctions. Rather, what King calls for is a theoretical framework that is attentive to the literature and not merely a means of dictating who can be an 'Indian author.'

This strategic rejection of extremely narrow notions of identity is especially crucial for King, given his own mixed-blood status. As Jace Weaver points out, 'King has always been intentional in identifying himself as of "Cherokee, Greek and German descent" so that the dominant culture' realizes that 'in him they are not getting their romanticized image of an "authentic Indian"' (149). Instead of viewing himself as inauthentic precisely because he doesn't conform to such a stereotype,

King emphasizes the positive dimensions of his situation: 'I'm in a position where I don't have anything to lose – or anything to gain – by asking some of the questions I ask. You know, in some ways, I'm this Native writer who's out in the middle – not of nowhere, but I don't have strong tribal affiliations. I wasn't raised on Cherokee lands ...' (Weaver 149). King takes what Weaver calls a 'pan-Indian' stance, concerning himself with issues that may span a variety of tribal groups, without necessarily being limited to one. Much like his desire to resist a definition of 'Native,' King, who was raised in an urban setting as opposed to a tribal community, recognizes the possibilities inherent in his position of literal and figurative 'in-betweenness.' Notably, King anticipates the problems with a pan-Indian perspective in his dissertation, in the chapter on oral creation stories, where he looks at 'over one hundred and fifty' narratives from different tribal traditions (73). There, he argues that the process of selection and problems of contamination, translation, and the questionable authenticity of some stories can make the task of surveying creation narratives seem 'worthless' (73). But instead of neglecting those stories altogether, King insists on examining their individual and collective significance, while retaining an awareness of the ways in which many of the narratives have been manipulated by Eurocentric informants and scholars.

Similarly, King's pan-Indian self-positioning becomes a powerful tool, which acknowledges post-contact interaction with non-Natives, yet focuses on the experiences of contemporary Natives:

> I think a lot of people think of pan-Indianness as a diminution of 'Indian,' but I think of it as simply a reality of contemporary life. Native culture has never been static even though Western literature would like to picture it that way ... [T]here are Indians upon Indians in novels who go off the reservation into the city and are destroyed, who come back to the reservation and can't make it. I think that's bullshit myself. In reality there are lots of Indians who go off the reserve, who come back to the reserve, who work, who go off the reserve again, who keep going back and forth and they manage. (Weaver 150)

And his creative work reflects his desire to explore the complexities of that 'in-between' space, within and without borders. King's latest novel, *Truth and Bright Water* (1999), for example, depicts this refusal to perpetuate the stereotype that Natives are static beings, who remain isolated from urban life off the reservation and cannot return once they have left. One of the central characters in his text is a famous Native painter, Monroe Swimmer, who has grown up in a tribal community, has gone off to work in Europe and the United States, and then moved home to continue his artistic pursuits, including a restoration project that, appropriately enough, involves resurrecting the presence of buffalo on the Prairies. Further, his return to Truth, an American border town, via Toronto, demonstrates his cross-border flexibility and his ability to adapt to and survive within a variety of social and political contexts.

King, like Monroe Swimmer, has continued to move between Canada and the United States: in the last decade of his career, he returned to the United States just before the publication of *Medicine River*, to join the faculty at the University of Minnesota. Even with his academic duties, King has continued to write fiction, producing both the highly acclaimed *Green Grass, Running Water* and a collection of short stories, *One Good Story, That One*. Notably, both works include examinations of how the forty-ninth parallel (with its national borders) has been imposed on Native North Americans. Eager to come back to Canada, King accepted an academic position in the Department of English at the University of Guelph in the mid-1990s. Since returning to Canada, he has cultivated a strong relationship with the Canadian Broadcasting Corporation, beginning in 1993 with the creation of a radio drama version of his short story 'The One about Coyote Going West.' King's work for CBC has included authoring and participating in the making of film and radio scripts, most notably a feature filmscript of his novel *Medicine River* and *The Dead Dog Café Comedy Hour* radio series. He has expanded the scope of his audience through his children's books, publishing the controversial *A Coyote Columbus Story* (1992) and *Coyote Sings to the Moon* (1998). Moreover, King's aspirations to become a photographer have motivated him to create several series of portraits, which have been exhibited at prestigious galleries in the United States and Europe, including the Ansel Adams Gallery in San Francisco. During this highly productive period, King also produced his third novel, *Truth and Bright Water*, which is set yet again on the Canadian-U.S. border.

Contextualizing King

Thomas King's biography provides one context for understanding his work; in turn, his 'in-between' position, as a part-White and part-Native writer, affords him a particular perspective into the foundations of borders – not only at the level of nation but also through the complex intersections and divisions between the oral tradition and the printed word. Weaver, in his study of Native American literatures and communities, contends that 'the importance of story for Natives cannot be overestimated' (40), precisely because First Nations identities are created through the process of storytelling, a process that brings otherwise displaced and fragmented individuals and communities together. Stories create a sense of belonging and facilitate the exchange of ideas. But these narratives also become spaces of debate and potential subversion, spaces to claim and refashion knowledge to reflect a past, present, and future otherwise elided by the dominance of national borders and a long-standing colonial rhetoric, in which Natives – and their stories – have been marginalized. As Weaver points out, 'The struggle may be land and sovereignty, but it is often reflected, contested, and decided in narrative' (41–2). King's narratives operate in the spaces between the oral and the written, offering a generous but thorough inquiry into the construction of history, culture, race, gender, sexuality, and genre, detailing the ways in which these issues intersect and inform one another.

Certainly King's writing, photography, and radio and television work is provocative and compelling, but why is it so timely? Given the infiltration of the concerns of Cultural Studies into traditional disciplines like English, any study of an author who enjoys popularity at a particular historical moment now invites larger questions such as Why this writer? and Why now? Or, more pertinent to this project, why Thomas King and why does his fiction rank above the works of other Canadian and Native writers in the contemporary cultural consciousness? Certainly, there are many First Nations authors who enjoy successful publication: on the American side, there are writers like Leslie Marmon Silko, Louise Erdrich, Michael Dorris, Sherman Alexie, and N. Scott Momaday, all of whom have received *international* recognition, perhaps as a result of the larger market in which they are situated. In Canada, however, writers such as Lee Maracle, Beatrice Culleton, Jeannette Armstrong, Tomson Highway, and Ruby Slipperjack generate local notice, but their works have not received the same transnational attention that has greeted Thomas King's. Without falling into the trap of rating the merit of the writers in question, we do suspect that King's popularity on both sides of the border is at least partially predicated on his U.S.-Canadian affiliations, and on the cross-national themes that pervade his fiction. And these themes, in turn, draw attention to the Canadian-U.S. borders that separate Native peoples from themselves.

Weaver argues that 'Natives have never been great respecters of national borders,' especially when they are predicated on the dismissal of tribal rights (23). King's focus on the forty-ninth parallel is, indeed, timely and relevant because it speaks to the issues of tribal identity and nationality that are at the centre of recent governmental negotiations in both Canada and the United States. Native tribes, on both sides of the border, continue to pursue land claims, the opportunity for self-government, and the recognition of their status as autonomous nations. Most 'American' First Nations writers focus on the status of individual tribes within and beyond the confines of the American federal and state governments. Their desire to acknowledge the 'nation-to-state' relation, through the recognition of borders that have been eradicated over time, tends to supercede discussions of other types of borders (Fleras and Elliott xi). When Native American authors do look beyond these 'internal' borders, they usually examine the 'wall' that separates the United States from Mexico, a military zone and graphic symbol of American attempts to keep so-called illegal aliens from travelling northward. For example, book 5 of Silko's *Almanac of the Dead*, called 'The Border,' traces the lives of two Native American sisters, one of whom profits from the Mexican-U.S. border by smuggling Native antiquities northward under the guise of a tour-bus business. A map, which appears at the beginning of Silko's novel, metaphorically documents the plethora of converging narratives in the text and visually conveys the impact of the border on various characters' lives. The border cuts across the centre of the page – dividing the United States from Mexico, but also separating Native lands, and keeping Indian populations from contact with other members of their tribal nations.

King, like these 'American' First Nations authors, explores the borders that have been eradicated over time within Canada by looking at the status of reserve[5] lands and the treatment of those who live on them, both at a provincial and federal level. Yet King also takes issue with the forty-ninth parallel, a political dividing line that systematically has erased prior tribal relationships and Native land claims. Importantly, King argues that one of his concerns is to stake 'out native literature as North American. I'm saying you can't divorce Canadian experience from American' (*Globe and Mail*, quoted in Beddoes 11). Rather than attending to the U.S. and Mexican borders, which are at the centre of contemporary border studies,[6] King directs readers to look northward to a boundary that embodies its own set of contradictions and conflicts. As a writer born in the United States, but who considers himself Canadian and holds Canadian citizenship, he embodies two nationalities. On a cultural level, moreover, his status throws those demarcations into question, since as a Cherokee who moved to Canada, he can be read as a Canadian writer and a Native writer, but he cannot be a Canadian Native writer because the Cherokees are not 'native' to Canada. Nonetheless, King insists: 'I guess I'm supposed to say that I believe in the line that exists between the US and Canada, but for me it's an imaginary line. It's a line from somebody else's imagination' (Rooke 72). His texts, by writing and transgressing the border that divides Canada from the United States, show the forty-ninth parallel to be precisely that: a figment of someone else's imagination. Thus, one of our tasks, here, is to consider the larger implications of King's focus on the Canadian-U.S. border. How does his interest in the forty-ninth parallel complicate recent work in the field of border studies and what questions does King's fiction raise for Canadians and Americans about the relationship of national borders to identity politics?

Part of King's popularity with Canadian and American readers may lie in his ability to examine the subject of the border and relay the stories of Native characters in an entertaining and accessible manner. Nowhere is that more evident than with King's radio show, *The Dead Dog Café Comedy Hour*, broadcast on the CBC, which during its six-year run (1995–2000) became enormously popular with Canadian audiences and forms the basis of King's national fame. For example, in a recent live performance of *The Dead Dog Café*, a Victoria Day special, cast members begin by debating whether Queen Victoria had an affair with George Washington, making Canada an illegitimate offspring. As one member of the show notes, the plethora of signs all over the United States attesting to the fact that 'George Washington slept here' becomes evidence of sexual consummation (Stackhouse A10); historical plaques are read as symbols of colonialism. The show, with its Native author and cast, reminds audiences of Canada's precarious position as a country vulnerable to the power of 'Manifest Destiny.' But it also plays with that claim by proceeding to examine the impact of Aboriginal colonization on Canada's development as a nation through a series of pointedly humorous sketches about 'Supreme Court decisions, colonial rule, bureaucratic incompetence, native corruption, and bingo' (A10).

Julie Beddoes has rightly argued that King's success may be the result of his reception as 'the good-news story non-native Canadians were looking for, a way for us to feel a little better about ourselves' (2). King's part-Cherokee background works to this purpose in both countries, since he can function both as a White and as a Native, making him an 'acceptable' proponent of Native values for a White audience. King himself has pointed out that he is really writing for two audiences: an ideal (Native) audience and those who can afford the book (composed primarily of non-Natives):

> ... with *Medicine River* I'm ... writing initially for a Native audience. It's a real irony because as I see my audience out there, and as I think about the Native audience and how much I hope they'll enjoy the book ... I'm also reminded that the book costs twenty-five bucks for the hard copy. And, you know, not a great many Native people are going to want or have twenty-five extra bucks to put out on the book. So the audience I write for is in many ways almost becomes a lost audience. I mean, the paperback may get out into the Native communities, but aside from that ... (Rooke 73)

Drawing on Francis's *The Imaginary Indian*, Beddoes suggests that King serves as the contemporary 'Imaginary Indian,' or, in her words, as the Indian who 'tell[s] us it is alright, we can keep what we have got and only need to be a little nicer for everything to be made right' (3). Beddoes is careful to limit her observations to the signifier 'Thomas King,' as opposed to the author or his writings, and in so doing refers to the 'Thomas King' of the cultural consciousness. But, while she makes perceptive points about King's reception, and is deeply concerned that reviewers tend to read King sociologically rather than as a serious literary figure, we think that there is more to this 'story' than the subtle marginalization Beddoes so astutely points out. We contend that another potential reason for King's popularity arises from his ability to found his politics on a comic platform. In other words, and to paraphrase Beddoes, King's fiction might make us feel good, but the sting that accompanies the laughter also makes us think.

Comedy provides a basis for King's politically charged narratives and facilitates his often bitingly ironic critique of the forty-ninth parallel. In *Borderlands: How We Talk about Canada*, William New discusses a well-known King short story, 'Borders,' in which a Blackfoot mother and son become trapped between the Canadian and United States borders because the mother won't declare herself to be Canadian, insisting instead that she be identified as Blackfoot. New argues that this is a useful example of how the emotional and intellectual borders between Canada and the United States generate texts that reflect the discomfort and complexities of being 'in-between' the nations. According to New, the comedy of 'Borders' 'does not hide the political ironies' of King's text (29). Further, and as we contend, the comic dimensions of King's rendering of the border, from a Native perspective, are precisely what make his works both palatable and subversive, entertaining and disturbing. Comedy is the foundation of his insightful commentary on life within Native communities and the complexities of Native-White relations.

Although King's writings do not conform to any specific genre, they employ techniques often associated with 'genre' or 'formulaic fiction' – like westerns, romances, and detective novels. As John G. Cawelti explains, genre works provide a social service, since, 'by their capacity to assimilate new meanings ... literary formulas ease the transition between old and new ways of expressing things and thus contribute to cultural continuity' (*Adventure* 124). It is important to note, here, that King's genre crossings enable him to transgress the borders (of genre, nation, and culture) at the same time that they contribute to his international popularity – largely because his works reside in that liminal 'in-between' space to which we have referred.

Interrogating the 'In-Between'

'In-betweenness' is a complex spatial, theoretical, and political concept. Thus far, we have used the term to refer to King's locus as inside and outside a variety of national and cultural boundaries. Yet this concept begs numerous questions, questions that include What are the boundaries? What do they demarcate? and How does King's 'in-betweenness' effect a counter or alternative perspective?

In their simplest construction, borders are those signs that divide one entity from another (the entities might be national, racial, or cultural, among others). Yet, while dividing lines or borders are often taken to be immutable, they are precisely the opposite. As Homi Bhabha, citing Heidegger, argues, a boundary is not just a line 'at which something stops' but a line 'from which *something begins its presencing*' (*Location* 1). Rather than understanding boundaries as merely defensive markers, then, these lines also create a space for the articulation of diverse viewpoints. What is striking about the categories mentioned above is that these entities are all culturally and socially constructed. One need only compare a 1940s map of Africa with one of the present day to trace how borders move – for political, racial, ethnic, and national reasons. And if a border is, in fact, inherently unstable and elastic, it follows that that which it demarcates is also flexible and rooted in particular historical and cultural moments. Consequently, national borders alter and what they delineate shifts. In North America, for example, borders divide Canada, the United States, and Mexico, but the traditionally accepted borders were constructed over a variety of different boundaries – Native boundaries – that served to distinguish one group's territory from another.[7] From a European cultural perspective, borders mark differences; from a Native view, borders are and always were in flux, signifying territorial space that was mutable and open to change. The borders that presently exist ignore the Native peoples, who are often cut off from one another as a result of a line that has been drawn through their lands.

Just as national borders separate First Nations people by ignoring (and erasing) their presence, so do those borders also obscure the acknowledged nations they outline. Robert Kroetsch has insisted that 'Canadian writing is not writing at the border ... Rather it is a writing *of* the border, the creation of a line that endlessly confounds itself into the conundrum (the riddle) of the other' (338). Undoubtedly, for Canada and the United States, the where of there is inevitably defined by somewhere else. Yet, there is also something paradigmatic about this complication. Both sides proclaim that theirs is the longest undefended border in the world; in so saying, however, both are wilfully oblivious to the consideration that borders exist only to the degree that they are defended and that this imaginary line is especially defended by the way that each side imagines an identity *in relation to* the other across it – but differently. The asymmetrical working of the imaginary border is especially evident in the way Canadians tend, somewhat dubiously, to view Americans as the rampant example of what they do not want to become, whereas the American tendency is to see, just as dubiously, Canada as already so much like the United States (except less interesting) that it is hardly there at all. In turn, that slippage in the very term 'American' as compared to, say, 'United Statesian,' conveniently posits 'American' as a governing adjective that merges country and continent. The envisioned border is thus cast as an asserted absence of borders – the comforting singularity of American exceptionalism, the endless promise of Manifest Destiny, even if (as Canadians believe) it still runs up against that forty-ninth parallel.

Timothy Brennan points out that the 'idea of nationhood is not only a political plea, but a formal binding together of disparate elements. And out of the multiplicities of culture, race, and political structures, grows also a repeated dialectic of uniformity and specificity' (62). Brennan goes on to suggest that this uniformity and specificity overlook the disparate elements that constitute it, and which are elided in the idea of nationhood itself. Likewise, Bhabha argues that borders and boundaries give rise to 'in-between' spaces that create alternative sites of meaning:

> The 'locality' of national culture is neither unified nor unitary in relation to itself, nor must it be seen simply as 'other' in relation to what is outside or beyond it. The boundary is Janus-faced and the problem of outside/ inside must always itself be a process of hybridity, incorporating new 'people' in relation to the body politic, generating other sites of meaning ... What emerges as an effect of such 'incomplete signification' is a turning of boundaries and limits into the *in-between* spaces through which the meanings of cultural and political authority are negotiated. (*Nation* 4)

In-between the traditional borders of the nation-state lie other nations, races, ethnicities, and cultures, such as those of First Nations peoples, which are divided by the traditional and imperialist demarcations. Native lands, in a sense, lie 'in-between' the borders of the nation-state – they are affected by them, but they are also independent entities. Bhabha's idea of the 'in-between' offers a different perspective and engenders other thresholds of meaning. For Native peoples, the space between the borders of the nation-state and the lands that were historically occupied by a tribe generate gaps in meaning that allow writers, like King, to explore oppostional definitions of identity and community. Borders are 'acknowledged as "containing" thresholds of meaning that must be crossed, erased, and translated in the process of cultural production' (Bhabha, *Nation* 4). To be 'in-between' the borders, therefore, suggests that one is able to recognize those borders and the 'identity' they distinguish, yet still hold another view that can encompass and subvert them. As a result, being inside/outside the borders allows for an understanding of what the borders are delineating, at the same time that it allows for a critique of their seeming stability.

More importantly, whether borders are imaginative constructs, or figments of someone's imagination, they have political and physical consequences, consequences to which King's fictions consistently draw attention. Being inside and outside the borders does not mean that one is immune to or from them; on the contrary, it suggests that from in-between, one can view either side, perhaps rejecting both, at the same time that those sides influence one's spatial position. Telling stories is one way to explore and reconfigure such complex interrelations from a position of in-betweenness. More specifically, as Michel de Certeau explains in *The Practice of Everyday Life*, 'what the map cuts up, the story cuts across' (129). Storytelling and the act of narration are primarily intended to 'to *authorize* the establishment, displacement or transcendence of limits' (123). Narratives can thus both affirm and contest the stability of borders and boundaries, those territorial lines on a map that confirm the ownership of space and the existence of nations. In King's texts, the process of finding and formulating places between those borders and boundaries, which are already institutionalized, means both accounting for and moving beyond the recognized limits, in order to create new terms for self-definition that do not merely replicate dominant (meaning Eurocentric) paradigms. Indeed, King rejects the term 'post-colonialism' as a new category to describe Native writing because it does exactly that – confines First Nations narratives to White conceptions of time and space in which certain borders and boundaries dominate:

> While post-colonialism purports to be a method by which we can begin to look at those literatures which are formed out of the struggle of the oppressed against the oppressor, the colonized and the colonizer, the term itself assumes that the starting point for that discussion is the advent of Europeans in North American. At the same time, the term organizes the literature progressively ... And, worst of all, the idea of post-colonial writing effectively cuts us off from our traditions, traditions that were in place before colonialism ever became a question, traditions which have come down to us through our cultures in spite of colonization, and it supposes that contemporary Native writing is largely a construct of oppression. Ironically, while the term itself – post-colonial – strives to escape to find new centres, it remains, in the end, a hostage to nationalism. ('Godzilla' 11–12)

Bearing this in mind, we wish to explore one of King's short stories, 'How Corporal Colin Sterling Saved Blossom, Alberta, and Most of the Rest of the World as Well,' republished in *One Good Story, That One*, which exemplifies the central concerns of our study. 'How Corporal Colin Sterling Saved Blossom' is a comic text about how Whites read Natives by imposing borders, borders that the First Nations characters and narrator subvert or ignore altogether to serve their own purposes. The story begins when a White Alberta hotel owner, Ralph Lawton, and his wife, Bella, awake after a noisy night at their aptly named Chief Mountain Motel, and speculate on who is to blame:

'Are you awake?'

Ralph grunted.

'Did you hear those damn Indians?'

'Coyotes,' said Ralph.

'I know Indians when I hear them. Drinking, I suspect.'

'Coyotes.'

'Did they pay you in advance?'

'It was the coyotes you heard last night.'

'Then they've flown the coop by now.' (49)

For Bella, the 'damn Indians' are clearly responsible for this nocturnal disturbance, a result of their heavy drinking. Her stereotypical assertions about Natives and her refusal to listen to her husband characterize her as a woman set in her ways, both blind and deaf, at least figuratively, to Ralph's suggestion that it may have been coyotes up to their trickster antics.

When Ralph finally goes to investigate room sixteen, where the Natives are staying, he discovers six bodies lying on the floor that appear to be dead, and he immediately calls the local RCMP detachment to report a mass murder. Shortly after, Corporal Sterling, a sixteen-year veteran of the force, who is more concerned about his morning doughnuts than Ralph's urgent call, appears on the scene and realizes: 'These fellows aren't dead. They're still breathing. This one's singing' (51). What is mysterious, however, is the rigid state of the bodies. Motivated by what he sees, the corporal makes a tactless and explicitly racist joke, recalling, 'When I was stationed at the subdivision at Lethbridge ... we picked up a fellow behind the Alec Arms who was so drunk ... well, he was ... "stiff"' (51). The humour of this joke is lost on Ralph, who immediately contests the clichéd idea that Natives typically are drunk and/or dead, and retorts: 'What are you, some kind of asshole comic?' (52). The corporal then calls in Dr Phelps, a local practitioner, to examine the rigid bodies; Dr Phelps determines that the Natives are, indeed, alive but cannot explain why they are in such a hardened physical condition. As Phelps tells Ralph, 'I've seen them drunk, beat up, suicidal, half-dead from drinking lighter fluid and vanilla extract. I've seen them broke and I've seen them rolling in money. But this is new' (52). Just as Sterling relies on stereotypical conceptions of what is perceived by Whites as 'normal' Native behaviour, the doctor provides a catalogue of 'typical' scenarios, none of which illuminates the current situation.

The Indians in King's story challenge the expectations of the locals precisely because their petrified state doesn't accord with a familiar template. Through the comments of Corporal Sterling, the text comically highlights the narrow White perceptions of 'appropriate' Native conduct, perceptions that promote a naive and vicious cycle that initially appears to reinforce White dominance but, in fact, reveals more about White stupidity. Such a strategy, however, has complex implications for King's readers. White ignorance is comically exaggerated and mocked within the story, offering an extreme vision of those who don't know any better. However, for those White readers who *do* get the joke, King's story gives them a reason to feel superior and to go out and behave more appropriately than individuals like Sterling. Thus, while King's text may delight in the ignorance of the fictional community depicted, it also conversely celebrates the insight of those White readers who see beyond the confines of racism and find such stereotypes ludicrous.

The corporal's self-absorbed and hierarchical vision of the world is furthered by Dr Phelps's medical exam. When he questions the corporal and Ralph as to whether the bodies have made any sounds, Sterling describes the chanting of one man who keeps asking, 'What took you so long?' a question that the doctor immediately assumes is directed at him: '"Well," said Doctor Phelps, "I got here as soon as I could"' (53). Like Bella, who thinks that she has all the right answers based on formulaic notions of Indianness, Dr Phelps also believes that he can read the situation correctly. Yet, as the story unfolds, King's narrative undermines the power and accuracy of these assumptions – the non-Native locals who know all become the butt of the joke.

Corporal Sterling, stymied by the fact that 'petrified' Natives are 'turning up all over Canada, the U.S., and parts of South America and Mexico' (53), eventually decides to stack the local collection of bodies in a warehouse, arguing that it will 'keep them out of harm's way' (55). But once the bodies are piled in the warehouse, the coyotes return again, lingering nearby and prompting the building manager, Mike Congistre, who has agreed to house the bodies over the winter, to comment: 'You believe those coyotes ... What a racket!' (56). Dr Phelps also hears the persistent noise of 'those damn coyotes,' a ruckus that notably is lost on Corporal Sterling, who insists that it is 'just the wind' (55). In an ironic repetition of the story's initial conversation between Ralph and Bella, certain individuals hear the coyotes while others remain oblivious to their presence.

Despite the doctor's selective perceptiveness regarding the Natives, and in an effort to ignore the coyotes and increase storage space, he allows a Blossom couple, the Bempos, to display two bodies in their living room. This gesture parodies historical attempts to assimilate and even eliminate Native North Americans by representing them as a dying race. Daniel Francis notes, in *The Imaginary Indian: The Image of the Indian in Canadian Culture*, that just as 'the government was trying to stamp out vestiges of traditional aboriginal culture in everyday life, it was creating a new institution [the ethnological museum] devoted to the preservation of that culture' in a contained and manageable form (103). The upright, seemingly lifeless bodies in the Bempos' home replicate this museological construction of Natives as on the brink of extinction, and enable Whites to gaze at the Indians, without having to interact with them. Notably, several recent Native North American artists have created their own parodic counterparts to these limiting representations, including James Luna, whose 1987 exhibition at the Museum of Man in San Diego, California, titled 'Artifact Piece,' parallels the physical appearance of Blossom's petrified Natives. During the exhibition, Luna performed the role of an apparently dead cultural object, lying prone in a display case, complete with various signs that provided ethnographic information about himself as 'artifact.'[8] What is especially comic about Luna's and King's pointed reworking of formulaic constructs is that the individuals who put the Natives on display seem unable to recognize that they are perpetuating the very same stereotypes. For example, when Corporal Sterling questions the appropriateness of this exhibition, Dr Phelps tells him: 'Running out of places to put them. They look alright' (55).

In the latter half of the story, the relentless objectification of the local Indians is unexpectedly twisted through a science-fictional dimension, which challenges at least some of the characters to radically rethink their perceptions of the hardened Natives. Shortly after the rest of the bodies are placed in the warehouse for storage, a spaceship arrives containing blue coyotes, who leave the ship long enough to gather up the petrified bodies and take them on board, a gesture that baffles those watching, including Dr Phelps and Corporal Sterling. When the corporal tries to take action by blocking the kidnappers physically, he runs into 'what felt like a sheet of glass' (58). He draws his gun and fires, but the bullet simply disappears, leaving him helpless to interfere with what seems to be an extraterrestrial invasion. Paradoxically, much of the conversation between the various locals rests on the assumption that the coyotes – whose abilities include being able to pass through solid walls – are not, in fact, the aliens. Several people watching the kidnapping speculate that there must be a group of beings inside the spaceship itself controlling their actions. This is yet another example of how the community has overlooked the importance of the howling coyotes that are present wherever the Natives go, but are actually heard by only a few individuals (namely Ralph, Dr Phelps, and Mike Congistre). The assumption that the coyotes are merely robots becomes increasingly ridiculous as the locals watch the coyotes methodically gather the Natives' bodies and successfully subvert the corporal's attempts to stop them.

Notably, the corporal reads the removal of the Natives in specifically nationalistic terms: 'What we have here are aliens disguised as blue coyotes who are taking advantage of helpless Indians, who, I might add, are Canadian citizens just like the rest of us here and who are entitled to the same protection as any Canadian gets' (60). Corporal Sterling's rhetoric shifts from pure practicality and a desire to distance himself from the 'undesirables,' especially when he is faced with housing them, to a claim that national identity and citizenship, as well as the unlawful behaviour of the coyotes, make the bodies worthy of the community's action. Desperate to halt the ship's departure, Corporal Sterling makes a final dramatic statement. He insists that the coyotes 'Stop, in the name of the Queen,' a command that creates an ironic parallel between Canada's historical status as a colonized country and the long-standing treatment of Native North Americans by European settlers and national governments (62). The absurdity of Sterling's assumption that the Queen will compel the coyotes to halt their trip underlines his own naive belief that Native North Americans still find such colonial figures authoritative and compelling. He overlooks the centuries of ill-treatment – the fact that Natives have been viewed literally and figuratively as alien 'others' – and the possibility that the Indians know better than to trust the word of a gun-toting officer who only recognizes them as Canadians when it suits his purpose. In a final desperate move, Sterling draws out his gun and commands: 'Bring back the Indians and surrender yourselves, or I will be forced to fire' (62). Not surprisingly, Sterling's efforts are unsuccessful, the ship departs, and one of the locals immediately complains to the corporal: 'Hey ... you scared them away' (62).

Though Corporal Sterling believes that a crime has been committed, Dr Phelps, who seems to change his viewpoint after observing the blue coyotes' actions, offers a different reading of the so-called kidnapping. He insists: 'They're probably up there somewhere laughing at us right now,' a comment that suggests the Natives are working in collusion with

the coyotes, and have successfully deceived the Blossom locals into
seeing them as victims (62). Sterling may want to believe that national
identity is central to the kidnapped Natives, yet his assumption is undermined by the Natives' treatment in Blossom. Only when a piece of property is threatened does the corporal start to acknowledge their legal
rights as citizens. Sterling does not consider the departure of their bodies in the spaceship as a positive event, which facilitates the Natives'
escape from a construction of identity that is circumscribed by Eurocentric conceptions of nation. Dr Phelps speculates, much to the corporal's
dismay, that the Indians 'may be better off with the blue coyotes' (63).

The story concludes with the discovery that Blossom is not the only
place that has been visited by spaceships filled with blue coyotes, coming
to take Native bodies on board. The narrator notes: 'By the end of the
week, all of the petrified Indians in North and South America and Mexico, and other places in the world where you wouldn't expect to find
Indians at all, had been loaded onto spaceships' (62). The discovery of
the existence of substantial First Nations populations around the globe
counters the assumption made by many Blossom residents, including
the corporal, that they are a dying people. When Mike Congistre mentions that fifty Indians have been picked up by the coyotes in Germany,
Corporal Sterling immediately insists that they were 'probably just there
on vacation' (63).

In contrast, once the Indians are gone, Dr Phelps re-reads his encounter with the hardened Native bodies, recalling the words of the Indian
in the hotel room, who asked: 'What took you so long?' (63). Phelps had
assumed that the Native man was speaking to him, but finally comes to
the realization, after watching the ship depart, that the man was likely
waiting for the arrival of the blue coyotes. Rather than presenting this
alterna(rra)tive to Sterling in an overt manner, Phelps merely says, 'See
... It's just as I thought,' leaving a sense of ambiguity that neither denies
nor supports the corporal's version of events, but acknowledges the
existence and viability of alterna(rra)tives that do not accord with the
discourse of nation and citizenship that is so selectively invoked (63).
The quietness of Phelps's revelation is contrasted with the concluding
lines of the story, in which a local man congratulates Corporal Sterling
on his heroic response to the spaceship, claiming, '... we're probably
alive because of your bravery' (63). The ludicrousness of this statement
is underlined by the fact that the blue coyotes have not tried to harm
anyone during their visit. They are simply rescuing the Natives, a point
the corporal misses entirely when he expresses his appreciation for the

local's compliment. At the end of the narrative, Corporal Sterling specifically laments his perceived lack of success: 'I just wish I could have saved the Indians, too' (63).

Clearly Corporal Sterling cannot imagine that his desire to keep the Indians in Blossom may not have been in their best interests. The title of King's story playfully mocks this blindness to other perspectives by claiming that 'Corporal Colin Sterling Saved Blossom, Alberta, and Most of the Rest of the World as Well,' a statement revealed as entirely misrepresentative at the end of the narrative. Appropriately, the title page to this King text juxtaposes the title, which appears in bold black print and occupies the upper half of the page, with the image of two coyotes, who sit back to back, one fuzzy but distinctly black and the other a mottled gray. This visual image, in which one coyote fades into another in a playfully incomplete mirror image, becomes a counterpoint to the title of the story. With its grainy quality and almost abstract appearance, the image demands that readers, and Blossom locals, look again.

Certainly, the narrative of this Indian kidnapping is all about borders, the political, economic, social, and cultural lines that are used to separate 'us' from 'them,' 'insiders' from 'outsiders,' and the 'right' to lay claim to those who are perceived as relevant to the community's or nation's identity. Even the borders between the two coyotes depicted on the title page are the subject of playful reconsideration; as noted, their behinds blend into each other, fusing together what should be two separate images and literalizing the question of exactly where the butt of the joke is located. Yet, 'How Corporal Colin Sterling Saved Blossom, Alberta' is also explicitly concerned with the act of reading, and, in particular, how many non-Natives perceive and define Natives according to our own needs and desires, rather than acknowledging and respecting the perspective of the First Nations themselves. Colin Sterling's lament at having let the Indians get away becomes a model of ignorance. Ultimately, he functions as the 'butt' of the story's comic message, in contrast to Dr Phelps, whose re-reading of the situation is also an acknowledgment that his initial interpretation of the Indian's words was likely wrong. The corporal's limited viewpoint becomes an impediment rather than a source of wisdom, a restrictive vision of the world that ultimately fails to comprehend the potentially positive outcome of the Natives' abduction.

The blue coyotes and their spaceships represent a rejection of the multiple, imperialistically ascribed political definitions that preclude their own self-definition. Sterling, unlike Dr Phelps, cannot see that the Indians' desire to leave may be a deliberate attempt to expose the hypocrisy of citizenship, at least as it is applied to Natives. The departing Indians literalize, for the audience within the story and those reading the text, their lack of recognition and belonging within the nation. Their departure can be read as a decolonizing border crossing, a crossing with a difference, precisely because the coyotes and their cargo restructure the terms of dominant discourse and definition, offering their own *counter* discursive definition. This alterna(rra)tive undermines the authority that Sterling attributes to Canadian citizenship and the figurehead of the Queen by opening both to question. While they may not explicitly relay a counter-narrative, the coyotes and their willing cargo function within King's story as an appeal to understand the complex workings of borders and boundaries – what they admit, what they impede, how they differently mediate what crosses or doesn't cross them.

The contrasting perspectives of Sterling and Phelps bring to mind Edward Said's argument, in *Culture and Imperialism*, that 'narrative is crucial' since 'stories are at the heart of what explorers and novelists say about strange regions of the world; they also become the method colonized people use to assert their own identity and the existence of their own history' (xii). As Said goes on to explain:

> The main battle in imperialism is over land, of course; but when it came to who owned the land, who had the right to settle and work on it, who kept it going, who won it back, and who now plans its future – these issues were reflected, contested, and even for a time decided in narrative. As one critic has suggested, nations themselves *are* narrations. The power to narrate, or to block other narratives from forming and emerging, is very important to culture and imperialism, and constitutes one of the main connections between them. Most important, the grand narratives of emancipation and enlightenment mobilized people in the colonial world to rise up and throw off imperial subjection; in the process, many Europeans and Americans were also stirred by these stories and their protagonists, and they too fought for new narratives of equality and community. (xii–xiii)

King's short story functions similarly. By drawing attention to historically demarcated borders and their imperialistic origins, his narrative points to what those borders elide and erase. As Phelps suggests when the spaceships disappear with the coyotes and the petrified Natives on board: 'They're probably up there somewhere laughing at us right now' (62). What is missing from the story are the voices of the Natives and their stories – narratives that we do not hear, except in the form of the question ('What took you so long?') that Dr Phelps initially assumes is for him. Clearly, Corporal Sterling and the community do not know what to make of the departed Natives and the counter-narrative that the spaceship visit suggests. Moreover, with the exception of Phelps, those who witness the spaceship are not willing to explore the possibility that the assertion of ownership and control of the Natives based on citizenship is inappropriate. Their very refusal to explore this possibility underscores the importance of the Natives' departure and the fact that the spaceship does not heed Sterling's invocation of colonial and national authorities, which have no relevance for the Indians or their rescuers.

The structure of this story, then, can be described as what George Lipsitz has called 'counter-memory':

> Counter-memory looks to the past for the hidden histories excluded from dominant narratives. But unlike myths that seek to detach events and actions from the fabric of any larger history, counter-memory forces revision of existing histories by supplying new perspectives about the past. Counter-memory embodies aspects of myth and aspects of history, but it retains an enduring suspicion of both categories. Counter-memory focuses on localized experiences with oppression, using them to reframe and refocus dominant narratives purporting to represent universal experience. (213)

In keeping with Lipsitz's definition, King's short story (and his fiction generally) undercuts authoritative accounts of the past and present by including stories from marginalized groups and individuals that highlight the precariousness of Eurocentric and Judeo-Christian ideologies. His works upset, in form and content, the historical linearity of traditional Western narratives and challenge the orderliness of events by questioning what constitutes the dominant discourse in an era of 'increasingly decentred and fragmented consciousness' (Lipsitz 214). In particular, King's incorporation of Native oral traditions demonstrates a desire to expand the scope of history to include those 'experiences and emotions rendered invisible by the ideology of individualism' (Lipsitz 218), and to acknowledge the important links between people and the stories they tell.

The 'counter-memory' format of King's texts also serves a political purpose, for it creates a gap that allows for cultural resistance. As de Certeau argues in *Heterologies*, this gap 'establishes the text's difference, makes possible its operations and gives it "credibility" in the eyes of its readers, by distinguishing it both from the conditions within which it arose (the context) and from its object (the content)' (68). King's texts, as they critique the context in which they are situated and question the object of colonization, create that space of interplay necessary to social change (de Certeau 68). In doing so, King's narratives become cross-cultural texts that demand a cross-cultural reading. In short, since all writing invokes and transgresses borders and since national writing particularly does so (however 'nation' is defined, which is always a problem in Canada),[9] the need for cross-border readings would seem obvious.

The following study is an effort to fill this need. Written by three Canadian scholars – one who lives in Canada, where she teaches *American* studies, another a resident of the United States, who worked in *Canadian* studies, and the third who lives in Canada and specializes in comparative *Canadian and American* studies – the book is a border-crossing venture. Like King's own narratives, this project too incorporates inside/outside perspectives (Canadian-U.S. and U.S.-Canadian), lending *Border Crossings* a cross-national viewpoint that illuminates many of the borders within his writing and media work.

But the authors of this study are not Native; nor would we want to claim 'insider' knowledge of Native North American cultures. As three White literary and cultural scholars, we are acutely aware of Native concerns regarding the appropriation and institutionalization of Native narratives to serve a Eurocentric agenda.[10] Lenore Keeshig-Tobias pointedly expresses this fear in 'Stop Stealing Native Stories,' when she states that 'the Canadian cultural industry is stealing – unconsciously, perhaps, but with the same devastating results – native stories as surely as the missionaries stole our religion and the politicians stole our land and the residential schools stole our language' (A7). Thus, rather than 'speaking for' the Native author and texts examined here and replicating the sense of exploitation articulated by Keeshig-Tobias, we see ourselves as 'speaking about' King's works, analysing rather than appropriating, and, in doing so, giving him the scholarly attention he deserves (Donovan 7).

Certainly, the ambiguity of territorial, racial, and cultural boundaries is critical to King's works, and the traditional boundaries that separate those categories are less static than they may at first appear. Hence, while racial borders may seem fixed at particular historical moments, in fact, they are far from constant. King is in a particularly complex situation because of his 'pan-Indian' self-identification, a position that makes him vulnerable to exclusion from both Native and non-Native arenas. It is our goal to explore the richness of this positioning and the relevance of his various border crossings. Such a mix of racial, cultural, and national definitions informs this study, which will demonstrate the ways in which the power of narration has the ability to contest and undermine dominant borders and boundaries.

The following pages comprise our efforts to analyse the complexity of King's fiction. Chapter 1 considers comedy's potential as a vehicle for shifting social awareness by exploring how Native writers use it as a political and artistic strategy. This chapter also outlines the theoretical (generic and literary) precepts of the study, and the methodological approach adopted. Chapter 2 reads King's texts as counter-narratives that explore alternative conceptions of identity through performativity. Chapters 3 and 4 explore King's genre crossings by contesting the seeming divisions between fiction and history, novels and short stories, television and literature; in turn, they trace how the author draws upon popular genres and inverts them. These chapters also consider how King's comic vision is developed through a variety of artistic forms, including photography, radio scripts, and television movies. The next two chapters focus on King's comic renderings of race, nation, gender, and sexuality. They, too, explore the construction of borders, and assess the relationships between national, racial, and gender concerns. Finally, chapter 7 considers how King's intertextual references to his previous narratives in his more recent fiction and photography can be read as a comic commentary on his own body of work and the complexity of his pan-Indian, cross-border positioning. This concluding chapter also suggests new directions for scholarly work on King.

Overall, our project considers how King explores political, social, and cultural possibilities through the use of alterna(rra)tives and counter-memories. In the following pages, we hope to foreground the ways in which nation is predicated upon narration, as well as the ways in which narration can transgress national, cultural, and social delineations. As one of the narrators of *Green Grass, Running Water* puts it, 'There are no truths ... Only stories' (326). As the novel suggests, however, the act of telling stories is by its very nature political, and carries with it social responsibilities. The ensuing study is our exploration of how King's texts exemplify these concerns.

CHAPTER ONE

Comic Contexts

In his examination of genre fiction, Cawelti argues that textual formulas 'serve both conservative and progressive functions, allowing culture to negotiate, through symbolic representation, both commonly shared values and the possibility of change' (*Adventure* 35–6). Audiences and readers may seek the conventionality of a familiar genre, for it is readily accessible and requires little effort to comprehend. But without some innovation, the genre becomes redundant and potentially unsatisfying. King's adaptation of comic formulations extends and revises the concept of comedy by integrating serious concerns about Native rights into his writings. Specific comic strategies characterize his works and alter the conventions of comedy, especially in relation to tragic issues, for they work to shift social perspectives in order to challenge dominant paradigms. In order to situate the readings that follow, this chapter explores Native North American conceptions of comedy and then considers the relationship of comedy to tragedy, which King sees as central to his methodology. In particular, we focus on how comedy, when mixed with tragedy, is employed by Native writers, like King, to undermine established beliefs and to introduce other, typically marginalized viewpoints.

Part of our task is to explore how King carefully couples selected aspects of traditional comedies with a distinctively Native sensibility to create his own subversively comic vision. Traditionally, Native humour has been dismissed or ignored altogether. According to Native American scholar and activist Vine Deloria, the cultivation and perpetuation of 'the image of the granite-faced grunting redskin' dehumanizes tribal populations and ensures a lack of sympathy from outsiders (146). Yet recent studies of everyday tribal interactions, and the written literature produced by Natives on both sides of the border, demonstrate that comedy is alive and well. Deloria, a Standing Rock Sioux, expresses the fundamental significance of a comic perspective to Indian life: 'I sometimes wonder how anything is accomplished by Indians because of the apparent overemphasis on humor within the Indian world. Indians have found a humorous side of nearly every problem and the experiences of life have generally been so well defined through joke and stories that they have become a thing in themselves' (146–7). Comedy, and the laughter it evokes, takes on a life of its own in a Native North American context by bringing communities together, facilitating conflict resolution, and establishing a common bond between otherwise divided nations.

This comic perspective is especially helpful to Native North Americans given the legacy of colonization and racial destruction that has shaped the history of various tribes over the past several centuries. Comedy may offer a basis for internal reconciliation amongst communities; however, the ability to joke about 'living as an exile in one's own land' also provides the First Nations with an opportunity to reconfigure their status as 'other' in relation to the White, Western settlers who came and claimed the New World for themselves (Allen 158). Kenneth Lincoln argues that comedy infuses contemporary Native life and can effectively bridge the gap between Natives and non-Natives, without ignoring the past: 'Indi'n humor is a way of recalling and going beyond tragedy, of working through the hurt of personal history, of healing old wounds and hearing the truth of what's happening among Native Americans. It is the most vocal and effective voice among Indians today ...' (116). Comedy is a particularly useful strategy for authors like King because it acknowledges the complex status of specific tribal communities and the pain of their histories.

In an interview with Hartmut Lutz, King suggests that 'it doesn't help the fiction if all you do is talk about the kinds of oppressions White culture has had on Natives. There are all sorts of other ways to do it which are much more powerful' (112). By developing his own comic vision, which marries aspects of the Western genre with various Native traditions, King's writing becomes accessible and even 'palatable' to many different audiences (McCormack 41). These intercultural aspects of King's comic texts, which we will explore in detail in later chapters, offer an invitation (rather than a threat) to non-Native readers – to participate in the text, and laugh with its various characters. At the same time,

King uses comedy to invert and contest the presumption of White dominance and to offer a different perspective on the world. His texts combine Native beliefs with an awareness of the contemporary complexities
of Indian identity, especially for those who have been raised off the
reserve.

Comedy: Definitions and Origins

Comedy, according to M.H. Abrams's *Glossary of Literary Terms*, 'is a work
in which the materials are selected and managed primarily to interest,
involve, and amuse us: the characters and their discomfortures engage
our pleasurable attention rather than our profound concern' (28).
Comedies can be aptly described as 'joking texts' or narratives that are
meant to be funny and deliberately structured to evoke laughter from
audiences (Purdie 71). Although there are distinct types of comedy,
which vary according to the aims and subject matter the writer chooses
to pursue (including 'romantic comedy,' 'satiric comedy,' and 'the comedy of manners'), comic works typically share the same, readily identifi-
able conclusion (Abrams 29). In most comedies, 'the story or plot ...
moves towards a laughable or celebratory ending' wherein 'the action
turns out happily for the chief characters' (Nelson 21; Abrams 29).
Northrop Frye's definition of (romantic) comedy, in *The Anatomy of
Criticism*, exemplifies this predominantly positive (and Eurocentric)
formulation of the genre's structure:

> What normally happens is that a young man wants a young woman, that his
> desire is resisted by some opposition, usually paternal, and that near the
> end of the play some twist in the plot enables the hero to have his will. In
> this simple pattern there are several complex elements. In the first place,
> the movement of comedy is usually a movement from one kind of society
> to another ... The appearance of this new society is frequently signalized by
> some kind of party or festive ritual, which either appears at the end of the
> play or is assumed to take place immediately afterward. (163)

But Frye also acknowledges that such a tidy model of comedy needs to
be expanded to encompass a range of variations on the ideal outcome.
He identifies six phases of comedy as it 'blends into irony and satire at
one end and into romance at the other,' which account for far bleaker
and uncertain endings (177).

Further, while the structure of a comedy may be mapped in ideal terms, the relationship between a text and its receivers (whether an audience or readers) also complicates theoretical treatments of the genre. The narrative context in which a work is presented and the make-up of those responding to it bring another dimension to discussions of comedy. Mary Douglas notes that for a joke to be 'received,' it must meet certain 'social conditions' (366). The population who hears the joke must recognize it as such and be open to it: 'Social requirements may judge a joke to be in bad taste, risky, too near the bone, improper, or irrelevant. Such controls are exerted either on behalf of hierarchy as such, or on behalf of values which are judged too precious and too precarious to be exposed to challenge' (366). Douglas insists that jokes only work when they mirror established 'social forms' and are congruent with 'the social structure,' assertions that prove especially problematic when studying comic texts, like King's, that overtly challenge the status quo (371, 372). King's work may play with Eurocentric traditions, but it does so deliberately to subvert their dominance. More specifically, his writings revise racial, sexual, and religious hierarchies by dismantling the authority of Judeo-Christian patriarchal belief systems and exploiting the ignorance of those who perceive themselves as knowledgeable.

Douglas's interest in the reception of jokes proves a useful starting point for examining King's work. The success of a comic or 'joking' text, for instance, depends on the audience's recognition of the work as having the potential to provoke laughter; what one reader perceives as funny may seem dull and formulaic to another (Purdie 73). One way to formulate comedy's complexity is to see it as shaped by two, potentially conflicted elements: the laughing responses of those reading and/or watching a comic work (which may range from pleasurable and sympathetic to mocking and derisive); and the progress of the narrative, which traditionally has moved toward resolution, through 'harmony, festivity, and celebration' (Nelson 22). This incongruous relationship between the structuring principles of, and audience responses to, a comedy means that studies of comic texts need to take different types of reception into account. Hence, our discussion of King's work in subsequent chapters relies, in part, on our subjective responses to his texts. These readings are situated within specific social contexts that combine a consideration of comedy – as a genre – with an exploration of how this Native writer adapts and revises various comic conventions to alter readers' perceptions of the world.

Scatology: Playing with the Body

Historically, scatology has played a central role within Native North American humour by levelling differences among groups of people, celebrating creativity in its basest forms, and depicting a playful mode of deviance and subversion. In his study of Native American humour, John Lowe argues that 'the origins of many oral comic narratives may be found in religious ceremonies involving sacred clowns' (193). Ritual clowns provided a 'comic counterpoint to sacral events' by mocking some of the most solemn rituals (193). The sexualized humour of these clowns often included grabbing the genitalia of spectators, performing acts of mock rape and masturbation, and 'throwing or even eating filth or excrement' (193). The opportunity to laugh was thought to prepare people for participation in the serious ceremony that was to follow. Similarly, the trickster, a chief mythological figure amongst Native North Americans, who crosses tribal boundaries, is often associated with acts of sexual and scatological transgression. Enlarged genitalia, a fascination with excrement and flatulence, and a constant drive to fulfil primal desires are central to the trickster's identity.

Mixed-blood Anishinaabe writer and scholar Gerald Vizenor has coined the term 'trickster discourse,' meaning 'a collection of utterances in [the] oral tradition,' to describe the uniquely comic spirit of Native texts ('Trickster' 191). Like the figure of the trickster, who is a cunning, playfully self-centred, impulsive, shape-shifting creature, trickster discourse is typically 'open-ended, unfolding, evolving, incomplete,' and can be 'imagined in numerous verbal and visual narratives and a multiplicity of ... voices' (Ryan xiii). This comic spirit shapes the work of many Native authors, including King, who combines a trickster aesthetic with literal representations of the trickster as a figure of play, infusing his work with irreverence and exploiting the possibilities of narrative chance.

In *Green Grass, Running Water,* for instance, Coyote – one version of this Native trickster – is depicted as a greedy lecher who is always eager to copulate and overeat. Coyote also continually interferes with the workings of the world by singing, dancing, meddling, and following his baser instincts. Here, Coyote impedes the work of the four Native elders, who are committed to 'fixing up this world' (348). The trickster proves to be a source of comic relief and offers a useful model of how individuals ought not to behave (348). But, at the same time, Coyote's presence in King's text provides an opportunity for readers to stretch their imaginations, and conceive of alternatives to the dominant social system. As the novel closes, Coyote is scolded yet again for interfering with the world, a charge that he initially denies:

> 'I didn't do it,' says Coyote.
> The Lone Ranger and Ishmael and Robinson Crusoe and Hawkeye looked at Coyote.
> 'It's a lot of work fixing up this world, you know,' said the Lone Ranger.
> 'Yes,' said Ishmael. 'And we can use all the help we can get.'
> 'The last time you fooled around like this,' said Robinson Crusoe, 'the world got very wet.'
> 'And we had to start all over again,' said Hawkeye.
> 'I didn't do anything,' says Coyote. 'I just sang a little.'
> 'Oh boy,' said the Lone Ranger.
> 'I just danced a little, too,' says Coyote. (348)

Coyote's conduct is treated with suspicion precisely because the four Native mythic figures know the power the trickster possesses. Yet Coyote's spontaneity, and his willingness to alter the world on a whim, opens up other possibilities and pre-empts a vision of the world as fixed and unchanging. By bending the rules, literally and figuratively, the trickster remains a key participant in the narrative and an example of how to survive and celebrate the disorderly aspects of life. More specifically, Coyote embodies the resistance and endurance of Native North American communities, whose belief systems have been marginalized or suppressed by White institutions.

Coyote's presence throughout *Green Grass, Running Water* exemplifies the kinds of symbolic inversion and transgression that characterize King's texts. His novels may be read as an example of Mikhail Bakhtin's influential notion of carnival, in that Bakhtin argues for carnival's symbolic importance as a period of celebration, instituted in the Middle Ages when the official order of Church and state, and their hierarchical status, were temporarily inverted by the general population. Integral to this concept of carnival is the presence of the grotesque body, usually a female body, whose physical excesses are seen as symbolic of liberation. However, critics of Bakhtin note that carnival 'often violently abuses and demonizes *weaker*, not stronger, social groups – women, ethnic and religious minorities, those who don't belong' (Stallybrass and White 19), and remains complicit with the dominant culture. Notably, King's comic texts do include clowns, tricksters, and a sustained interest in the grotesque body (with its orifices and excrement); but, rather than targeting racial and ethnic minorities, he employs comedy to explore the interactions of Native peoples within their communities. Hence, his comic contestation of norms is based on the invocation and exploration of a different social order.

King challenges the legitimacy of Eurocentric paradigms by installing a framework of Native beliefs and perspectives that reveal the absurdity of specific aspects of the former, from divergent viewpoints. Here, Barbara Babcock's notion of 'symbolic inversion' helps to explain King's brand of comedy. Babcock describes symbolic inversion as 'any act of expressive behavior which inverts, contradicts, abrogates, or in some fashion presents an alternative to commonly held cultural codes, values, and norms, be they linguistic, literary or artistic, religious, or social and political' ('Introduction' 14). Symbolic inversion, according to Babcock, is closely related to irony, parody, and paradox. It repeatedly tests the limits of discourse and challenges human understanding by crossing categorical boundaries. Those who encounter symbolic inversion in a text, for example, may be presented with disorderly or contradictory materials that do not neatly adhere to the established social system. Such contradictions and incongruous juxtapositions encourage readers to explore alternative viewpoints and incorporate new roles and ideas. In turn, symbolic inversion is linked to what Babcock calls 'a central and ancient principle of comedy,' or the sudden switching of conventional roles (e.g., prisoners lecturing judges) ('Introduction' 17). As Henri Bergson explains, in his famous essay 'Laughter' (1899), this kind of 'topsyturvydom' (118) is 'an attack on control, on [those] closed systems' which reinforce the notion that phenomena cannot be reversed or altered (Babcock, 'Introduction' 17). A comic approach to such rigidity makes the seriousness of the challenge to dominant paradigms much easier to accept and enjoy, even for those who may support the status quo.

Much of King's work relies on the comic premise of inversion and incorporates elements of paradox, irony, and parody to undermine some of the standard clichés about Native peoples. As the creator of his own 'trickster discourse,' King invokes and alters Eurocentric narrative conventions in a deliberately provocative manner, which moves to dismantle the hierarchical relationship between Natives and non-Natives living in Canada and the United States, and to displace perceptions of 'difference' onto the dominant population. He also demonstrates how powerful certain negative images of Indians have become, even within Native communities.

King's comic inversions do not merely involve replacing Eurocentric perspectives with Native alternatives (e.g., God with a Native female goddess, citizenship with tribal identity). Instead, King's texts cultivate a sustained interaction between these conflicting perspectives, a strategy that conveys the complexities of being located 'in-between' non-Native and Native worlds. This layering of various perspectives is considered to be a 'defining aspect of a widespread Native [North] American aesthetic' (Ryan 64). The act of combining and making connections, as well as recognizing differences between diverse points of view, allows writers like King to challenge the supremacy of Western paradigms in an overtly comic manner. Babcock notes that such inversion involves the infusion of actuality with reality and emphasizes the conditional nature of *any* reality. To clarify the meanings of actuality and reality, Babcock cites the work of Erik Erikson, who contends that 'if reality is the structure of facts consensually agreed upon in a given stage of knowledge, actuality is the leeway created by new forms of interplay. Without actuality, reality becomes a prison of sterotypy, while actuality must always resist reality to remain truly playful' (Babcock, 'Introduction' 25).

King's texts are structured by this interaction between reality and actuality, a juxtaposition of often conflicting ideas that pose a challenge, particularly to those non-Native readers who rely on their version of 'reality' to relegate Native peoples to the margins of a society or a narrative framework. The interactions between so-called reality and actuality highlight how certain accounts of reality typically prevail and engender their own set of stereotypes, conceptions of the 'other' that are accepted and even reproduced by the minority populations they are intended to mock. In *Medicine River*, for instance, Will's presumption that Harlen Bigbear has resumed his drinking highlights the pervasiveness of negative images of Native alcoholism. But King also structures his novel to undercut and mock the naïvety of protagonists (and readers) like Will, who assume they know what is wrong with Harlen based on rumour, and have accepted that characterization without question. Will's assertion that Harlen is 'still pretty drunk,' when Harlen asks for chicken soup and a bucket to throw up in, is exposed as absurd by Bertha Morley, who tells Will: 'Harlen's not drunk, Will. He's just got the flu' (101). In this case, King pointedly employs comic strategies to shift the social awareness of those reading

Medicine River. The drunk Indian is exposed as a sick Indian, and Will's unquestioning acceptance of the negative construct becomes the object of laughter. Thus, King inverts conventional paradigms in a playful and often surprising manner, designed to make readers laugh by catching them off guard and presenting a set of unexpected incongruities. He also uses comedy to pose questions about readers' willingness to follow Will's lead without first examining his claims. Laughter may be liberating or corrective, apologetic or derisive, but, at least in the case of King, it comes with a certain responsibility, namely to understand the power relations that underlie a comic text and to consider both whom that laughter serves and whom it may hurt.

Pairing the Comic and the Tragic

Not surprisingly, the ability to interweave comic and serious perspectives is central to the work of many Native North American writers. In an interview with Laura Coltelli, Paula Gunn Allen explains how and why serious issues are so often part of contemporary Native comic texts: 'There's this tradition of humor, of an awful lot of funniness, and then there's this history of death. And when the two combine, you get a power in the work; that is, it moves into another dimension ... And so when you laugh you know perfectly well that you are laughing at death' (Coltelli 22). The legacy of attempted extermination, which has shaped the history of Indians on both sides of the forty-ninth parallel, casts a dark shadow over Native comedic traditions, but it also justifies and strengthens First Nations' wills to survive and flourish.

Blending the comic and the tragic is a Native tradition that existed long before colonization. As Leslie Marmon Silko, when describing Laguna tales, points out, 'often in the stories there will be a movement toward a balance – the funny with the serious – and this goes back ... to the Creation' (cited in Lincoln 31). Thus, comedy, tinged with seriousness, provides a platform on which to rebuild tribal communities, while retaining traditional links to the past and preserving valuable aspects of pre-contact cultural beliefs.

The communal nature of Native societies and the Eurocentric perception of Indians as 'tragic' have shaped the manner in which comedy is tempered by authors like King. Vizenor describes the power of the comic spirit within Native communities and speculates on why, historically, non-Native critics have assumed that Indians possess a predominantly tragic vision of life:

... tribal cultures are *comic* or mostly comic. Yet they have been interpreted as tragic by social scientists ... Not tragic because they're 'vanishing' or something like that, but tragic in their worldview – and they're *not* tragic in their worldview ... In a tragic worldview people are rising above everything. And you can characterize Western patriarchal monotheistic manifest-destiny civilization as tragic. It doesn't mean that they're bad, but they're tragic because of acts of isolation, their heroic acts of conquering something, always overcoming adversity, doing *better than* whatever ... usually doing it alone and almost always at odds with nature. Part of that, of course, is the idea of the human being's divine creation as superior. The comic spirit is not an opposite but it might as well be. You can't act in a comic way in isolation. You have to be included. There has to be a collective of some kind. ('Follow' 295)

By focusing on group interaction, rather than the supremacy of a single individual, Native writers move away from hierarchical models of thinking and, instead, focus on the collaborative, communal possibilities that comedy creates and sustains. Yet what is 'tragic,' as Vizenor puts it, remains an integral part of these same texts precisely because of the desire to find a balance between extremes and to acknowledge both the celebratory and disturbing aspects of Native North American tribal histories.

The seriousness of Native comedy is not surprising, given the comments of Allen and Silko. It also coheres with Freud's famous study *Jokes and Their Relation to the Unconscious* (1907), in which the psychoanalyst contends that humour involves the repudiation of suffering:

Humour can be regarded as the highest of these defensive processes. It scorns to withdraw the ideational content bearing the distressing affect from conscious attention as repression does, and thus surmounts the automatism of defence. It brings this about by finding a means of withdrawing energy from the release of unpleasure that is already in preparation and of transforming it, by discharge, into pleasure. (233)

In a subsequent essay on 'Humour,' written in 1927, Freud broadens his primarily economic view of humour to show how it, too, can be a form of liberation. As he explains, 'The grandeur in it [humour] clearly lies in the triumph of narcissism, the victorious assertion of the ego's invulnerability' (428–9). Humour becomes, in this context, 'rebellious' and 'signifies ... the triumph of ... the pleasure principle, which is able here to assert itself against the unkindness of the real circumstances' (429). Freud's observations about humour are particularly relevant when he notes that, while 'humorous pleasure ... never finds vent in hearty laughter,' humour remains 'especially liberating and elevating' precisely because it mediates conflicting emotions and allows those who create humour to challenge the status quo (432).

In this latter essay, Freud returns to the concept of what he calls 'Galgenhumor' or gallows humour, first mentioned in his 1907 study, in which a rogue, being led to his execution on a Monday morning, remarks, 'This week's beginning nicely' (229). The rogue's comment deliberately disregards the uniqueness of this Monday morning – the date of his death – and demonstrates his refusal to give in to the fear and sadness one would expect. Likewise, the audience who hears the joke is, according to Freud, 'infected by the rogue's indifference,' and laughs off whatever pity might have been invoked initially (286). The ability to find pleasure through pain, to look beyond the conventional reaction to such bleak situations as Native genocide, explains why so many First Nations writers blend the comic and the tragic in their works. The texts produced by these authors take Freud's psychoanalytic reading a step further by exploring the pain *and* pleasure of a situation in which Natives, in particular, have been relegated to the underclass, or left for dead. Rather than presenting an exclusively tragic scenario or reducing the depiction of individuals and tribes to a formulaic narrative of destruction and extermination, however, authors like King place tragic issues within a comic framework that invites action and encourages imaginative play. Without losing sight of the so-called serious or potentially tragic aspects of their narratives, these writers recognize and exploit the 'psychic' wealth of comedy for a number of purposes: to entertain; to draw readers into the mindset of the narrator and/or characters; to offer another perspective on the world; and to affirm the strengths of a community by dispelling animosity between groups of people (Lincoln 46).

King himself is someone who is situated 'in-between' fixed identities, and thus his alteration and merging of genres reflects his efforts to create and maintain a liminal space that both acknowledges the historical struggles of Native peoples and also examines their day-to-day lives. Such a blend of the comic and the tragic resists a simple replication of conventional notions of 'Nativeness' and retains an awareness of Native history. By cultivating a healthy balance between the comic and the serious, King's texts employ the same survival tactics that have characterized

Native communities for centuries. His writings affirm Deloria's assertion that 'one of the best ways to understand a people is to know what makes them laugh. Laughter encompasses the limits of the soul' (146).

Using comedy to ensure a population's survival and affirm the bonds of a community characterizes the work of many different ethnic[1] minority writers; however, studies of the kinds of comic strategies employed by minority authors are virtually non-existent. Most examinations of ethnic humour involve 'jokes directed against the out-group by the in-group, or by one out-group against another, or "self-deprecating" jokes told by members of the group itself' (Lowe, 'Theories' 439). These jokes ensure that the group in power retains control. The desire to be taken seriously has likely precluded extensive studies of the comic texts produced by ethnic minorities: if being 'funny indicates a lack of seriousness,' it is not surprising that authors and scholars who write from a marginalized perspective or study the works of minority authors often avoid discussing comedy (439), for to do so is to threaten the credibility of the community and the artist. Nonetheless, as Lowe points out, humour 'is absolutely central to our conception of the world' and proves especially useful to those minorities who have 'shortened and sweetened' the struggle to achieve 'full citizenship' by making 'up their minds to enter laughing' (439).

Comic laughter becomes an important part of identity formation for ethnic minorities by establishing boundaries between those who 'get' the joke and laugh, and those who do not.[2] Such laughter, according to Konrad Lorenz, 'forms a bond and simultaneously draws a line' (253). But this line continually changes as ethnic identities are reformulated to accommodate different concerns and groups within the larger population. King is particularly skilled at manipulating and revising the boundaries between Natives and non-Natives; he plays with a combination of commonalities and differences that reflect the multiple dimensions of a person's identity (constituted by race, sexuality, religious beliefs, gender, class, and ethnicity). King's works bring disparate groups of characters together, and instil respect for the individuality of various tribes and communities, each with its own heritage. The problems of approaching comedy in this manner are described by Lowe, who notes that 'ethnic humorists, when writing for both ethnic and nonethnic audiences, are in one sense walking a high wire aesthetically, subject to falling into disfavor with their ethnic group on the one side, and with the dominant culture on the other' (440). However, Lowe further suggests that by taking such risks, minority writers also maximize the possibility of permeating the mainstream and interacting with audiences who might not otherwise be aware of, or willing to listen to, minority perspectives. Through employing an apparently disarming approach and utilizing aspects of a well-known genre, King creates a buffer zone of sorts for audiences, who may find the subject and viewpoints offered up in his texts to be otherwise unfamiliar and potentially disconcerting.

Some critics of King have suggested that to appeal to a broader cross-section of readers via comedy creates another set of contradictions. The Native writer who successfully markets him- or herself to a non-Native audience – a pragmatic move given the difficulties of finding a publisher for Indian-authored texts (especially when written in a tribal language) – runs the risk of obviating differences between the two groups and merely affirming similarities. As Daniel Francis explains, in his study of how many non-Natives have represented Indian culture within Canada, 'the "exceptional Indian"' is one who 'plays ... a dual role. He or she is an interpreter and defender of Native culture. At the same time, by succeeding so well as a White Man's Indian, the "exceptional Indian" implicitly confirms the superiority of White society' (129). King's comic strategy and pan-Indian status may be seen as an easy way to win non-Native readers over and to avoid some of the more serious and pressing issues facing specific tribal communities in Canada and the United States. Yet, to dismiss King's brand of comedy as simply a means of reaching a broader audience is to miss the complexities of his work, which continually walks a tightrope between inclusion and exclusion.

In particular, King's novels, short stories, poems, and other writings possess an 'edge' or 'bite' that links the author to humorists of other ethnicities and races who use comedy, especially when blended with aspects of tragedy, to expose oppressive ideologies, subvert conventional assumptions, and acknowledge the challenges of representing a minority perspective (Hutcheon, *Irony's Edge* 26; Lincoln 26). Rather than simply offering comic texts that follow standard generic formulations, these writers incorporate oppositional techniques that alter the expected outcome of the plot, and reflect the particular cultural and linguistic heritages of their communities. For example, King adds an ironic dimension to his comic works, which enables him to continually undercut the dominance of Eurocentric assumptions without simply installing another equally inflexible structure. Moreover, this ironic aspect of his texts foregrounds his own status as a writer who lives and circulates between several cultures and regularly crosses national borders and boundaries.

The presence of irony in King's works is not surprising. Irony is an important aspect of 'trickster discourse' and has been recognized as a defining feature of Native North American writing. The trickster, for example, binds contradictions together, bringing 'chaos and order, sacred and profane, farce and meaning ... food and waste ... play and reality' into the same realm (Sullivan 238). As with comic incongruities, irony usually involves the layering of different perspectives to create a double voice or vision. Allan Rodway's photographic analogy is helpful in this respect: 'irony is not merely a matter of seeing a "true" meaning beneath a "false," but of seeing a double exposure ... on one plate' (113).

When paired, humour and irony generate texts with linguistic and situational incongruities that encourage readers to negotiate multiple – often conflicting – perspectives, to interpret the work without necessarily reaching any definitive answers, and to take pleasure in this challenge. Ironic humour, as Michael Fischer calls it, is a sophisticated mode of discourse that 'deconstruct[s] and comment[s] upon itself' (224; Babcock, 'Arrange' 124). Together, humour and irony facilitate cognitive play and, as we will see in later chapters, allow King to avoid simply lecturing his audience. Instead, he offers readers an opportunity to participate in the making of various different texts. Comedy, in this case, may be fun, but it is also sustained by the author's refusal to 'serve a symbolic agenda' that is not his own or to play Indian by adhering to a non-Native version of a comedy (Atwood 250).

King's comic vision also reworks a variety of generic conventions, including the Western linearity of most comedies. In 'Godzilla vs. Post-Colonial,' King lists some of the key characteristics that he sees as distinguishing the wide range of Native-authored texts produced in Canada and the United States. These descriptions are especially helpful when looking at how King deviates from, inverts, or alters comedy as a genre. One of the terms he proposes bears direct relevance to our readings of King's texts: what he calls 'associational literature,' or 'the body of literature that has been created, for the most part, by contemporary Native writers' (14). As he explains:

Associational literature, most often, describes a Native community ... [c]oncentrating ... on the daily activities and intricacies of Native life and organizing the elements of plot along a rather flat narrative line that ignores the ubiquitous climaxes and resolutions that are so valued in non-Native literature. In addition to this flat narrative line, associational literature leans towards the group rather than the single, isolated character, creating a fiction that de-values heroes and villains in favour of members of a community, a fiction which eschews judgements and conclusions. (14)

King's description of associational literature elucidates why some aspects of his own texts (e.g., a non-linear plot-line, the lack of focus on individual characters) do not conform to established comic models like Frye's.

Although the hero and heroine of a traditional Eurocentric comic plot may take centre stage, comedy tends to be an inclusive rather than an exclusive vision of societal harmony; 'as many people as possible' are brought into the plot at its conclusion, either through reconciliation or conversion (Frye 165). Some comedies depend upon the 'blocking characters,' rather than the protagonists, to amuse and delight the audience. In a comedy of manners, for instance, the 'technical hero and heroine are not often very interesting people,' and hence audiences shift their attention to the cast of characters, whose actions are far more absurd and memorable (167). Similarly, most of King's comic texts lack a single, clear protagonist. His heroes and heroines, if they can even be called that, do not adhere to traditional roles. Instead, the relationships among various community members form a web of interactions that are potentially funny.

In his book *Indi'n Humor*, Lincoln claims that, generally, 'Native [North] American patterns appear more cyclical, periodic, and composite – less historically progressive, less personally transformational, less structurally end-stopped' (32). In other words, the outcome of a traditional comedy, with the emergence of a 'new society,' signalled by a festival or marriage ceremony, calls for an ending that is not usually part of Native-authored texts. King's *Medicine River*, for example, undercuts the typical conclusion of a comedy. The desire of young lovers to be together, a wish that is fulfilled in many formulaic versions of comic texts, is replaced by a somewhat different scenario in *Medicine River*. The so-called heroine of King's text is an independent woman, Louise Heavyman, who dates Will, a local photographer, but remains ambivalent about marriage or even the possibility of living together. In the latter part of the novel, Louise enlists Will's help to buy a house, a gesture that Harlen perceives as an invitation for Will to act: 'You've got to get moved in right away, Will. Women have a way of taking over. Man's got to mark out his territory or there won't be anything left. You give your notice yet?' (226). When Louise finally purchases a home, it has a darkroom that both Harlen and Will mistakenly assume is 'symbolic' of her interest in Will (233). Ironically, however, Louise has the darkroom torn out to make room for another bathroom, and thus inverts the masculine assumption that she has purchased the home for her lover. Even in its final pages, the text resists traditional comic closure: Louise rejects a marriage proposal from Harold, the father of her little girl, South Wing, whom she is raising on her own, and Will spends Christmas Day alone. Although Will plays with the musical top he is giving to South Wing, a loving gesture that reverses his own father's numerous promises to deliver toys that never appeared, the 'marriage' plot remains unresolved and lacks the kind of overtly celebratory conclusion of a conventional comedy. Here, closure is provisional and tentative, rather than festive and clearly defined by marriage.

Associational Literature and Native Languages

For King, associational literature, comic or otherwise, is empowering for Native audiences because 'it reinforces the notion that, in addition to the usable past that the concurrence of oral literature and traditional history provide us with, we also have an active present marked by cultural tenacity and a viable future' ('Godzilla' 14). Although a contemporary Native storyteller is self-appointed, and does not necessarily participate in 'a traditionally sanctioned manner in *sustaining the community*' (Weaver 42), the commitment to a living First Nations culture and the ability to transform oral practices into written texts demonstrate the strong ties between the past and the present. The form and subject matter of the stories may have changed, but the sustained interest in generating narratives that begin between and on the borders of the oral and the written is a powerful reflection of the continued relevance of story to Native peoples. In particular, by incorporating oral storytelling techniques and structures into written texts, authors like King can cultivate the comic aspects of those narratives, which originally were a significant part of the interactions of the storyteller and the audience. One of the most effective ways to affirm the existence of a tribal community is to relay stories in a Native language or dialect. Lowe points out that 'ethnic writers' pride in folkspeech stems from their ... awareness that dialect is rich, humorous, laden with metaphor, and therefore tactile and appealing' (448). Moreover, since 'dialect, at least to the oppressor, is part and parcel of the negative stereotype, pride in dialect constitutes inversion, transforming an oppressive signifier of otherness into a pride-inspiring prism' (448). King's works follow this model by including phrases from the Cherokee language in selected texts (e.g., *Green Grass, Running Water, Truth and Bright Water*) and using a dialect version of 'red English' throughout his writings (Lincoln 15).

Influenced by the stories of Harry Robinson, a member of the Okanagan tribe, whose narratives create an 'oral syntax,' which 'encourages readers to read the stories out loud' (King, 'Godzilla' 13), King plays tricks with the written word in order to retain this oral tradition and to sustain a comic vision through his use of language.[3] Robinson's ability to create 'the sense of an oral storytelling voice in a written form' provides an important model for King's own work, and challenges Eurocentric distinctions between literary genres (King, 'Peter Gzowski' 72). By re-ordering sentence structure, repeating key words and phrases, incorporating idioms and puns, employing 'irregular grammar, reverse twists on standard English,' and sticking primarily to present-tense 'terse' sentences, in which subjects and verbs do not always agree (Lincoln 15–16), King creates texts that incorporate traditional Native storytelling techniques and offer modern responses to the challenge of straddling the Native and non-Native worlds, especially when English is perceived as the dominant language. As Blanca Chester explains, 'King's translation of oral performance into writing reveal[s] the complexity of the relationship between the English language and Native cultures. King uses the English language to translate Native worldview' (54). This translation between 'the oral and the written suggests the same kinds of meaningful displacements that occur in the translation between different languages' (54).

King's comedy, at the level of language, derives primarily from the incongruities between conventional English and his non-standard renderings of it. The richness of this linguistic play is evident throughout his works. In *Green Grass, Running Water,* for instance, the biblical Adam is renamed 'Ahdamn,' signifying his literal damnation (33). The repetition of certain phrases at the beginning of the novel signal its circularity ('And here's how it happened'); the interweaving of multiple stories in short vignettes create an interactive, dialogic experience for readers; and the use of dialect throughout conveys a sense of orality. The opening lines of *Green Grass, Running Water* exemplify this skilful reworking of English:

So.

In the beginning, there was nothing. Just the water.

Coyote was there, but Coyote was dreaming. That Coyote was asleep
and that Coyote was dreaming. When that Coyote dreams, anything can
happen.

I can tell you that. (1)

The comic aspects of these opening lines derive from the colloquial
tone of the text, which replicates, on paper, the feel of a spoken narrative. Phrases and individual words blend into a pattern of repetition and
revision that tests some of the laws of English grammar and, thus, literally enacts, at the level of language, the idea that 'anything can happen'
(1). What makes these lines funny is their deliberate irregularity and
twisting of conventions as well as the creation of a speaking voice, which
invites immediate interaction but may not tell the tale readers expect
to hear. This use of language reflects both 'a trickster's tolerance for
deviance and a survivalist's native humor' (Lincoln 12). Language, especially when used to create a comic vision of the world, brings the community together and affirms tribal bonds, even when breaking the rules
of logic and order.

Discourses of the 'Other'

As studies of comedy have begun to acknowledge the contributions of
women and ethnic minority writers, discourse has become an important
focus of discussion. Our examination of King's work is no exception.
Language is a means of attaining 'full subjectivity' (Purdie 128), of creating a cultural context, and giving meaning(s) to the world in which
one lives. However, access to this tool of self-definition has been repeatedly denied to women and other 'abjected groups,' including Native
peoples (128–9). In her aptly titled book *Comedy: The Mastery of Discourse,*
Susan Purdie argues that 'jokers' are the '"masters" of discourse'
because they are 'able to break and keep the basic rule of language' (5).
Accordingly, 'joking not only effects immediate discursive control but
also appropriates wider power ... by denying other people's behaviour
such propriety when they form the Butt of a joke' (5). When Purdie
turns to an examination of comic texts and their language, she is primarily concerned with the patriarchal dimensions of discursive authority,
which underlie traditional comedies and ensure a return to a particular

kind of social order (where Eurocentric and decidedly patriarchal perspectives prevail).

Purdie never specifically mentions Native comedy, yet her interest in how discursive power can be used to create or impose a definition of what is right and real proves useful in our study of King. Notably, King's works employ discourse (or language-in-use) to deconstruct the exclusivity of various Eurocentric viewpoints. His narratives offer a vision of reality that is mixed with the actuality experienced by the Native characters. The more recent novels establish a different set of boundaries around language access. Cherokee words and phrases frame the four sections of *Green Grass, Running Water* and thus cultivate an 'in-group' of readers who are familiar with this Native language and can comprehend its significance in the context of King's narrative. Each section begins with a colour (red, white, black, blue) and a cardinal direction (North West, East, South) written in Cherokee, which represent the four sacred directions of the earth and the cycle of life, giving a symbolic circularity to the novel that complements the various levels of narrative.[4] Even the Cherokee divination ritual, which the four Native figures recite to get the story 'right,' appears in King's text in Cherokee, without any explanation or translation (10–11). This ritual, which involves observing the direction that pine needles take when floating on water, becomes a way to read the future that is privy only to those familiar with Cherokee tribal practices. The ceremony cunningly subverts the fixity of Western history in its official (meaning written) form by focusing on the possibilities yet to come, possibilities that English may not have the capacity to inscribe or explain. Moreover, the ritual is invoked after several failed attempts to use clichéd dominant narrative formulas, including '*A long time ago in a faraway land*' (8) and the first line of Genesis ('In the beginning'), to mark the beginning of the story. As Ishmael notes when the Lone Ranger quotes the Bible, 'That's the wrong story ... That story comes later' (10). In this case, language becomes a way to reorder time and historical priority. By pre-empting English with Cherokee, the Native runaways can begin to relay their own, Native-centred version of the past, present, and future.

This linguistic technique, known as 'code-switching,' is an 'indirect form of social commentary' that allows for an ironic redefinition of what constitutes the dominant group (Basso 9). In this case, it is English-speaking readers who remain excluded from full participation in the novel, an ironic reversal or inversion of the linguistic hierarchical relationship, relegating English speakers to the status of 'outsiders.'

Such discursive moves form the focus of the next chapter, which looks at how inversions and reversals, at the level of language and narrative conventions, are an important part of King's comic technique, particularly when read in relation to performativity. If comedy, as Purdie suggests, is dependent upon the ownership of discourse, how does King use his own 'trickster discourse' to overthrow dominant paradigms, shift power relations, and present counter-narratives, without resorting to an overtly polemical stance or abrogating the playful aspects of his works?

CHAPTER TWO

Comic Inversions

As King's works suggest, counter-narratives or, in Lipsitz's terms, 'counter-memories' are forceful means of opening discourse to question. That is, shifting the terms of homogeneous narratives can unsettle their seeming 'normality,' at the same time that it can create a space, as de Certeau has noted, for interrogating and re-imag(in)ing their production. Relying upon the inversion of such constructions, the comic surface of King's fictions enables pointed political critiques.

Through their counter-narratives, King's texts work to overturn the dominant discursive field. In theoretical terms, Foucault argues that this is a crucial step in disrupting master-narratives:

> Discourses are not once and for all subservient to power or raised up against it, any more than silences are. We must make allowance for the complex and unstable process whereby discourse can be both an instrument and an effect of power, but also a hindrance, a stumbling-block, a point of resistance and a starting point for an opposing strategy. Discourse transmits and produces power; it reinforces it, but it also undermines and exposes it, renders it fragile and makes it possible to thwart it. (100–1)

Here, the focus of the original discourse is thrown into relief through the inversion, which highlights the terms of the 'normative' constructions and then employs those terms to assert an oppositional statement.

King's strategy often depends upon the recognition of dominant discourse conventions, and their systematic overturning and refashioning. The resulting counter-narrative serves a political purpose quite different from the movement of the originary discourse, for it comprises a 'taking back' gesture that redirects the trajectory of the initial formulation. Since, read on its own, a counter-narrative does not change or reconfigure anything, its very efficacy depends upon readerly recognition of the inversion it embodies. This inversion speaks back to an existent situation and must be placed in context because it is a response, not an assertion on its own. It should be noted, therefore, that counter-discourse is not in itself a subversive gesture – it can be articulated by the marginalized, as outlined above, or by the dominant to suppress marginal voices.[1]

Because discourses are not stable or simplistic constructions, easily recognized and categorized, their cultural location and political intent require analysis. As Foucault argues:

> There is not, on the one side, a discourse of power, and opposite it, another discourse that runs counter to it. Discourses are tactical elements or blocks operating in the field of force relations; there can exist different and even contradictory discourses within the same strategy; they can, on the contrary, circulate without changing their form from one strategy to another, opposing strategy ... [W]e must question them [discourses] on the two levels of their tactical productivity (what reciprocal effects of power and knowledge they ensure) and their strategical integration (what conjunction and what force relationship make their utilization necessary in a given episode of the various confrontations that occur). (101–2)

Given that discourse can be used to resist or to assert a dominant norm, the placement and the operation of discursive constructions need to be unpacked to assess their cultural implications. This is not to suggest that these formulations cannot be read oppositionally by different readers; readers can always read 'against the grain.' However, the two levels Foucault highlights in the above quotation – 'tactical productivity' and 'strategical integration' – help to locate the primary movement of the discourse in question. They point to the motivation and, hence, the direction of the interventionist strategies.

The level of 'strategical integration' (or the reasons why a counter-discourse is necessary and what it accomplishes) clarifies some of the critical divisions effected by Native (and other anti-hegemonic) writings. King's work, for example, is 'talking back' to a dominant discourse that has demeaned, trivialized, and even demonized Natives. The efficacy of the reverse discourse depends upon the cultural placement of the speakers (a Native writer speaking back to racist conventions) and on the recognizability of this counter-movement.

In King's texts, counter- or reverse discourse is employed in a number
of ways. Some passages play upon Eurocentric assumptions about Native
culture and invert them in order to dislocate commonly held White perceptions; some play 'tricks' on readers; some create an 'inside' and an
'outside' readership ('sides' that are rendered permeable). These various strategies will be explained in more detail below, but it should be
noted, at this point, that their execution makes the texts accessible at
the same time that it allows for performative political critiques.

Green Grass, Running Water, for example, plays upon presumptions of
Native habits and turns them to advantage by reversing pervasive stereotypes. Commonly held beliefs are rearticulated clearly within the text,
and their readerly recognizability renders their inversion all the more
forceful. In one of the magic realist interludes that inflect *Green Grass,
Running Water*, Thought Woman floats ashore, accompanied by Coyote,
and meets A.A. Gabriel. Gabriel promptly hands her a business card that
identifies him, on one side, as a spy employed by the Canadian Security
and Intelligence Service and, on the other, as the 'Heavenly Host.'
When he flips the card to the side that identifies him as a servant of
God, the card itself begins to sing:

'I know that song,' says Coyote. 'Hosanna da, in-in the highest, hosanna da
forever ...'
'You got the wrong song,' I says. 'This song goes "Hosanna da, our home
on Natives' land."'
'Oh,' says Coyote, 'That song.' (226)

This passage pointedly reorders the words of 'O Canada' and flips them
to make a political statement about the land on which 'Canada' stands,
land that was originally settled by Natives and then taken from them as
part of the colonial endeavour. More broadly, King's representation of
A.A. Gabriel's card suggests that the White, patriarchal, and nationalist
agenda that led to the colonization of Native peoples throughout Canada clearly parallels the White-dominated, masculinist hierarchy of the
Judeo-Christian Church. Shortly after the singing of this ironically
altered version of the Canadian national anthem, A.A. Gabriel asks for
Thought Woman's name and proceeds to substitute the name Mary – an
allusion to the Virgin Mary – into his entry. He then quizzes Thought
Woman about her social insurance number, whether she possesses firearms, cigarettes, or alcohol, and if she has ever been associated with the
American Indian Movement, all questions commonly posed by border

guards at the Canadian-U.S. border. But the nationalist discourse that underlies Gabriel's queries quickly shifts focus when he insists that Thought Woman sign a 'Virgin verification form' and then has her pose for a photograph next to a snake – acts that allude both to the birth of Jesus, who was produced through immaculate conception, and Eve's fall into temptation in the garden of Eden when lured by the snake to eat an apple (226). Here, the value granted to Eurocentric Christian paradigms is shown to be ludicrous in the eyes of many Native peoples, who see through a rhetoric that justifies the subordination of ethnic minorities and women based on religious principles and nationalist ideologies.[2] Thought Woman refuses to be party to either and inverts the standard, sexist presumption that 'no' means 'yes' in order to prove her point:

> So, says A.A. Gabriel, you really mean yes, right?
> No, says Thought Woman.
> But that's the wrong answer, says A.A. Gabriel. Let's try this again.
> Let's not, says Thought Woman, and that one gets back in the water. (227)

In keeping with the theme of inversion, one of the characters in the novel, Latisha Red Dog Morningstar, runs a restaurant that she calls the 'Dead Dog Café.' As the narrator explains:

> Latisha would like to have been able to take all the credit for transforming the Dead Dog from a nice local establishment with a loyal but small clientele to a nice local establishment with a loyal but small clientele *and* a tourist trap. But, in fact, it had been her auntie's idea.
>
> 'Tell them it's dog meat,' Norma had said. 'Tourists like that kind of stuff.'
>
> That had been the inspiration. Latisha printed up menus that featured such things as Dog du Jour, Houndburgers, Puppy Potpourri, Hot Dogs, Saint Bernard Swiss Melts, with Doggie Doos and Deep-Fried Puppy Whatnots for appetizers. (92)

This passage depicts White assumptions about Native culture, and then effectively pokes fun at (and 'cashes in' on) them. Through puns and the deliberately provocative renaming of traditional Native foods, Latisha plays with the English language as she simultaneously entices and mocks her non-Native clientele. Latisha's menu manifests a counter-discourse in action: the assumptions of the dominant discourse are already culturally inscribed, and the texts play upon these inscriptions and overturn them, thereby opening them to question.

Telling Tales

More sustained critiques are effected in various passages in King's works, which expand singular flips or inversions into counter- or reverse discourse. That is, the texts not only play upon dominant discursive constructions but also offer their own oppositional accounts. Stories are told and retold, or in some cases, pointedly not told at all. In *Medicine River*, for instance, Lionel James, a Native elder, travels all over the world to tell stories:

> 'You know, sometimes I tell stories about today, about some of the people, on the reserve right now ... But those people in Germany and Japan and France and Ottawa don't want to hear those stories. They want to hear stories about how Indians used to be. I got some real good stories, funny ones, about how things are now, but those people say, no, tell us about the olden days. So I do.' (172–3)

This bittersweet episode not only points to the ways in which Natives are slotted into the past and erased from the present, a typical tactic of Canadian and American government assimilation policies, but also demonstrates Lionel's performative strategy. If old stories are what the Whites want to hear – those are the stories he will tell. Like Latisha, he thereby 'profits' through the telling of the tales, even though these are not the tales he wants to relate. In King's novel, the very absence of the tale that is not told assumes far more importance than those that Lionel recounts, generating a desire, on the part of the reader, to hear that which is lost.

In a similar fashion, lost tales about 'origin' are refigured and inserted into the texts. The master-narratives of Christianity provide a rich field for subversion in King's works, which proceed to demonstrate the exclusivity of Christian constructions. In *Green Grass, Running Water*, Christian mythology is resituated when the Native elders and Coyote attempt to tell counter-na(rra)tive versions of the creation story. The inherent racism and sexism embedded in the myths are highlighted as they are retold. When Old Woman helps calm the waves for Young Man Walking on Water, he rejects her assistance, and his response underscores the masculinist basis of Christianity:

Hooray, says those men. We are saved.

Hooray, says Young Man Walking on Water. I have saved you.

Actually, says those men, that other person saved us.

Nonsense, says Young Man Walking on Water. That other person is a woman. That other person sings songs to waves.

That's me, says Old Woman.

A woman? says those men. Sings songs to waves? They says that, too.

That's me, says Old Woman. That's me.

By golly, says those men. Young Man Walking on Water must have saved us after all. We better follow him around.

Suit yourself, says Old Woman. (293)

As Thomas Matchie and Brett Larson explain, King stages a confrontation between Old Woman and the New Testament Christ, and 'updates the Gospel story where Christ takes the Apostles out into a boat and then calms the water so that his disciples believe in him' (162). In King's novel, a Native version of this story is told, one that undermines the control Christians assume they have over the origins of the world. In turn, however, when, in the same text, Coyote helps Alberta Frank, his assistance, too, is treated cautiously by the Native elders: '"I was helpful, too," says Coyote. "That woman who wanted a baby. Now, that was helpful." "Helpful!" said Robinson Crusoe. "You remember the last time you did that?" ... "We haven't straightened out *that* mess yet," said Hawkeye' (348).

The use of Coyote in the above passage exemplifies the ways in which King's texts utilize counter-narratives to embody 'tricksterish' elements – elements that are part of the 'trickster discourse' that characterizes Native storytelling in its oral and written forms. The trickster is, itself, a Native performer of those strategies labelled by scholars as 'counter-discourse,' 'reverse discourse,' 'counter-memory,' or 'counter-narratives,' terms denoting the deployment of dominant discourse conventions other-wise. Trickster stories serve several important functions in Native communities: for example, they offer an 'outlet for voicing protest,' provide a source of entertainment and release, and can provoke a 'reexamination of existing conditions ... [which may lead] to change' (Babcock-Abrahams 183). These narratives, by 'effecting an inversion of ... assumed values ... expose "the arbitrary quality of social rank"' and other measures of 'difference' that have oppressed Native peoples (183). If comedy is, according to Matchie and Larson, 'less about loss than it is survival ... that is why the role of the trickster is so important' (164–5). In this context, trickster stories like King's serve a corrective function and vent social tensions, even as they test the boundaries of propriety and amuse audiences. But more broadly, by inverting and reversing audience expectations and assumptions, King's writings, as a whole, perform as tricksters which lure (at least many readers) into believing one thing at their own expense. Often King's fictions exploit commonly held constructions in order to generate laughter on the part of the unsuspecting reader

'One Good Story, That One' is a reversal of both the Genesis myth and a trickster tale. Its trickster nature highlights the trick embedded in Genesis, which is manifested in God's testing of Adam and Eve. The tricks in King's text, however, are apparent on several levels. The story itself is a trickster tale in that it deceives the reader, who comes to understand that what is presented is not a Native legend, but an inversion of the Genesis myth. The narrator becomes a trickster when she tricks the White anthropologists who come to hear her story. Within the story, Ah-damn is tricked by Coyote, a trickster figure with whom the narrator associates herself in the conclusion, and the trick is in the tale, itself, which is able to pluralize Genesis.

'One Good Story, That One' begins with the narrator preparing to tell her story. The time-frame of the narrative is indicative of her philosophy since it does not move from one point to another in a direct line. It has no specific (or overriding) purpose (or Truth). It is merely a good story. The narrator is visited by her friend, Napiao, and 'those ones': 'You know, they come to my place. Summer place, pretty good place, that one. Those ones, they come with Napiao, my friend' (3). 'Those ones' are the White anthropologists who have come to hear a Native story. That they are White is an important element in the text, and the narrator perceives their colour as exclusive: 'Napiao comes with those three. Whiteman, those. No Indianman. No Chinaman. No Frenchman. Too bad, those' (3). The absence of colour, here, is significant because it emphasizes the Whiteness of the anthropologists, and highlights the racially specific nature of their perspective. The views of the anthropologists, which are 'bereft' of colour, are identified as distinctively White, and hence not universal at all. In this way, the tale suggests that there are many different ways of viewing, and that this is but one of them.

The anthropologists ask to hear a story. They have not come to visit the narrator, but to gather information. The information they desire is of a particular sort, and the narrator, much like Lionel James, is unable to tell the story she wishes to tell. The anthropologists want to hear a 'traditional' narrative:

How about a story, that one says.

Sure, I says. Maybe about Jimmy runs the store near Two Bridges. His brother become dead and give Jimmy his car. But Jimmy never drives.

Napiao hold his hand up pretty soft. My friend says that good story, Jimmy and his car. Those ones don't know Jimmy. (4–5)

When the narrator is hindered from telling her tale, which becomes the 'real' Native tale absent from the narrative, she seemingly capitulates to the anthropologists' wishes. Yet she also subverts their efforts. What she tells is not an 'original' Native story at all, but a traditional Judeo-Christian story. Nonetheless, the tale that is to come is Native American in its neo-colonial play upon and subversion of the Judeo-Christian myth.

The tale begins with one person walking around, 'call him god' (5). God creates the world: 'They look around, and there is nothing. No grass. No fish. No trees. No mountains. No Indians, like I says. No white-man, either. Those come later, maybe one hundred years. Maybe not. That one god walk around, but pretty soon they get tired. Maybe that one says, we will get some stars. So he does. And then he says, maybe we should get a moon. So, they get one of them, too' (5). The slippage between singular and plural, here, suggests that god is both one and multiple. This slippage is also indicative of the narrator's reluctance to posit a source, a source from which everything else derives, and hence a source that is privileged. Although god is posited as the origin, his authority is undercut by the rest of the tale. Indeed, this god is not benevolent, but rather an acquisitive consumer.

The narrator begins her tale with a litany of names – in Cherokee, and then English – that highlight the ways in which White culture, as represented by god and Ah-damn, has tried to lay claim to everything:

Me-a-loo, call her deer.
Pa-pe-po, call her elk.
Tsling-ta, call her Blue-flower-berry.
Ga-ling, call her moon.
So-see-ka, call her flint.
A-ma-po, call her dog.
Ba-ko-zao, call her grocery story.
Pe-to-pa-zasling, call her television. (6)

In particular, Adam's naming in Genesis is an effort to incorporate what he sees into his discourse, thereby interpellating it into his ideology.[3]

This process is highlighted in the above passage, which moves from natural objects to specific products of White culture: 'grocery story' and 'television.' The narrator ironically points out: 'Pretty long list of things to get, that. Too many, maybe those ones say, how many more that one needs for world. So' (6).

Naming becomes important in 'One Good Story, That One,' and the Genesis characters are renamed in the narrator's story. Her tale plays upon the names of the Genesis text when Eve becomes Evening and Adam becomes Ah-damn. The two live in Evening's garden (as opposed to God's), which is 'pretty nice place, that one. Good tree. Good deer. Good rock. Good water. Good sky. Good wind. No grocery story, no television' (6). What follows inverts the order of the Genesis narrative. Whereas the traditional myth focuses on Adam, the Native text focuses on Evening, the female figure.

In 'One Good Story, That One,' it is Evening who is responsible for the movement of the story: 'That woman, Evening, she is curious, nosy, that one. She walk around the garden and she look everywhere. Look under rock. Look in grass. Look in sky. Look in water. Look in tree' (6–7). Evening's adventures lead her to a big tree: 'This one have lots of good things to eat. Have potato. Have pumpkin. Have corn. Have berries, all kind. Too many to say now' (7). And, as in the traditional story, this tree bears 'mee-so' or apples: 'This good tree also have some mee-so. Whiteman call them apples. This first woman look at the tree with the good things and she gets hungry. Make a meal in her head' (7).

Unlike Eve, Evening is not breaking a treaty (so to speak) with god, who has not told her that the tree is sacrosanct. She is hungry and she eats. Hence, in 'One Good Story, That One,' it is not Evening's desire but god's request that is disreputable: 'Leave that mee-so alone. Someone says that. Leave that mee-so alone. Leave that tree alone. The voice says that. Go away someplace else to eat! That one, god. Hello, he's back' (7). There is no ostensible reason for god's position, and Evening questions his dictate: 'Hey, says Evening, this is my garden' (7). In King's tale, god's infallibility is not an accepted fact, and the narrator's story both challenges god's authority and undercuts the idea that issuing commands, especially those regarding access to the riches of the natural world, constitutes acceptable behaviour. When god continues to threaten Evening, his conduct reflects poorly on him, not on her:

You watch out, says that one, pretty loud voice. Sort of shout. Bad temper, that one. Maybe like Harley James. Bad temper, that one. Always shouting.

Always with pulled-down mean look. Sometimes Harley come to town, drives his truck to town. Gets drunk. Drives back to that house. That one goes to town, get drunk, come home, that one, beat his wife. His wife leave. Goes back up north. Pretty mean one, that one. You boys know Harley James? Nobody there to beat up, now. Likes to shout, that one. (7)

Evening ignores god, whom she perceives as bad-tempered, and eats an apple. Since she 'is generous, Evening, good woman, that one,' she takes 'mee-so' to Ah-damn. Whereas, in Genesis, Adam is the noble father-figure and Eve is his appendage, in 'One Good Story, That One,' Ah-damn is held up to ridicule. While Evening is gathering food, Ah-damn is 'busy then, writing things down. All the animals' names he writes somewhere, I don't know. Pretty boring that' (7–8). In this passage, Ah-damn's affinity with White culture, which is written, is contrasted with Evening's affinity with Native culture, which is primarily oral and closely allied with nature.

King's story does prioritize Evening's perspective – 'Ah-damn not so smart like Evening, that one thinks Blue-flower-berry is animal, maybe' (7) – and, when the animals come by, the text undermines Ah-damn's position by casting him as the butt of a joke, coordinated by the trickster, Coyote. The narrator observes: 'That Ah-damn not so smart. Like Harley James, white man, those. Evening, she be Indian woman, I guess' (8). Evening, however, is not fooled by Coyote, and she 'come back. Hey, she says what are all these coyote tracks come around in a circle. Not so smart, Ah-damn, pretty hungry though' (8). This passage privileges the stance of Evening, the 'Indianwoman'; yet, when one bears in mind that this is a reverse discourse, a reinscription of master-narratives, the effects of the tale's prioritization are mitigated and diffused.

'One Good Story, That One' reverses the order of the original myth in order to deflate it. It does not assert itself as Truth, as do biblical books like Genesis. What is important in this passage is that Evening feeds Ah-damn because he seems incapable of looking after himself. Since King's text posits Evening's actions as practical rather than seductive, it undercuts Eve's traditional role as *femme fatale*. In turn, while the story emphasizes Evening's practicality, it also throws god's conduct into question, especially when he becomes angry with her: 'You ate my mee-so, he says. Don't be upset, says Evening, that one, first woman. Many more mee-so back there. Calm down, watch some television, she says' (9).

God's position, here, when situated in a Native text and in light of Native history, effects another level of signification. There are enough apples for everyone, but god has decided they are his. His request lacks logic, for there is no reason behind it that is intelligible to Evening. When she ignores him, god asserts his power and ejects Evening and Ah-damn from what is Evening's garden: 'But they are upset and that one says that Evening and Ah-damn better leave that good place, garden, Evening's garden, go somewhere else' (9). King's text foregrounds the repercussions of such a gesture when the narrator wryly adds: 'Just like Indian today' (9). Evening accepts god's dictates, but Ah-damn wants to stay, and the narrator notes: 'But that fellow, god, whiteman I think, he says, you go too, you ate those mee-so, my mee-so' (9). God's Whiteness is highlighted, here, for the first time in the story, and this spotlights the parallel that exists between god's actions and the actions of White culture. Both issue edicts, and then both remove people who do not conform to them.

While King's text draws attention to certain elements of Genesis, it also elides or ignores others, and this contributes to the parodic nature of the story. When the narrator is concluding her tale, she adds, as an afterthought:

> There is also a Ju-poo-pea, whiteman call him snake. Don't know what kind. Big white one maybe, I hear, maybe black, something else. I forgot this part. He lives in tree with mee-so. That one try to get friendly with Evening so she stick a mee-so in his mouth, that one. Crawl back into tree. Have trouble talking, hissss, hissss, hissss, hissss. Maybe he is still there. Like that dead-river pig and Billy Frank lose his truck. (9)

The serpent loses its importance, therefore, just as God's wishes are trivialized, and the structure of Genesis is inverted. The two higher beings of Genesis, who manipulate Adam and Eve, are minimalized in 'One Good Story, That One.' Evening is not a pawn of the gods, although she is a victim of god's frivolous wishes and demands. God's manipulations are thrown into relief when he remains in Evening's garden with the serpent and, hence, shares in the traditional connotations of deceit and guile associated with snakes:

> Evening and Ah-damn leave. Everybody else leave, too. That tree leave, too. Just god and Ju-poo-pea together.
>   Ah-damn and Evening come out here. Have a bunch of kids.
>   So.
>   That's all. It is ended. (10)

Evening and Ah-damn leave Evening's garden, and leave behind the culture that has excluded them. The contest in 'One Good Story, That One' is not between good and evil, then, but between practicality and acquisitiveness. Whereas, in Genesis, Adam and Eve were tricked, for the Tree of Knowledge was God's test (or his trick), in King's text, the trick lies in the tale itself. The anthropologists, who have come to study a 'primitive' culture, get their information. At least, it appears this way when

> those men push their tape recorders, fix their cameras. All of those ones smile. Nod their head around. Look out window. Shake my hand. Make happy noises. Say goodbyes, see you later. Leave pretty quick. (10)

The anthropologists beat a hasty retreat after hearing the narrator's story. The purpose of their visit has been to collect a 'true' Native legend. But the joke is on them, since 'we watch them go, My friend, Napiao, put the pot on for some tea. I clean up all the coyote tracks on the floor' (10).

The tale thus deconstructs Genesis and tricks the unwary reader who has made the mistake of underestimating the narrator. Such a reader is implicated in the anthropologists' dismissal of her. The story is a hoax, as well as a good story, because its teller gets the last word. By transposing the biblical narrative, 'One Good Story, That One' foregrounds the monologism of Genesis and pluralizes it by opening it to include people of different colours and genders. King's tale foregrounds the culture- and gender-specificity of Genesis, and, as a result, it also draws attention to its own. 'One Good Story, That One' becomes an/other account, an account that is different, and an account that manifests an alternative to the singular and exclusive Truth of Genesis. In refusing to proffer itself as Truth, like the Bible, King's tale becomes more inclusive than the latter, and thus more indicative of the heteroglossia of Native culture.

Texts that utilize a trickster figure or tricksterish elements tend to create an 'inside' and an 'outside' readership: the 'inside' audience is aware of the trick at play, while the 'outside' falls prey to the trick. This effective strategy generates laughter on the part of those who have been 'had,' at the same time that it affirms the positions of the 'insiders.' Since, in King's case, the 'inside' readers are frequently social 'outsiders' (Natives) and the 'outside' constitutes cultural 'insiders' (non-Natives), the position of the 'insiders' is acknowledged because they are privy to the trick, and the 'outsiders' have their cultural familiarity disrupted over the course of the work. In this way, the strategy affirms the position of those who have been socially marginalized and ostracized. Providing both 'inside' and 'outside' looks at social constructions through the presentation of significant issues, the texts serve as springboards from which to examine dominant cultural assumptions and such issues as bigotry and stereotyping.

Rediscovering America/s

The 'discovery' of America is lampooned in a similar fashion in *Green Grass, Running Water* when four stolen cars resurface on a dam that has been erected on the Blackfoot reserve. Several of the Whites responsible for constructing the dam are the first to spot the cars, and immediately note their brand names: "'Let's see," said Lew. "There's a red Pinto. And ... a blue Toyota, no, no ... a Nissan, a blue Nissan. And a ... hey, that's nice. Look, it's a Karmann-Ghia. The white one. A convertible, too." "A Nissan, a Pinto, and a Karmann-Ghia?"' (339). These modern-day puns on the *Pinta*, the *Niña*, and the *Santa María* – the names of the ships used by Columbus – signal a repetition of the voyage, five hundred years later. The new tall ships sail into the dam and destroy it, thus generating a reversal of the paradigm implemented through the Columbus story, wherein the appearance of the tall ships led to the devastation of Native cultures. By 'taking back' the original narrative and playing upon it in order to effect the destruction of the dam, the text posits counter-memory as an effective strategy of resistance.

Additionally, through readerly identification with the main characters, King's works invite readers from all backgrounds to familiarize or re-familiarize themselves with the problems in question, thus rendering the 'outside' and the 'inside' permeable spaces.[4] Normative cultural artifacts like cookbooks are parodied when Lionel's mother, who loves to cook and to try new recipes, adapts her recipes to conform with the food she has on hand:

> The Hawaiian Curdle Surprise was a big surprise. Lionel didn't know exactly what was in it, but he was able to identify the pineapple and the fish ...
>
> 'I got the recipe out of the cookbook on Hawaiian cuisine that Harley gave me for Christmas. You're supposed to use octopus for the stock, but where are you going to find octopus around here? ... Moose works just as well.' (143)

Rather than feeling compelled to replicate the recipe exactly, Lionel's mother freely improvises with the ingredients according to her own cultural context, reversing the priority of the written word by producing her Native-inflected version of this traditional Hawaiian dish. Instead of positing herself as an 'outsider' in relation to Hawaiian culture, Lionel's mother adapts and reconfigures the recipe in a manner that confirms her 'insider' status, without excluding or dismissing the legitimacy of other versions of Hawaiian Curdle Surprise.

One of the means through which the fictions achieve a 'familiarity' with their readers, and thus bring 'outsiders' in, is through the use of a naïve protagonist. In *Medicine River*, Will Horse Capture inhabits both an inside and outside position. Will is part-Native, but has rejected his Native heritage and lived in the world beyond the reservation. Thus, when he returns to Medicine River, Will is introduced to various situations (and tricks) for which he falls – along with the unsuspecting reader. Readers are closest to Will because he narrates the story, and, thus, the sting of being 'had' is lessened (in that he is 'had' too), while the 'lesson' is highlighted. As already noted, Will hears rumours that Harlen Bigbear has resumed his drinking and accepts them as true. Like many readers, Will is caught within the dictates of the dominant discourse of alcoholic Natives.

In another example of the power of stereotypes, Will, near the beginning of the novel, learns about the 'suicide' of tribal member Pete Johnson from Floyd, a fellow player on the Medicine River Friendship Centre Warriors basketball team:

You knew Pete Johnson, didn't you?

Rodeo?

Yeah. Got busted up by a bull in Calgary. Couldn't rodeo any more, so he took up stock-car driving.

So?

So, he killed himself. Couldn't rodeo, wasn't much of a stock-car driver. One night he just drove his truck off Snake Coulee.

Floyd, I saw Pete last week.

What? ... Oh, yeah ... I remember now, it wasn't Pete, it was Jimmy Bruised Head.

Jimmy's in law school. (19)

Here, the presumption of high suicide rates on the reserve, a part of the dominant discourse that is accepted and recirculated by some members

of the Native community, becomes an object of ridicule. Will's response
to these rumours offers a cautionary tale for readers who might otherwise continue to cultivate the stereotype of the self-destructive Indian.
Will corrects Floyd twice and refuses to sustain the illusion of Natives as
a dying race. Nonetheless, he is repeatedly 'had' throughout *Medicine
River,* along with readers of the novel, for making similar assumptions
about Native peoples (such as Harlen Bigbear). The novel continually
reveals the ease with which such stereotypes circulate, and how they
need to be countered in order to break down the clichés that relegate
Natives to the status of 'outsider' or 'other.'

In this way, King's fictions employ conventions primarily used to marginalize Native characters in order to counter readers' perceptions. His
texts empower those disempowered by the originary formula. Many
writers take the subject of Native mistreatment as the topic of their
works, and, indeed, are most effective in their portrayal. King's works,
however, because they use comedy to convey the tragedies of Native life,
tend to attract a broader readership, and, thus, they expose a wider
audience to the plight of Native peoples. Whereas many political writings are dismissed as 'polemical,' King's fictions avoid this trap precisely
because of their comic approach. Comedy is the means through which
the political statement is made in these texts, which, as a result, avoid
the charges of 'proselytizing' often levied at critical writings. Rather
than being merely corrective, King's comic writing also entertains readers and draws them into the text, encouraging active participation and
enjoyment as Native stereotypes are pointedly debunked.

Refashioning Discourse

From a theoretical perspective, Teresa de Lauretis's argument, in *The
Practice of Love,* foregrounds how such a performative operation functions in works like those authored by King:

> Foucault's term *'reverse' discourse* actually suggests something of the process
> by which a representation in the external world is subjectively assumed,
> reworked through fantasy, in the internal world and then returned to the
> external world resignified, rearticulated discursively and/or performatively
> in the subject's self-representation – in speech, gesture, costume, body
> stance, and so forth. (308)

For de Lauretis, representations can be reconfigured via fantasy and then, when returned to the external world, pose serious challenges to the fixity of preconceptions. De Lauretis focuses on sex and gender identities, but her approach is also readily applicable to the issue of race. Expanding on her contention, she stresses 'the importance that fashion and social performance have, in all cultures and cultural (self-)representations, for the normative sexual identity of their subjects' (308). De Lauretis's stance signals how fantasy and costume can disrupt normative gender and sexual representations, since they enable subjects to imagine themselves in alternative positions. At the same time, the cultural placement of the subject disrupts the normative designations because it shifts their significations.

Medicine River provides an obvious example of this performative operation in racial terms through the character of David Plume, who takes enormous pride in his AIM (American Indian Movement) jacket. This jacket is woven into a tale of violence, a trait commonly associated with Natives, and especially with Native activists. Indeed, the inscribed violence draws readers into the text by playing upon and inverting their expectations. The episodes of violence turn out to be more rumour than 'fact,' rumours that arise and are granted credence because of the discourse surrounding Native behaviour, a discourse that informs readers' expectations of the text. In this way, the reader is implicated in the construction of the 'Native,' as is Will, the Native protagonist.

Within the text, David Plume is arrested for shooting Ray Little Buffalo, and the *Medicine River Herald* carries a story that Will summarizes for readers: 'Ray Little Buffalo had been shot in the stomach. He was found in Chinook Park by the river. David had been arrested and held for questioning' (251). David is found guilty by that voice of White authority – the newspaper – which contributes to the myth of the violent and explosive Native. In particular, the seriousness of the incident is measured by the fact that Ray is thought to have been wearing David's much-coveted jacket when he was discovered, wounded in the park, a detail that baffles Will and Harlen. As Will tells Harlen: 'That's crazy. David wouldn't let Ray wear his jacket. David wouldn't let *you* wear his jacket' (252). Nonetheless, Will's expectations (and the readers') are raised and seemingly confirmed when Harlen, the character who is the focal point of the novel, expands upon the rumour:

Ray and three of his friends caught David behind the American Hotel and beat him up. 'Damn, Will,' Harlen told me, 'after they beat him up, Ray took that jacket. Ray's a lot bigger than David, and when he tried to put the jacket on, you know, just to tease David, he ripped it.'

According to Harlen, David jumped back up and started swinging again, and Ray beat on him some more. After it was over, David went into the American to wash the blood off, and then went to his apartment and got his deer rifle. He found Ray down by the river drinking and throwing rocks at the empty bottles. (253)

That Will, and unsuspecting readers, do not question the story is evidence of the power and pervasiveness of the dominant discourse that surrounds Native subjects. But, by accepting the story, the text implicates them in the proliferation of what are destructive cultural stereotypes.

Harlen, the one character who is in doubt about the veracity of the story, discovers that

'David found him [Ray] and started shooting at him. But he missed. When he ran out of bullets, he went home.'

'Who shot Ray?'

'Ray wasn't shot. The papers sort of got that mixed up. When David started shooting, Ray tried to get out of the way, but he slipped and fell on the bottle he had in his pocket. Cut his stomach pretty bad. At first, everybody thought Ray had been shot, but he was just cut and drunk.' (254)

This passage demonstrates how minor incidents of Native violence are often over-dramatized in the non-Native media. King also suggests that even those who are Native, like Will, tend to accept Native stereotypes without question, despite knowing intellectually that the stories presented by the media make no sense. In this case, David's attachment to his AIM jacket becomes his means of defying hierarchical power. The credibility of the story hinges on David's surrender of his jacket, an act that neither Harlen nor Will believes could have happened. Although there is some question about David's actual activism, the jacket does serve as his way of asserting resistance. David may be ridiculed for wearing a jacket with the letters 'AIM,' which, according to Ray, refers to 'Assholes in Moccasins' (252), but, paradoxically, the novel suggests that the people who generate such reductive stereotypes are those, like Will, who cannot see beyond the White media's manipulation of Native identities. The jacket thus becomes a costume that, when worn by David, performatively helps to undermine and contest these fabrications.

Lionel Red Dog's story provides another example of how 'fashion' generates a subversive space. Lionel had always admired John Wayne and aspires to be like the movie star cowboy. Hence, Lionel is delighted when the Native elders give him a birthday present: a leather jacket that magically resembles the one Wayne wore in his films. But Lionel begins to reject his media-fostered desire to emulate White heroes when he realizes that such a desire is culturally destructive for him; the jacket begins, literally, to strangle him. Shortly after receiving the jacket, Lionel finds that it becomes increasingly uncomfortable to wear: 'In fact, Lionel felt as if the jacket was suffocating him. Worse, the jacket had begun to smell. A stale, sweet smell, like old aftershave or rotting fruit' (318). Lionel discovers that the Native elders have simply 'borrowed the jacket' in an effort to make him feel better, and he happily removes it (318). He returns the jacket to its rightful owner, a non-Native man who is caught trying to photograph the Sun Dance in order to sell the results for profit. As the elders tell Lionel, the jacket is intended to make him 'feel better,' but it does not always work (318). Ironically, in this case, the jacket clearly *has* done its job. By rejecting the jacket and all that it represents (as a symbol of Eurocentric values that confine and suffocate Native peoples), Lionel also begins to accept the culture he has been taught to repudiate.

Judith Butler's work is important, here, in explicating how performative acts – like Lionel's rejection of Wayne's jacket, or David's attachment to his – can become radical gestures within a matrix of power relations. For Butler, performance can complicate and potentially undermine the power balance affirmed through dominant discursive constructions. Performativity also complements reverse discourse, for it too depends upon originary significations, which it then throws into question. As Butler explains, performativity is not merely a moment of free play but rather a complex 'reiteration' and resignification of normative values (94). In her words:

> I would suggest that performativity cannot be understood outside of a process of iterability, a regularized and constrained repetition of norms. And this repetition is not performed *by* a subject; this repetition is what enables a subject and constitutes the temporal condition for the subject. This iterability implies that 'performance' is not a singular 'act' or event, but a ritualized production ... (*Bodies* 95)

If a repetition of forms both enables and constitutes the condition in which the subject performs, then re-figuring those forms puts pressure on them, and allows for their re-visioning. And, using Butler's work in tandem with de Lauretis's suggestion that fantasy is a crucial component of reverse discourse, these theoretical arguments foreground how fantasies, advanced by a mode that shifts the power balance from non-Natives to Natives, relate to assumptions of normative roles by non-normative subjects.

Specifically, by shifting what constitutes normative values and characters, King's novels perform the exclusivity of stereotypical formulations. In one of the mythic passages of *Green Grass, Running Water,* Changing Woman and Moby-Jane, the great (black and female) whale, travel together and share a sexual interlude. By offering an alternative version of Melville's *Moby Dick,* in which the great white male whale dominates, *Green Grass, Running Water* highlights the homoerotic subtext of Melville's novel, as it shifts the gender of the characters from male to female:

> Changing Woman presses herself against that whale's soft skin and she can feel those waves rock back and forth. Back and forth. Back and forth.
>
> This is very nice, says Changing Woman.
>
> Yes, it is, says Moby-Jane. Wrap your arms and legs around me and hold on tight and we'll really have some fun.
>
> It is marvellous fun, all right, that swimming and rolling and diving and sliding and spraying, and Changing Woman is beginning to enjoy being wet all the time. (187)

Margery Fee and Jane Flick argue that to understand this allusion to and reconfiguration of Melville's text, readers have to 'juxtapose knowledge from different sources ... Most readers will ... get the "Look, look, see Dick and Jane" allusion to the perfect white family of the Ginn readers' (135). However, 'Dick and Jane also establish the difference between a Moby with a dick and a Moby without one (or any interest in one) and so we can make the jump to lesbian, too' (135). In this case, ethnic minority women come together, both literally and figuratively, to undermine the fixity of race, gender, and sexuality as represented in 'classic' works.

As the novel moves to decentre the origins of master-narrative texts (like Melville's 'great American novel') and to relocate them in Native culture, it also points up the cultural specificity of dominant-discourse versions of history, which present a White and decidedly male viewpoint as the source of authority. When the mythic characters engage in a further discussion of *Moby Dick*, Coyote explains: "'I read the book. It's Moby-Dick, the great white whale who destroys the *Pequod*.'" "You haven't been reading your history," I tell Coyote. "It's English colonists who destroy the Pequots'" (164). Coyote's presumption that he is getting the whole story is sharply undercut by King's narrator, who reminds the trickster of the ways in which history can be used to obscure or silence alternative accounts of the past. Clearly, Coyote 'ought to have been reading Native history' (Fee and Flick 136). Moreover, fantasy facilitates this reverse discourse in King's novel as a non-normative subject, Moby Jane, takes on a normative position.

As Butler has suggested in the above quotation, the reiteration of dominant discourse in another fashion effects a performative subversion. Thus, in King's works, when the normative object of the performance becomes the subject, the trajectory of the master-narrative is redirected. For example, in *Green Grass, Running Water*, Eli Stands Alone is reading a formulaic romance of brawny braves and nubile White captives, which is so familiar that it puts him to sleep:

> Eli opened the book and closed his eyes. He didn't have to read the pages to know what was going to happen ... There would be a conflict of some sort between the whites and the Indians. And Iron Eyes would be forced to choose between Annabelle and his people. In the end, he would choose his people, because it was the noble thing to do and because Western writers seldom let Indians sleep with whites. Iron Eyes would send Annabelle back to the fort and then go to fight the soldiers. He'd be killed, of course, and the novel would conclude on a happy note of some sort. (166)

As Eli suspects, the novel conforms precisely to his predictions. And in so doing, the ludicrous nature of the constructed 'Noble Savage' is held up to ridicule in the performative space afforded by reading the romance 'through' Native eyes. Eli's boredom with standard representations of Native men is a source of comic relief as well as a critical commentary, because, clearly, Eli no longer has to read the text to know what is coming:

> Eli should have kept his eyes closed.
>   Chapter fourteen.
>   Iron Eyes and Annabelle were standing on the bank of a beautiful river.

It was evening, and in the morning, Iron Eyes was going out with his men to fight the soldiers.

'It's such a beautiful evening,' said Annabelle, brushing a wisp of hair from her glistening cheeks. 'I don't want to leave,' she said, trembling. 'I don't want to leave this land. I don't want to leave you.'

Eli shifted his body on the sofa. His left leg was going to sleep.

'Tomorrow is a good day to die,' said Iron Eyes, his arms folded across his chest, etc., etc., etc.

Eli flipped ahead, trying to outdistance the 'glistenings' and the 'tremblings' and the 'good-day-to-dyings.'

Flip, flip, flip. (167)

These performative interludes become more pointed as they illuminate the effects of the imposition of cultural stereotypes on Native peoples. When Portland Looking Bear goes to Hollywood to play Indians, he has to change his name to appear more authentic, and becomes 'Iron Eyes Screeching Eagle.' His son, Charlie, asks his mother about Portland:

'Did he ever play the lead? You know, the hero.'

'He could have,' Charlie's mother told him. 'But that was back before they had any Indian heroes.'

'I mean, did he ever play a lawyer or a policeman or a cowboy?'

'A cowboy.' And his mother had laughed. 'Charlie, your father made a very good Indian.' (127)

Despite Mrs Looking Bear's assurances, Portland does not make a 'good' cinematic Indian since his nose is not deemed 'Indian' enough for White Hollywood producers: 'Portland's nose wasn't the right shape ... The director ... told Portland that he could have the part but that he would have to wear a rubber nose' (128–9). Out of frustration, Portland brings the rubber nose home and nails it to the bathroom wall. As Charlie's mother explains, 'It was the silliest thing you ever saw. Portland put it on and chased me around the house. He only caught me because I was laughing so hard' (129). Although Portland eventually dons the nose in order to earn a living, his private display of mock savagery – running around the living room – and his initial refusal to wear the nose are acts of resistance that subvert the dominant representations of the Indian, as depicted in Hollywood westerns.

Performative Problems

While Portland's nailing of his fake nose to the bathroom wall may provoke laughter and afford delight in the power of altering, if only temporarily, the terms of dominant narratives, shifting significations may appear a simplistic solution to normative constructions, since the process seemingly negates cultural placement and extant power relations. Natives may hold dominant positions in these texts, but if they are posited as 'inferior' in dominant culture, dominant culture will dictate how they are to be treated, regardless of their actions. Butler, for instance, is aware of this problem in *Gender Trouble*, and she turns to considerations of cultural placement in her later study, *Bodies That Matter.* The theorist continues to maintain, however, that playing with ideological imperatives is crucial to destabilizing their construction:

> Performativity describes this relation of being implicated in that which one opposes, this turning of power against itself to produce alternative modalities of power, to establish a kind of political contestation that is not a 'pure' opposition, a 'transcendence' of contemporary relations of power, but a difficult labor of forging a future from resources inevitably impure ... This *resignification* marks the workings of an agency that is (a) not the same as voluntarism, and that (b) though *implicated* in the very relations of power it seeks to rival, is not, as a consequence, reducible to those dominant forms. (241)

In this passage, Butler both stresses the significance of deconstructing gender roles, and points to their operative difference in reverse discourse. That is, the inverse assumption is not the same as the originary inscription, for it is a play on, rather than an assertion of, dominant norms. The reverse may be implicated in the reiteration of the dominant, but it is not a simple reinscription of it. Butler's contentions also underscore the agency of the subject who performs, for the assumption of the role points to the subject's active engagement in transfiguring power relations, and the subsequent alterna(rra)tives opened by and through that act.

Green Grass, Running Water, for instance, insists on the stories *it* wants to tell, and does not simply constitute a counter-cultural challenge to dominant boundaries. This text displays a distrust of the postmodern delight in decentring and transgressing borders, and in doing so, offers a meta-critique of its own formulaic strategy. The space of interplay that is effected through the counter-memory process allows for the affirmation of subject positions denied in dominant discourse, and foregrounds the need for a more careful consideration of identity politics as a series of constructed representations, which favour certain groups over others. Indeed, *Green Grass, Running Water* suggests that one can disrupt and dissolve borders to a certain point, for such an action only resonates if, as Nancy K. Miller has argued in relation to women, one *has* a subject position to begin with (53). Moving to affirm marginal subject positions, King's transgressive writing goes on to advocate political agency. As his text indicates, some boundaries must be maintained, for without them, the marginalized become hegemonized within the dominant. The Native content of this novel points to the very problems inherent in shifting borders, for it foregrounds the historical significance of boundary abrogation for Native peoples in a very tangible and yet complex manner.

At the centre of the text is the story of Eli Stands Alone. Eli refuses to relinquish his mother's homestead to the hydro company that has built a dam on Native lands, without Native permission. His reiterated 'No' – which King acknowledges was inspired by Elijah Harper's 'No' to the Meech Lake Accord – underscores the pressing subject matter that propels this novel. *Green Grass, Running Water* risks aborting postmodern play, therefore, when Eli stops and refuses to allow the boundaries and the borders to be shifted any further.

Eli provides the focal point of the text. A Native who has attempted to escape from his past by moving to Toronto and becoming an English professor (specializing in the study of famous dead European male authors, including Shakespeare), Eli returns to the reserve in later life and commits himself to his mother's tribal legacy. He adamantly refuses to have his rights undermined any further. Every morning, he engages in conversation with the dam supervisor, and every morning he says 'No' to the supervisor's request that he relocate his mother's cabin. Another character recalls a conversation with Eli:

'Wouldn't be hard to move the cabin ... Probably get the government to move it to higher ground for free.'
    'Cabin's just fine right here.' ...
    'Can't stay there forever.'
    'As long as the grass is green and the waters run.'
    As long as the grass is green and the waters run. It was a nice phrase, all right. But it didn't mean anything. It was a metaphor. Eli knew that. Every

Indian on the reserve knew that. Treaties were hardly sacred documents. (223–4)

Eli's commitment to halting the dam is fuelled by childhood memories of non-Native appropriations of Native culture. Eli remembers how, as a child, he was tricked when he attempted to stop a White man from taking pictures of the Sun Dance. Deceived into accepting blank film at that time, Eli draws upon the memory to bring a halt to the further desecration of Native ceremonies:

> Eli released the camera from its mount, opened the back, and took out a roll of film .. He held the film canister in his hand. 'What's this?' ...
>   'Undeveloped film. Just blank film.'
>   Eli reached into his pocket and pulled out a ten-dollar bill. 'Then this should cover it,' he said, and he caught the end of the film between his thumb and forefinger and stripped it out of the canister in a great curling arc. (321)

Ultimately, Eli's refusal to be compromised costs him his life, since the flood, which the Native elders unleash to destroy the dam, kills Eli in the process. But his commitment has secured the desired result, for the dam is destroyed. As his sister summarizes at the end of the novel: 'Eli's fine. He came home' (352).

Eli 'comes home' in a myriad of ways, for his 'No' is reiterated throughout the text, and resonates in other boundary and border constructions. His refusal to acquiesce to the demands of the Eurocentric world quickly becomes emblematic of other marginalized people and their acts of resistance. That is, the man to whom Eli says 'No' at the Sun Dance is George Morningstar, who has been brutalizing his wife, Latisha Red-Dog Morningstar. Latisha's marriage to the White, American-born George has resulted in physical and emotional abuse, and her story encompasses both cultural imperialism and sexual dominance. On a cultural level, George delights in belittling Canada to his Canadian spouse, but despite her apparent acquiescence, Latisha ultimately refuses to allow him to trivialize her nationality:

> George's comparisons became even more absurd ...
>   Americans were modern, poised to take advantage of the future, to move ahead. Canadians were traditionalists, stuck in the past and unwilling

to take chances. Americans liked adventure and challenge. Canadians
liked order and guarantees.

'When a cop pulls a Canadian over for speeding on an open road with
no other car in sight, the Canadian is happy. I've even seen them thank the
cop for being so alert. What else can I say?'

In the end, simple avoidance proved to be the easiest course, and whenever George started to warm up, Latisha would take Christian into the bed-
room and nurse him. There, in the warm darkness, she would stroke her
son's head and whisper ferociously over and over again until it became a
chant, a mantra, 'You are a Canadian. You are a Canadian. You are a Canadian.' (134)

Latisha repudiates George's racist and sexist assertions, and articulates
an alternative for her children. She identifies them as Canadian citizens
and resists her husband's desire to colonize their family, an act that
allows for a parody of Canadian fears of Manifest Destiny, but with an
added twist. In this case, Latisha, who is multiply marginalized within a
nationalist discourse, both upholds and deconstructs the virtues of Canada. She may consider herself to be a Canadian citizen willing to battle
the imperialism of the United States, but she also comes to recognize
that she is Native and, hence, belongs to a group that has been traditionally ignored within constructions of national identity on both sides
of the border. Saying 'No,' here, becomes a gesture of resistance against
erasure on numerous levels for Latisha. When George returns to her, at
the end of the novel, she is able to reject his efforts to reincorporate
himself into her life *and* she is able to preserve the sacredness of the
Sun Dance, a ceremony that no one, neither Native nor non-Native, is
allowed to photograph.

Holding to principles is also a theme that resurfaces in Alberta
Frank's story. Alberta, who desperately wants a child, also wants to be a
single mother and continually eludes her suitors' efforts to marry her.
Although her resolve generates complications with artificial insemination officials, she is adamant that she wants a baby without a husband.
Coyote's intervention enables Alberta to get pregnant, through an alternative 'immaculate conception,' and she therefore achieves what she
desires without conceding her position.

As *Green Grass, Running Water* works to deconstruct dominant-
discourse master-narratives by providing counter-memory re-visions,
then, it also upholds the maintenance of some boundaries, which it

argues must not be dislodged. The subversive trajectory of the novel moves to the point where it meets Eli Stands Alone at the centre of the text. Through Eli, the novel affirms the necessity of maintaining some crucial borders, including the lines that designate reserve lands. For Eli, it is essential to acknowledge that these reserve lands are the rightful property of individual tribes, who should determine their use, as opposed to natural resource areas waiting to be exploited by the federal and provincial governments. The preservation of specific borders offers one way to ensure that Native rights are respected. While, initially, Eli 'stands alone,' he also stands firm and refuses to be dislodged. When his resistance serves to generate further resistance, King's textual strategy and the space of interplay his novel engenders allow not only for the creation of counter-memories, but also for the affirmation of political agency. As this text demonstrates in relation to Native land claims, the transgression of boundaries can serve as a tool for the maintenance of the status quo. Political agency and identity politics must be employed to combat the abrogation of borders which serves to marginalize and to re-marginalize dominated groups. Through its postmodern meta-critique, therefore, *Green Grass, Running Water* provides a twist to post-modern writings, a twist from which postmodern theory, itself, can ben-efit. The assumption that postmodernism's pluralistic vision is indisputably positive is put to the test yet again by King's novel. *Green Grass, Running Water* suggests that such postmodern models, though seemingly generous and egalitarian, often cultivate 'indifference' or complete ignorance of those borders and boundaries that actually pro-tect and sustain otherwise marginalized populations. In doing so, King's novel, with its deliberate eradication of some borders and pointed main-tenance of others, 'takes back' a form and a theory, which potentially allows for co-option, and engages in a performance that offers a marked potential for strategic cultural resistance.

CHAPTER THREE

Genre Crossings

If, as we have been arguing, King's fictions concentrate on various border crossings for political and cultural reasons, his texts also incorporate a number of disciplinary, genre, and media crossings to similar effect. Kings works serve as performative 'hybrid' texts, or works that combine diverse modes and forms as they venture across cultural and literary boundaries – boundaries, it is worth noting, that have been in place for decades, and boundaries that influence the ways in which writings are read and categorized. The inversion of such academic categorizations may not seem as socially relevant as some of the other subversions we have discussed, but they are no less limiting and restricting, and they, too, have serious cultural repercussions. In King's hands, academic and institutional 'rules' are broken, and in the process are shown to be homogenizing and exclusive in many of their practical applications. Consequently, by crossing these borders, King's texts reflect on such constructions and uncover their political ramifications. His works challenge conventional definitions, open them up to questioning, and offer alternative visions.

As a means of distinguishing between academic boundaries, some writings and disciplinary styles have been severed from others. Certain works, therefore, are delineated differently, or fall into disparate categories: some are labelled 'History,' while others 'Literature,' and texts are broken down further to accord with genre definitions within their disciplinary status. Disciplines, traditionally, have been denoted as separate and distinct; indeed, Umberto Eco argues that aesthetic 'rules' mark off a singular work from the disciplinary body of which it is a part. Social and cultural norms are central to the formulation of these 'rules.' Eco describes this 'modern conception of aesthetic value' and endows it with two characteristics:

1. It must achieve a dialectic between order and novelty – in other words between scheme and innovation;
2. This dialectic must be perceived by the consumer, who must not only grasp the contents of the message, but also the way in which the message transmits these contents. (173, 174)

For Eco, aesthetic value is inherently contradictory. In order for a work to be taken seriously, it must appear unique as well as familiar, for readers must recognize it in order to determine its 'novelty.' In other words, the work must be recognizable and innovative – simultaneously.

Of course, if a work is to be recognizable, it must conform to particular accepted customs and practices. Janice Radway outlines these conventions in her introduction to *Reading the Romance.*

A theory in which genre is conceived as a set of rules for the production of meaning, operable both through writing and reading, might therefore be able to explain why certain sets of texts are especially interesting to particular groups of people (and not to others) because it would direct one's attention to the question of how and where a given set of generic rules had been created, learned, and used. (10)

Radway's analysis points to a provocative means of uncovering institutionalized 'rules,' for she contends that one should avoid the aesthetic distinctions and values that have motivated critical reading, and turn, instead, to the works themselves to understand the ways in which they produce meaning. To take this idea a step further, such an analysis should also consider the particular cultural and social norms that have shaped the texts in question.

King's works invite readers to do just this. As they cross disciplinary boundaries, they do so in a variety of ways: some through a composite re-vision, some by a disciplinary conflation, some through an integration of diversity, and others by a subversion of recognizable academic conventions. As discussed in chapter 2, King's can be described as postmodern texts, or texts that self-reflexively play upon cultural and artistic practices for different purposes, and they incorporate a number of divergent strategies as a means of challenging various disciplinary limitations. In turn, King himself is a newsworthy figure, who does not simply write books, but also is a frequent presence on radio programs, an occasional actor, and a sometimes critic. His work as a whole, therefore, breaks with disciplinary boundaries in order to capture a diverse audience, an audience that, as we have mentioned, his fiction might not otherwise reach.

One of King's texts, *A Coyote Columbus Story*, illustrates the ways in which the author conflates disciplines and genres as a means of raising political issues for a readership often ignored by political activists. *A Coyote Columbus Story* is a children's book that revises the historical record. The story mixes history and fiction, blurring the divisions drawn between them. Like other Native responses to the quincentenary (Michael Dorris and Louise Erdrich's *The Crown of Columbus* among them), *A Coyote Columbus Story* retells the tale of Columbus's journey to the Americas from a Native North American perspective; in so doing, it refashions the standard Eurocentric narrative of exploration and conquest. King's book, through its shift in focus, reveals the racial and cultural specificity of the traditionally accepted version of Columbus's voyage, subverts the authority of European history, and deflates any glory surrounding Columbus in his 'discovery' of the New World. The world Columbus discovers, here, is not 'new,' and it is not discovered, but rather disrupted as a result of his voyage.

Despite *A Coyote Columbus Story*'s effort to offer an alternative to Columbus's triumphant arrival in America, the text has been criticized for its attack on Euro-American culture. In April of 1992, the *Globe and Mail* ran an article on the book's reception at the Bologna Book Fair, and reported that

> Groundwood Books went to Italy to sell foreign rights to several books, including a funny, angry attack on the 'discovery' of America, *Coyote Columbus*, written by native author Thomas King and illustrated by Métis artist Kent Monkman. One U.S. publisher called the book 'hateful.' Another said: 'American kids have enough depressing news. We need to lighten up!' (Ross, 'Book' C14)

A Coyote Columbus Story's status as a children's book lends a certain moral imperative to the U.S. publishers' assertions, for if it is 'hateful,' it has the potential to 'corrupt' its young audience. Not coincidentally, the audience constructed through the *Globe and Mail*'s report is nativistically Canadian, for the newspaper assumes a nationalist stance in defending this 'Canadian' writer's book against its American critics. The

U.S. publishers, as they condemn King's text for its depressing subject matter, ignore the cultural relativism of their own perspective and, thus, inadvertently draw attention to the power imbalance that has generated King's alterna(rra)tive.

Clearly, King's children's book is threatening to proponents of dominant discourse (it would be interesting to see how the *Globe and Mail might* have responded if the text had not been criticized by the Americans) because dominant discourse is unable to entertain alternative views – to do so would foreground its own specificity. The dominant ideology has always presented itself as The Norm, a position that legitimizes its perspective and works to trivialize and dismiss those that differ from it. Should dominant discourse open itself to other points of view, it would lose its ideological mandate as the authoritative Norm. In other words, the act of inclusion would necessitate a relaxing of its stronghold on centricity. As the *Globe and Mail*'s report on the U.S. publishers' dismissal of King's book demonstrates, alternative perspectives continue to be deemed intolerable; indeed, in this time of cultural confusion, the assertions of the dominant norm as The Norm are all the more in evidence.

While the U.S. publishers who condemned *A Coyote Columbus Story* at the Bologna Book Fair drew attention to the political implications of King's counter-narrative, they elided the possibility that canonical children's literature might itself display a certain cultural specificity. Popular opinions aside – and as studies of race in children's literature have demonstrated – such writing is hardly free of political motivation. The suspension of disbelief required by these largely Realist texts frequently depends upon the maintenance of clearly demarcated race, class, and gender boundaries in order to effect the ideological coherence on which they rely and to which they contribute through their affirmation of Normative values.

There is another article in the *Globe and Mail* on *A Coyote Columbus Story* that illustrates our point. This article describes how Tom Mashler of Jonathan Cape 'sniffed when he took a look at a children's book by native writer Thomas King,' and 'told Groundwood publisher Patsy Aldana, "This is just about as far as it could be from a Cape book."' The *Globe and Mail* goes on to ask:

So what *is* a Cape book? An example arrived this week, an edition of Hilaire Belloc's classic cautionary poem *Matilda, Who Told Lies and Was Burned to Death*. The amusing illustrations, by Posy Simmonds, culminate in drawings of a raging inferno, with the text 'For every time she shouted "Fire!"/ They only answered "Little Liar!"' The last page in the book shows Matilda's faithful pug dog crouched over the little girl's smouldering remains.

Oh, so *that's* a Cape book ... ('Diamonds' C6)

This summary of *Matilda, Who Told Lies and Was Burned to Death* describes what has been deemed acceptable in children's literature by publishers like Jonathan Cape, and provides an apt contrast to that same publisher's condemnation of *A Coyote Columbus Story*. Perhaps one of the reasons for the condemnation arises from the ways in which King's text highlights how children's literature functions as an enculturating and normalizing agent of dominant discourse. Indeed, *A Coyote Columbus Story* opens children's literature as a body to scrutiny, at the same time that it foregrounds the cultural relativism of legitimizing select versions of history.

The narrative manifested in King's counter-discourse underlines the cultural specificity of those select historical versions. It plays upon imperialist discourse and re-contextualizes it, as becomes apparent when *A Coyote Columbus Story* is juxtaposed with representations of canonical children's literature.

J.M. Barrie's *Peter Pan* is perhaps a less obvious example of what has been deemed acceptable in children's literature than *Matilda, Who Told Lies and Was Burned to Death*, but it is more apt as an intertext for *A Coyote Columbus Story* because of its imperial perspective. The content of the play is telling, for it depicts a struggle for dominion over Never-Never Land between Peter Pan and the Lost Boys and Captain Hook and the Pirates. And its content is hardly devoid of racism. Never-Never Land is inhabited by a Native band led by Tiger Lily, and the Natives are dismissed as suitable contenders for the territory because they are 'morally unsound.' The Natives are bloodthirsty and vengeful, as becomes apparent when Tiger Lily asks: 'Have um scalps? What you say?' A member of the band replies: 'Scalp um, oho, velly quick,' and the rest chime in 'Ugh, ugh, wah,' before they 'crawl off like a long snake that has not fed for many moons' (58).

Perhaps the most famous line of Barrie's text lies in Peter's Pan's question: 'Do you believe in fairies? Say quick that you believe! If you believe, clap your hands!' (119. In order to save the fairies, as Peter points out, one must believe in them, for without belief, the fairies cannot function. And audiences, watching the play, allow for this suspension of disbelief. But, self-reflexively, as a narrative, *Peter Pan* demands that its readers or viewers share more than a belief in fairies: the audience must also accept the play's premise in order for it to function as a Realist narrative as well as an ideological tool. To question the legitimacy of Peter Pan's and the Lost Boys' 'natural' right to Never-Never Land would be to read against the textual grain, and to produce a very different story.

King's *A Coyote Columbus Story*, in effect, does just this, for by decentring the *Peter Pan* fantasy of imperialism, it calls into question the 'truth' of Eurocentric versions of history and their claims. To put it another way, when King's book is criticized for its negative portrayal of Columbus, such a criticism draws on the 'do you believe in fairies' question that underpins the narrative structure of *Peter Pan*. Like the fairies, if one does not believe in the Columbus myth, the myth no longer works, and this traditionally accepted narrative is undercut. King's story, by resisting the benevolent historical version of Columbus as courageous explorer, and by undermining racist characterizations of Native people (like Tiger Lily in *Peter Pan*), opens normative ideology up to questioning, for it reverses the discourse of homogenizing sameness. Indeed, as it resists the imperial thrust, this narrative actively works to bend and diversify all singularizing conceptions.

A Coyote Columbus Story provides an alternative belief system, apparent in its opening pages. The story begins by introducing readers to Coyote, the trickster figure, who is posited as the centre of origin. It was Coyote 'who fixed up this world, you know. She is the one who did it' ([1]). That it is Coyote who is the creator figure undermines the assumption that 'civilization' is the product of European culture kindly bestowed upon the 'savages.' King's text shifts the paradigm, since Coyote, as a Native creator figure, gives birth, as it were, to the Europeans. Because Coyote is the founder, or the originating source, in the story, she functions in opposition to the White patriarchal god of Judeo-Christian culture; unlike this god, Coyote does not demand obedience or service. And her antithetical stance is suggested by her gender – in *A Coyote Columbus Story*, the creator figure is female.

Initially, we were troubled by Coyote's feminine status, because it is her seemingly frivolous desire to play baseball that generates the problems in the story. However, as a colleague pointed out, to condemn frivolity is to accept the hierarchical value system of Eurocentric culture that dictates what is and is not important. Coyote, in fact, works against the black and white moral structure of imperialist ideology. She is both good and bad, creator and disrupter, as signified in *A Coyote Columbus*

Story when the world she creates is filled with a mixture of useful and silly objects:

> She made rainbows and flowers and clouds and rivers. And she made prune juice and afternoon naps and toe-nail polish and television commercials. Some of these things were pretty good, and some of these things were foolish. ([1])

Coyote is not a moral force; hence, she does not effect a binary structure of good and evil in the text. Lacking the imposition of a 'good' norm, *A Coyote Columbus Story* is able to resist the structure of imperialist narratives that posit Truth, and thus avoids the pitfalls inherent in assertions of moral centricity. There is no norm established in this text. Rather, there is an allowance and a respect for differences, a situation that subverts the Western ideological insistence on hegemony. This shift in ideological stance is crucial, since it reverses the imperative of the *Peter Pan* fantasy. In refusing to posit a norm in which we must all believe, *A Coyote Columbus Story* subverts established hierarchies.

For example, Coyote's approach to creation differs dramatically from Judeo-Christian conceptions of divinity. Indeed, Coyote's approach to creation in itself marks her difference. Unlike the patriarchal male god of Judeo-Christianity, Coyote's feminine creative process is devoid of the imperialistic drive for power. Coyote is not interested in power – she is interested in playing baseball. And her lack of adherence to any given structure, later apparent in her shifting rules, allows for further creation. Coyote's hit-and-miss approach may engender problems, as is evident in her creation of Columbus, but it also allows for diversity and multiplicity.

Coyote's respect for difference is apparent early in the narrative. She loves to play ball but tires of playing alone, and so begins to create others to join in her game. She first creates the beavers, who refuse to play with her:

> We've got better things to do than play ball, says those beavers. We have to build a dam so we'll have a pretty pond to swim in.
>
> That's all very nice, says Coyote, but I want to play ball.
>
> So Coyote sang her song and she danced her dance and she thought hard, and right away along came some moose. ([4])

Coyote is not interested in obedience, and she does not insist on her own objective; she accepts the beavers' choice and turns to the creation of new beings. When the moose she makes exhibit little interest in sport, Coyote makes turtles, with the same result. Coyote formulates without interest in controlling the outcome. When her creations refuse to behave as she desires, she simply creates something else. She does not force her creatures to do her bidding. It is noteworthy that, in *A Coyote Columbus Story*, the animals are presented as beings with rights and privileges; they do not serve as commodities to be exploited.

Since Coyote has 'struck out' with the animals, she turns her attention to a new creation and devises human beings. These first human beings are Indigenous people, indicated through the historical positioning of the text and through its illustrations, a situation that further upends the White norm. The human beings agree to play ball with Coyote, and

> Coyote and those human beings become very good friends. You sure are a good friend, says those human beings. Yes, that's true, says Coyote.
> But you know, whenever Coyote and the human beings played ball, Coyote always won. She always won because she made up the rules. That sneaky one made up the rules, and she always won because she could do that. ([7])

Coyote does not operate in a realm above the people, but rather is directly accountable to them for her actions. When the human beings complain about her shifting rules, they argue 'that's not fair ... Friends don't do that' ([9]). Notably, Coyote does not have a mandate for governing those around her. Hence, the idea of governance itself is deconstructed and the desire for sameness displaced. The emphasis in this text is on family and friendship, not on domination and division.

While there is no division in Coyote's world, there is diversity. Difference is accepted and even fostered, for the human beings are perfectly free to engage in their own pursuits when they tire of playing ball with Coyote:

> Some of them go shopping.
> Some of them go sky diving.
> Some of them go to see big-time wrestling.
> Some of them go on a seven-day Caribbean cruise.
> Those human beings got better things to do than play ball with Coyote and those changing rules. ([10])

The Native peoples indulge in a plurality of leisure activities, none of which is prioritized over others, and, hence, no activity is posited as normative. As the textual illustrations indicate, these human beings are having fun.

In marked contrast to the Native peoples is Coyote's next creation, Columbus and his crew, who provide Coyote's world with a normalizing force. All of the explorers engage in the same pursuit. They reject Coyote's invitation to play ball, since, unlike the First Nations people who are having fun, these Europeans are instilled with an overpowering work ethic. They tell Coyote:

> We got work to do ... We got to find India. We got to find things we can sell.
>
> Yes, says those Columbus people, where is that gold? Yes, they says, where is that chocolate cake?
>
> Yes, they says, where are those computer games?
>
> Yes, they says, where are those music videos? ([13–14])

The explorers are blind to the alternative lifestyles apparent in Coyote's world, and impose upon it their own values and belief system. Because they perceive North America through their expectations of Europe, they find in it little of interest or worth. As a result, they attempt to assess the New World in terms of the Old:

> I see a four-dollar beaver, says one.
>
> I see a fifteen-dollar moose, says another.
>
> I see a two-dollar turtle, says a third.
>
> Those things aren't worth poop, says Christopher Columbus. We can't sell those things in Spain. Look harder. ([16])

Columbus and his crew, not conditioned to delight in difference, seek sameness in the world they have 'discovered,' and that which they find to be somewhat the same, the human beings, become worth/y of notice. Columbus's assessment of value is highlighted when he exclaims:

> I'll bet these are Indians. And he looks at his friends. I'll bet we can sell those Indians.
>
> Yes, says his friends, that's a good idea. We could sell Indians. And they stop trying to catch those beavers and moose and turtles.
>
> Whew! says those beavers and moose and turtles, that was close. And they run and hide before Columbus and his friends change their minds. ([18])

Columbus and his crew have come to North America to exploit it for

Europe, and what they deem valuable they appropriate and remove to Spain. When Coyote begs them to reconsider and to let her friends go, Columbus responds: 'I'm going to sell them in Spain ... Somebody has to pay for this trip. Sailing over the ocean blue isn't cheap, you know. Grab some more Indians!' ([1]).

Coyote's ideology of collective diversity is openly contrasted with Columbus's belief in singularizing sameness. King's story foregrounds the difference between the two cultures early in the narrative when Coyote creates the explorers while preoccupied with the idea of shifting rules: 'That silly one sings a song and she dances a dance and she thinks really hard. But she's thinking about changing those rules, too, and she doesn't watch what she is making up out of her head' ([11]). As a result, Coyote literally changes the rules with her new creation. And the 'game' that results has severe repercussions for the Native peoples, who reproach Coyote for bringing Columbus to America:

> You're supposed to fix up this world, cry those beavers and moose and turtles. You're supposed to make it right. But you keep messing it up, too.
>
> Yes, says the human beings, you better watch out or this world is going to get bent. ([25])

Unlike Columbus, who feels he is above the rules, Coyote is accountable for her behaviour and must answer to the population. She accepts responsibility for her actions, acknowledges her error, and attempts to rectify her mistake.

Notably, Coyote's effort to fix the problem she has generated, so that 'everything will be balanced again' ([26]), does not involve changing the people she has created, nor changing the collective approach she favours. Hence, she does not force Columbus to return the Natives, and she does not destroy him. Rather, she conjures up Jacques Cartier. Refusing to compromise her belief system, she creates another singularizing force to counter the singularizing force of Columbus. The Native people and the beavers, moose, and turtles find this to be an equally problematic resolution, arguing that Coyote's 'done it again,' and escaping from the newcomers by catching 'the first train to Penticton' ([28]). Coyote, however, insists that 'everything is under control' and gives the newcomers a chance. She greets their queries about India by making 'a happy mouth. And that one wags her ears. Forget India, she says. Maybe you want to play ball' ([29]).

While Coyote refuses to compromise the world she has created, and accepts responsibility for the advent of a new and totalizing belief system, her story dramatizes the repercussions of the imposition of singularity upon a collective society. King's text signals the difference between Eurocentric and Native cultures, one of which insists upon a homogenizing sameness while the other resists such homogenization. That the Natives are comically displaced to Penticton (a famous enclave of Native writers and artists and the home of Theytus Books, a pioneering First Nations press) draws attention to the historical displacement of Native peoples, who were forced to flee west to avoid the encroachers.

Although it is difficult for Native culture, as it finds voice in King's text, to parry the European assaults because it refuses to posit a counternorm to offset the thrust of the Eurocentric Norm, Native society nonetheless manifests an alternative ideology. This ideology, with its plurality of points of view, works, on a philosophical level, to undermine the structure of dominant discourse by decentring it as an authoritative Norm. Indeed, by revealing the dangers inherent in positing a Norm, *A Coyote Columbus Story* dramatizes the negative effects of singularizing hegemony, and draws attention to the ways in which that homogenizing force can be deflected and dismantled. Proponents of dominant discourse condemn *A Coyote Columbus Story* precisely because it provides an alternative to the ideology they seek to uphold, and as they do so, they highlight the ways in which the very provision of an alternative actively challenges the conceptualization of imperialist ideology. By celebrating the alternatives that dominant discourse rejects, this resistant narrative not only opens a space for alternative theorizing, but also, potentially, paves the way for an alternative practice.

Mooning As Meta-narrative

King has subsequently published a second children's book, *Coyote Sings to the Moon* (1998), which avoids the openly controversial subject matter of *A Coyote Columbus Story* and offers a more gently humorous look at Coyote's antics. This latter text, however, retains an equally irreverent attitude toward Eurocentric value systems. King dedicates the book to his two children, Elizabeth and Benjamin, 'who think Coyote's singing got a bum rap' ([1]). As it turns out, Coyote is a terrible singer, whose dismissive attitude toward the Moon and arrogance about the wonders of his own voice lead to a variety of mishaps. Most importantly, the Moon hides from the local animal population, depriving them of their main source of light, and instead illuminates the depths of a pond. Ironically, in order to bring the Moon back to the sky, Coyote is enlisted to sing her out of hiding. His voice is so powerfully awful that he manages to drive Moon to desperation – she either disappears from the sky or hurries back to the pond. Eventually, the community reaches a compromise. Coyote will sing just enough every night 'to keep Moon in the sky,' an exercise that explains why coyotes, in general, howl at the moon ([36]).

This text, though not overtly concerned with traditional versions of history, advocates a similar kind of diversity and plurality to that which is presented in *A Coyote Columbus Story*. Rather than presuming that the natural world can be colonized, Coyote comes to realize that the Moon, with its autonomy, needs to be respected and wooed accordingly. Coyote's singing may simply deter the Moon from hiding, but, in doing so, Coyote also demonstrates his unwillingness to assume, immediately, that others are wrong. In this case, the trickster makes an effort to fix the problem he has created without placing blame on those around him. Moreover, Coyote's compromise does not necessitate changing the Moon itself; instead, Coyote learns how to influence the Moon's behaviour for the benefit of the community as a whole.

Coyote's selfishness and egotism, which initially annoy the Moon, are repeatedly mocked in this cautionary tale. Although at the beginning of the story, Coyote tells his fellow animals 'that silly Moon is so bright, I can hardly sleep' and insists 'I wouldn't sing with you if you begged me,' he soon discovers that this arrogance is not only unhelpful but also makes him the butt of various jokes within the community. When Coyote walks into a Tree, unable to see his way home because the Moon has disappeared and left the area in darkness, the trickster is openly ridiculed:

'Hey!' says Tree. 'Watch where you're going.'
'Sorry,' says Coyote, 'but it's dark.'
'That's because some fur-brain insulted Moon,' says Tree, 'and she has gone away.'
'I can see just fine,' says Coyote, and he walks into a large boulder.
([13])

Coyote's insistence that he 'can see just fine' leads ultimately to a rather stinky encounter with a skunk, which he mistakenly identifies as a pillow, and an accidental visit to the pond, where he discovers Moon ([13]). Even here, Moon laughs at Coyote's naivety, pointing out to him that 'you're underwater,' and that he should head to the surface for some air to avoid suffocating ([18]). Despite the fact that Coyote is a constant source of humour in the story and has created 'a fine mess' for the community as a whole, he also becomes part of the collective solution, a strategy of accommodation and negotiation that provides an alternative to the imposition of a singular vision in which control of the natural world is the goal ([21]).

Fictive Histories, Historic Fictions

Alternatives – be they practical or theoretical – serve as the performative focal point of King's work. Indeed, as his texts criss-cross conventional subject matters, and rewrite authoritative accounts, they provide alterna(rra)tives, at the same time that they point to the permeability of disciplinary and cultural boundaries. Through a number of strategic revisions, King invites readers to see through a different lens, and to assess some of the consequences of Eurocentric master-narratives, which themselves have long gone unquestioned.

King's texts often play upon the constructs and the content of nineteenth-century novels. Edward Said, in *Culture and Imperialism*, discusses the ideological operation of these novels and underscores three of their major functional strategies. He suggests:

> There is first the authority of the author – someone writing out the processes of society in an acceptable institutionalized manner, observing conventions, following patterns, and so forth. Then there is the authority of the narrator, whose discourse anchors the narrative in recognizable, and hence existentially referential, circumstances. Last, there is what might be called the authority of the community, whose representative most often is the family but also is the nation, the specific locality, and the concrete historical moment. (77)

King's fiction transposes the traditional author, narrator, and communal factors that Said highlights. As a Native author, King approaches the forms and subject matter of these narratives from an alternative subject position; consequently, his narrators differ from those his audiences have been conditioned to expect (by the novel tradition, among other things) and, thus, offer an amended perspective to the reader. The community, as the authoritative structure of the texts, adheres to a disparate pattern, since it is not nuclear, and the construct of 'nation' is dissimilar from that in dominant discourse. By changing these conventions, King's works assume a different locus – they recreate various normative scenarios, which, through their placement in a Native writer's texts, are recontextualized and thus opened to question.

In *Green Grass, Running Water,* for example, narrators assume the position of various historical figures at different points in time. At the beginning of the novel, the four elders who have escaped from the asylum are named, respectively, 'Hawkeye,' the 'Lone Ranger,' 'Ishmael,' and 'Robinson Crusoe' – all characters of imperial master-narratives. The novel flips the position of these characters, for, in *Green Grass, Running Water,* they are Native figures, who have masqueraded as Whites and, ironically, become White heroes. The elders explain their 'mission' when Lionel and Norma pick them up hitch-hiking:

> Norma leaned her head toward Lionel. 'This is my nephew Lionel. I'm Norma.'
>   'Yes' said the Lone Ranger. 'I'm the Lone Ranger.'
>   Lionel snorted. Norma whacked him in the ribs with her free arm. 'Nice to see our elders out on vacation,' she said.
>   'Oh, we're not on vacation,' said Ishmael.
>   'No,' said Robinson Crusoe.
>   'We're working,' said Hawkeye.
>   'Working, huh?' said Lionel, and he dropped his arm to protect his side.
>   'That's right,' said the Lone Ranger. 'We're trying to fix up the world.'
> (104)

As it transpires, the Native elders have tried to fix up the world before, but their efforts were always turned to other ends, which is how they have become White heroes. This process of inversion reveals the problems with the conventional historical record, which has only provided one point of view.

In another passage, First Woman and Ahdamn are taken to the notorious Fort Marion. Despite Coyote's enthusiasm ('I always wanted to go to Miami' [82]), the narrative inverts the origin of the historic Trail of Tears: 'So First Woman and Ahdamn are on that train and there are a bunch of Indians on that train with chains on their legs. First Woman and Ahdamn have chains on their legs too. Everybody is going to Florida' (82). The heroic First Woman liberates the Natives by putting on her 'black mask' and walking out the front gate:

It's the Lone Ranger, the guards shout. It's the Lone Ranger, they shout
again, and they open the gate. So the Lone Ranger walks out of the prison,
and the Lone Ranger and Ishmael and Robinson Crusoe and Hawkeye
head west ... 'Wait, wait, wait,' says Coyote. 'Who are those other people
walking out the gate with the Lone Ranger?'
'We'll meet them later' (83)

Freeing the Natives from Fort Marion and beginning the march to Oklahoma, this narrative reposits agency with the Natives, taking away the
momentum from the White American hero. (Ironically playing on the
Trail of Tears, in an early version of *Truth and Bright Water*, King penned
the following passage regarding the potential construction of a road:
'"Miles says the smart money is in real estate." "Ask the tribes back east,"
said my father. "One day a couple dozen Europeans show up on your
doorstep in Georgia, all smiling and good will, and the next thing you
know, you're walking to Oklahoma"' [MS 22]).

As Fee and Flick demonstrate, many of the characters in King's second novel are historical figures. Clifford Sifton, the man who represents
the company that is trying to build the dam on Native territory, is drawn
from history. Fee and Flick point out that the actual Sifton, who lived
form 1861 to 1929, was an active promoter of 'white settlement (and
Native displacement) through the Prairie West Movement' (132). Since
the actual Sifton was deaf, his placement in King's novel is all the more
resonant, in that, like many other characters, he can't *hear* what he is
told.[1] In King's works, history is fiction, and fiction history, both inter-
mingling and overlapping – yet always with a critical difference.

The narratives that weave throughout *Green Grass, Running Water* work
to reposition historical characters whose literary works have been instru-
mental in the construction of Native subjects for dominant discourse. In
one scene, customers enter Latisha's restaurant and introduce themselves: 'My name is Jeanette, and this is my friend Nelson. This is Rose-
marie De Flor and her husband, Bruce' (110). Jeanette (MacDonald)
and Nelson (Eddy) proceed to make fools of themselves. Jeanette asks
Latisha, '... may we assume that you are Indian?' and, receiving Latisha's
answer, Nelson pipes up: 'Damn fine tribe.' All the while, Nelson leaves
'his hand on Latisha's arm and tri[es] to reach her hip with his thumb'
(110). Jeanette and Nelson bicker throughout the meal, and as Latisha
helps Jeanette into the bathroom (she has a bladder problem), Jeanette
whispers of her husband, 'He'll die before I do ... There's some consola-

tion in that' (113). The filmic characters are caricaturized in this scenario, and the romantic love they cinematically shared is rendered
ludicrous by extending it to its potential yet likely conclusion.

In another episode, different tourists enter the Dead Dog Café. These
characters are identified as 'Canadian' since they are tight with money.
When Latisha goes to serve them, she notices name tags, which identify
the customers as 'P. Johnson' and 'S. Moodie.' With the women are 'A.
Belaney' and 'J. Richardson.' The four customers' names play on the
legacies of various nineteenth- and early twentieth-century Canadian
writers: Archibald Belaney (a.k.a. Grey Owl) actually masqueraded as a
Native, while Susanna Moodie's *Roughing It in the Bush* and John Richardson's *Wacousta* include depictions of Native characters, who are generally treated as a threat to the survival of English colonists attempting
to 'civilize' pre-Confederation Canada. Conversely, Pauline Johnson is a
mixed-blood writer who composed poetry and prose, and marketed her
Native roots to audiences all over North America through readings
of her works. Thus, when 'Sue' Moodie strikes up a conversation
with Latisha, the conversation highlights both Latisha's ignorance of
Johnson's writing and the politics of colonization:

> 'With the exception of Archie,' said Sue, 'we're all Canadians. Most of us
> are from Toronto. Archie is from England, but he's been here for so long,
> he thinks he's Canadian, too.'
>
> 'It's nice to meet you.'
>
> 'None of us,' said Polly, looking pleased, 'is American.'
>
> 'We're on an adventure,' said Sue.
>
> 'We're roughing it,' said Archie.
>
> 'That last motel was as rough as I want it,' said John, and Polly and
> Archie and Sue laughed, though not loud enough to disturb the other peo-
> ple at the other tables.
>
> 'Well, there's lots to see around here.'
>
> 'What we really want to see,' said Archie, 'are the Indians.'
>
> 'Mostly Blackfoot around here,' said Latisha. 'Cree are a little farther
> north.'
>
> Sue reached over and put her hand on Polly's arm. 'Polly here is part
> Indian. She's a writer, too. Maybe you've read one of her books?'
>
> Latisha shook her head. 'I'm sorry, I don't think I know them.'
>
> 'It's all right, dear,' said Polly. 'Not many people do.' (133)

Poking fun at major Canadian literary figures, their construction of

Canada, and its subjects, *Green Grass, Running Water* defines their perspective as specifically Eurocentric, complicating this with the mention of Johnson's mixed-blood writings, the impact of which are explored in chapter 6. But the novel does not stop here: it then turns to British literary figures, whose imperial constructs informed the basis of Canadian and American dominant discourses. Thought Woman's encounter with Robinson Crusoe casts Defoe's hero in a rather different light:

> So Thought Woman floats along and pretty soon she hits an island ... Say, says that cranky Island, I'll bet you've come to visit Robinson Crusoe, the famous shipwrecked writer.
>
> Does he write novels? says Thought Woman.
>
> No, says that Island. He writes lists.
>
> 'Hey,' says Coyote, 'haven't we seen that guy before?'
>
> 'They all look the same,' I says.
>
> 'But isn't that ... ?' says Coyote.
>
> 'No,' I says. 'That's Robinson Crusoe. You're getting him mixed up with Caliban.'
>
> 'Who's Caliban?' says Coyote. (244–5)

When Thought Woman meets with Crusoe, he says, 'Thank God! ... It's Friday,' to which Thought Woman responds, 'No ... it's Wednesday' (245). Crusoe then explains his plans for her: 'as a civilized white man, it has been difficult not having someone of colour around whom I could educate and protect. What's the point? says Thought Woman. Now you're here, says Robinson Crusoe' (245).

By placing the Defoe narrative within a particular context, King is able to point up the singular perspective proffered by this imperial master-narrative. Consequently, the text invites readers to rethink a fiction that has become normative. Turning, then, to canonical American texts, *Green Grass, Running Water* focuses on Melville's *Moby Dick.* King's novel includes an encounter between Changing Woman and a man who asks her to 'call me Ishmael.' After asking for her name, he tells Changing Woman:

> That just won't do either, says the young man, and he quickly thumbs through the book again. Here, he says, poking a page with a finger. Queequeg. I'll call you Queequeg. This book has a Queequeg in it, and this story

is supposed to have a Queequeg in it, but I've looked all over the ship and there aren't any Queequegs. I hope you don't mind.

Ishmael is a nice name, says Changing Woman.

But we already have an Ishmael, says Ishmael. And we do so need a Queequeg. (162–3)

Positioned as Queequeg (the Native character in *Moby Dick*), Changing Woman shifts the locus of Melville's novel, for she perceives Ahab as a monster when she discovers the purpose of a whaling ship:

And.

When they catch the whales.

They kill them.

This is crazy says Changing Woman. Why are you killing all these whales?

Oil. Perfume, too. There's a big market in dog food, says Ahab. This is a Christian world, you know. We only kill things that are useful or things we don't like. (163)

Ahab's statement (that the whalers only kill things 'we' don't like) allows the narrator to outline the dangers inherent in his position. Consequently, Changing Woman proceeds to conflate whales and lesbians (people whom, historically, 'we don't like') when she spots 'Moby-Dick':

Blackwhaleblackwhaleblackwhalesbianblackwhalesbianblackwhale, they all shout.

Black whale? yells Ahab. You mean white whale, don't you? Moby-Dick, the great male white whale?

That's not a white whale, says Changing Woman. That's a female whale and she's black.

Nonsense, says Ahab. It's Moby-Dick, the great white whale.

You're mistaken, says Changing Woman, I believe that is Moby-Jane, the Great Black Whale. (164)

All the White sailors bail out in terror at the sight of the Whale, at which point, as noted earlier, Coyote breaks in: '"She means Moby-Dick ... I read the book. It's Moby-Dick, the great white whale who destroys the *Pequod.*" "You haven't been reading your history," I tell Coyote. "It's English colonists who destroy the Pequots."' By examining the consequences of both White-washing and masculinizing history, the narrative proceeds to trace how Changing Woman and Moby-Jane frolic together in the water. By rewriting and resituating these authoritative narratives, therefore, King strategically inverts traditional binaries, and makes a pointed statement about the adverse impact of this dominant discourse.

Contemporary Crossings

In 'A Seat in the Garden,' included in *One Good Story, That One*, King turns to contemporary subject matter. Although the story's title bears no indication of its intertextual play, that play is clear in its opening pages. The narrator begins the tale with a description of the protagonist, Jo Hovaugh, who notices a 'big Indian' in his garden:

> The big Indian was naked to the waist. His hair was braided and wrapped with white ermine and strips of red cloth. He wore a single feather held in place by a leather band stretched around his head, and, even though his arms were folded tightly across his chest, Joe could see the glitter and flash of silver and turquoise on each finger. (83)

Surely this is the 'Indian' that King discusses in *The Native in Literature*, in relation to Wayland Drew's *The Wabeno Feast*: 'As MacKay and his voyageurs make their way up the rivers, they pass among familiar Indians. It is not that MacKay has seen these Indians before; he has not – but we have' (7). The big Indian in Hovaugh's garden is also the Indian 'we have' seen before – the Indian presented in countless adventure narratives, most the products of non-Native writers. Sure enough, King's big Indian begins to repeat the phrase that W.P. Kinsella made famous: 'If you build it, they will come' (83).

'A Seat in the Garden' reinscribes yet another text, which those who attended the 1990 Annual Convention of the Canadian Learned Societies in Victoria will recognize. The character 'Red Mathews,' who is introduced in the second page of the tale, bears a remarkable resemblance to Robin Mathews, a noted Marxist Canadian nationalist, who attacked King at that conference for being 'American' and for ignoring not only Canadian Native peoples but, in particular, colonial contact narratives in his discussion of First Nations literature. Mathews suggested that King's inability to recognize imperialism was typically American, and countered this neglect with the assertion that he himself had done much for those in question, offering up as proof the bench he had built in his garden for Indians to rest upon while 'drinking their Lysol.' This remark by Mathews becomes a significant intertext in King's short story, which describes Natives who collect bottles for an environmental group.[2] When Jo Hovaugh queries these people about the big Indian in his garden, the tale's joke hinges upon the racist bias of the non-Native nationalist. In the story, the Natives are not alcoholics, nor do they see the big Indian. They simply admire the bench to humour Joe:

'Boy,' said the first Indian, 'that's a good looking bench.'
   'You think this will take care of the problem?' asked Red.
   'That Indian still in the cornfield?' said the second Indian.
   'Of course he's still there,' said Joe. 'Can't you hear him?'
   'I don't know,' said the third Indian, and he twisted the lid off the bottle and took a drink. 'I don't think he's one of ours.'
   'What should we do?'
   'Don't throw your cans in the hydrangea,' said the first Indian. 'It's hard to get them out. We're not as young as we used to be.' (94)

The story concludes with a pointed (for those 'in the know') final paragraph, a paragraph that highlights the cultural origin of the 'big Indian' in a final description of Joe and Red Mathews:

Joe and Red spent the rest of the day sitting on the porch, drinking beer, and watching the big Indian in the garden. He looked a little like Victor Mature, Red thought, now that he had time to think about it, or maybe Anthony Quinn, only he was taller. And there was an air about the man that made Red believe – believe with all his heart – that he had met this Indian before. (94)

The nubile young brave of Eurocentric traditions reappears here with 'a critical difference' – in 'A Seat in the Garden,' the big Indian is the product of a Native teller, who uses these non-Native constructions to mock them and their creators. The worm has turned, as it were, and the story, given its intertextual and meta-textual movements, becomes a postmodern pastiche of non-Native stereotypes of Native peoples. In the next chapter, we will trace the ways in which King draws upon other contemporary venues, in his non-written work, to cross divergent borders and boundaries for similar purposes.

CHAPTER FOUR

Comedy, Politics, and Audio and Visual Media

Just as the movement afforded by short stories can be used to political ends, so can that of other artistic forms. Indeed, in King's hands, visual and audio media become loci for collective action. The author integrates these venues into his texts, at the same time that he utilizes the space they provide to include audiences that might not have access to his works. Branching out from the written word, then, King uses technology to traverse and encompass alternative locales. In particular, his photography, radio work, and television writing are sites of political articulation for King, who depicts and subverts stereotypical assumptions about Indians in a comic manner that challenges audience expectations and crosses genre boundaries.

In his study of American popular culture and memory, George Lipsitz explores the ways in which 'the commercial context of commodified mass culture' can operate as a site of subversion for ethnic minority populations (4). He argues that pop cultural forms, such as television, radio, movies, and photography, may be used to create narratives that refuse to conform with mainstream or conventional versions of history – complete with footnotes – and instead provide a documentation of experience that resists such 'linearity and teleology' (4). If culture, as we have been arguing, often operates as a form of politics, which can be used to reshape 'individual and collective practices for specified interests' (17), King's decision to work in various mass media becomes a political act with important ramifications. Through his radio shows, television scripts, and photographs, King self-reflexively revisits media forms that have been used to marginalize Natives and in many cases to construct them as a dying other.

For example, photography has traditionally functioned in an imperialistic fashion with respect to Native North Americans. As Lee Clark Mitchell explains in a recent study of the relationship between American Indians and photography, the desire of Whites to photograph Native Americans was 'no mere accident' (xi): 'Long before colonialists had actually settled their various continents, then, a "colonization through photography" had successfully confirmed the very process of decline and extinction that the photographic record was meant to forestall' (xi). Ironically, photography became a tool that legitimized colonization by depicting the First Nations as a disappearing race. In recent years, however, Mitchell notes that such subjugation has been reversed, as Native photographers have begun to 'bridge two disparate cultures [in their own work], transforming a tool that initially bore witness to their demise' (xi). Will Horse Capture, a central character in *Medicine River*, takes on this very role: he has worked in Toronto as a portrait photographer and then returns to the reserve, where he begins to examine his values and beliefs through a camera lens.

Likewise, as King so aptly demonstrates in *Green Grass, Running Water*, television and film traditionally have been equally powerful media for depicting Native subjugation to stereotypes, especially through the Hollywood western. In *Tonto's Revenge: Reflections on American Indian Culture and Policy*, Rennard Strickland contends that 'surely, no racial, ethnic, or political group has been subjected to as much or as frequent on-screen stereotyping than the Native American' (24). Strickland supports his argument by noting the abundance of westerns produced since the advent of film: 'forty single-spaced and double-columned pages are required to list Indian films and actors portraying Indians' in a book on the subject published in 1972 (24). Yet Strickland also points out that, despite the wealth of films, most are 'non-Native portrayals of Native Americans' that continue to replicate the same stereotypes and clichéd depictions of Natives first introduced during the silent picture era (24–5). In *Green Grass, Running Water*, however, the four Native runaways take control of both the videotape and television versions of a John Wayne western and revise aspects of the picture in subversively comic ways. Their alterations of the movie undermine the underlying message of White western male superiority by showing the Indians defeating the cavalry, as led by Wayne and Richard Widmark. Widmark wets his pants and both men die from their wounds, adding a surprising twist to the conventional ending of the western by making Natives rather than Whites the heroes of the narrative.

Given King's fictional interest in various media, it is fitting that he has also begun to explore these forms independently, as the writer of a radio show aptly called *The Dead Dog Café Comedy Hour,* broadcast by the CBC, as a photographer who has exhibited several series of prints, and as the writer of television scripts and made-for-television movies. No doubt, such diversity can be seen as one way to pay the bills, a difficult task for most writers. But King has held academic positions since 1986, and thus is likely not as concerned with the economic benefits of these multiple projects as he is interested in the creative and political dimensions of his endeavours. By using different media, King makes his work accessible to a wider variety of (potentially Native) audiences, audiences other than the book-buying public (which, he acknowledges, is mostly non-Native). His efforts in these various arenas, by forcefully asserting and comically reflecting on his position as a Native artist in his 'texts,' contest the imperializing tendencies that shape even popular forms. As Susan Sontag explains in *On Photography*:

> Superseding the issue of whether photography is or is not an art is the fact that photography heralds (and creates) new ambitions for the arts ... (Such developments as film, TV, video, the tape-based music of Cage, Stockhausen, and Steve Reich are logical extensions of the model established by photography.) The traditional fine arts are elitist: their characteristic form is a single work, produced by an individual; they imply a hierarchy of subject matter in which some subjects are considered important, profound, noble, and others unimportant, trivial, base. (149)

Through moving away from 'the traditional arts,' King returns to media that overtly lend themselves to the collective process, which is an integral part of Native communities and identity. His fiction may challenge Eurocentric models, but it remains primarily a solitary artistic endeavour, since the novel form is generally the published work of a single author. In contrast, his television scripts, photography, and radio shows rely on collaboration for their creation, whether it involves using a production crew, hiring radio actors, or finding subjects to pose for portraits.

As with his fictional endeavours, King infuses the work that he does in the fields of photography, radio, and television with a comic edge that foregrounds and mocks Eurocentric assumptions. By reconfiguring the 'imperial aspirations of the mass media' when using these forms, King accomplishes several tasks at once (Lipsitz 69). He dismantles the hierarchical relationship between Native and non-Native audiences, and displaces perceptions of 'difference' onto the dominant population. At the same time, he shows how powerful certain negative images of Natives have become – even within Native communities – and offers a counternarrative that comically contests such limited representations. Moreover, much like King's writing, his visual and audio works are layered with incongruities that invite audiences to participate and take pleasure in the making of new and different texts, without simply serving the symbolic agenda of conventional narratives.

Photographic Collectivity

King incorporates photography into his first novel, *Medicine River*, and opens the conventions of the artistic form. Traditionally, as Linda Hutcheon points out, photography comprised an effort to confine and to frame, since 'the camera records and justifies, yet it also imprisons, arrests and thus falsifies the fleeting moment. Taking pictures is a way of both certifying and refusing experience, both a submission to reality and an assault on it' (*Politics* 47). King's assault focuses on the singular efforts photography has tended to generate in non-Native hands. Since, according to Arnold Krupat, Native experience is collective in nature (331), the photographs in *Medicine River* are a consolidation of multiple forces. Within the novel, Will Horse Capture is a photographer, and the photographs he produces begin to push at the boundaries of their frames. When he poses Joyce Blue Horn's extended family, for example, the photograph becomes a self-reflexive portrait of a collective event:

> As soon as Harlen explained, in detail, just what a time-delay device was, everyone insisted that I had to be in the picture too. Jasper's granny even got up and moved her chair over, so I'd have a place to sit. (214)

Will is both the author of the photograph and a participant in it, and the resulting artifact resists containment. Instead, the collective photograph assumes a comprehensive impetus:

> Then, too, the group refused to stay in place. After every picture, the kids wandered off among their parents and relatives and friends, and the adults floated back and forth, no one holding their positions. I had to keep moving the camera as the group swayed from one side to the other. Only the grandparents remained in place as the ocean of relations flowed around them. (214–15)

This photograph, which has no centre and no margin, works against efforts to reify or limit, in the same fashion as does King's text. Because the photograph, here, is constructed through language, readers are also included within its frame, for they are asked to visualize the textual photograph, which comes to life only through readerly interaction with the printed page.

The text offers a variety of readerly interactions, however, and readers can be included in a number of ways. They can act as the camera, and try to fix and control the collective photograph by freezing it in a singular interpretation; or, they can be included within it like Will, who learns that one cannot limit a collective experience, for this would be to restrict others' participation in the project. The picture spills out of its frame since it is an inclusive, not an exclusive, endeavour, and as it does so, it dramatizes a communal moment, a moment that inspires further collaboration.

King's collaborative efforts at photography have led to a series of projects that incorporate text and image in an ironic fashion. He has worked with Greg Staats, a Canadian fine-art photographer, on a collection of portraits of Native Canadian contemporary authors, which was published in a 1994 issue of *Books in Canada*. The portraits themselves consist of twelve black and white photographs, mostly close-ups of the writers' faces. The photographs seem minimally stylized, with the exception of Lee Maracle's portrait (taken by King), in which the backdrop is covered in wall art, including a cartoon animal head with a large, open mouth, wide eyes, and sharp, visible teeth (see fig. 1). This trickster-like figure is on Maracle's right in the photo, gazing at the viewer and seemingly undermining Maracle's own direct and almost defiant look outward. The seriousness of Maracle's stance and her body language – her arms are tightly wrapped around her body in a self-protective fashion – is countered by the larger-than-life presence of this cartoon character, who can be read as both invoking and mocking the idea that Native peoples lack a sense of humour.

The underlying comic message of Maracle's photograph is replicated in King's self-portrait, which appears on the back-flap of his short story collection, *One Good Story, That One* (see fig. 2). Published by HarperCollins, King is clearly credited as the photographer of what is usually a standard shot of the author's face. In this case, however, King uses the photograph as a performative tool that both depends upon the repetition of norms and turns that normativity into the focus of his presentation. King's image is juxtaposed with that of a (stuffed) coyote, which is

Figure 1

positioned reaching up, mouth open and tongue extended, to lick the author's face. The photograph plays tricks with the eye by aligning King with the coyote in his own visual form of trickster discourse, a discourse that refashions normative constructions of Indians in a technologically sophisticated fashion. As King explains in an artist's statement that accompanied another set of his photographs: 'Edward Curtis, when he went off on his photographic expedition at the turn of the century, took along boxes of Indian paraphernalia (blankets, wigs, etc.) in case he ran into Indians he wanted to photograph who didn't look Indian enough' ('Artist's Statement' 1). The tradition of framing and containing 'other-ness' through photographic means is both invoked and subverted in King's self-portrait. He alters the subject matter of the photo through the use of an unusual accessory: a stuffed coyote. In doing so, King draws attention to the ways in which Natives have been confined by the gaze of White photographers like Curtis, and offers his own version of

Figure 2

reality, a reality that includes and celebrates a distinctly Native sense of humour (through this animal trickster's interactions with the author).

King's brand of photographic play is also at work when he brings pictures and text together, a genre-crossing venture that he pursues in his joint project with Staats. The portraits that appear in *Books in Canada* are accompanied by an essay, written by King, which provides a context for the collaborative series and jokingly mocks his own lack of talent:

> Greg wasn't all that impressed with my cameras or my technique.
>
> 'You a photographer?'
>
> 'You bet,' I told him.
>
> Well, it wasn't a lie. I had worked as a photo-journalist for a rather dreadful magazine in Australia and gone on from there to do some rather dreadful work for several better magazines.
>
> One hundred and fifty years ago. (12)

Through his own self-deprecating stance, King critiques the history of photography as a technology first made available to the public in 1839, which was subsequently used in North America to 'document' the existence of Indians. Most of these early photographs, taken by White North Americans and intended for White viewers, were treated as an anthropological record of a 'vanishing race.' In discussing the oddities of the photographic medium, John Berger notes that photographs appear to halt time; as a result, viewers often have the strange impression that 'exposure time [in which the camera is taking the image] *is* the lifetime' of the photo's subject (47). Thus, photography may be perceived as a record of 'relics of the past, traces of what has happened,' that no longer exist in the present (57). The subject is figuratively killed off via the photographic image. Such representations of Indians by non-Native photographers justified the mass relocations of tribes and the genocide that occurred as a result of these policies. The camera's paternal gaze fixed power relations between Natives and non-Natives, relegating Indians to the role of the savage 'other' and subordinating them to the much-needed authority of civilizing (White) forces (Tagg 12). The dying breed of Native North Americans was a sustained subtext of these photographs, and the nostalgia for a disappearing population made these images valuable. They became a testament to the fact that Indians no longer had the skills to survive and, conversely, a romantic record of a primitive past. Part of what gets lost in these images are the stories of the subjects being photographed; the images reveal more about 'the photographers and the times they lived in than the subjects themselves' (Katakis 2). This earlier photographic tradition provides a useful intertext for the project that King and Staats have decided to undertake. But rather than merely being corrective in their approach, King's essay – and the photographs themselves – redirect the trajectory mapped out in these Eurocentric master-narratives about Indians by combining genres and self-consciously reclaiming the collectivity of Native experience.

King evokes the orality and vernacular style of his literary texts in the essay that is woven, literally, amongst the various portraits, a strategy that conveys the strength of tribal communities and traditions through the banter between himself and Staats. When King and Staats agree to turn a 'continuing conversation' into a book project on 'traditional and contemporary Native artists in North America,' Staats attempts to narrow down the field of potential subjects by asking King 'just the right questions': '"What do you do when you're not pretending to be a photographer?" "I pretend to be a writer"' (14–15). King creates a story that slyly and subversively frames the pictures as a legitimate scholarly endeavour that also becomes an exercise in recording and acknowledging a living Indian tradition in a collaborative manner. The photographs gather together a selection of what he calls 'the first wave of Native writers in Canada,' a group that is 'alive and well' (15). As King points out, these authors exist in direct contrast to 'the general backdrop of literature, where most of the writers we chase in high school and university have been dead for a couple of centuries' (16). At the conclusion of his essay, King outlines the plans that he and Staats have made to travel through Canada and the United States, 'cameras in tow, to visit Native artists and writers where they work' (18), a trip that Staats approaches with caution because of the delight King takes in mocking the legacy of Edward Curtis:

> 'You're not going to make any dumb Edward Curtis jokes on this trip, are you?'
>
> 'Why would I do that?'
>
> 'Meanness,' he said, 'I've read your novels.'
>
> So I promised Greg no Curtis jokes – I had a couple of good ones, too. I'm a man of my word. But, say, did you hear the one about the Mohawk from Brantford and the ...? (18)

The portraits, like the text, invert formulaic assumptions about Native writers and artists by alluding to *and* refashioning the objectification of

Natives both in discourse and through photographic representations that work together to counter lost histories and celebrate the collective richness of the present.

Cur/tailing Curtis

As Vizenor points out in a recent catalogue of Native American photographs taken by Whites from the end of the nineteenth century to the middle of the twentieth, Edward Curtis used his treasure chest of objects in order to achieve the desired image of 'simulated *Indianness*' in his photographs (*Excavating* 11). Most of the photographs Curtis took typically involved one or two Native subjects in what Vizenor has called 'the fugitive warrior pose' (11). Those who were selected to pose took on the role of the 'tribal other.' Vizenor explains that 'Curtis removed umbrellas, suspenders, the tracks of civilization, and any traces of written language' from the photographs and replaced them with decorative tribal dress. Nor did Curtis usually depict his chosen subjects with their 'families, children, or in situations of humor and chance' (11).

In contrast, the portraits of the twelve writers, taken by Staats and King, show people in casual modern clothing, located in a variety of settings, looking directly at the camera, and often smiling: Jordan Wheeler is photographed in a coffee shop, with his sunglasses on, and coffee cups in plain view; Ruby Slipperjack sits on a park bench; and Basil Johnston wears a tweed jacket and Indian bolero tie, in an overtly cross-cultural blending of traditions. Even Maracle's grimly defiant gaze at the camera is undercut by the cartoon character that appears beside her, a comic gesture that parodies the 'fugitive warrior pose' by juxtaposing Maracle with a caricatured trickster figure within the photographic frame. Moreover, the choice of subjects for this project – Native writers – undermines Curtis's romantic construction of Indians as illiterate by depicting authors who have published works in English and French, as well as (in some cases) Native languages.

The collection of photos, when coupled with the essay, criss-cross genre borders and counter the legacy of non-Native photographers, who photographed Indian subjects in order to create their own narratives about the 'other.' In this case, King and Staats work together to reconfigure power relations behind and in front of the camera. As Native photographers, taking pictures of Native subjects, and dialoguing about the project with an awareness of how photography has been used to objectify Indians in the past, the ventriloquism which so often characterized earlier photographs of Indians is reversed, and the 'other' has the opportunity to 'talk back' in a variety of forms, through text and image. Without discounting the power of the camera, which fixes an image and potentially threatens to eliminate the need for memory and continuity, tools that are an essential part of Native North American survival, King and Staats are able to reclaim a technology that, historically, has been used to silence Indians, and to provide an entrée into the lives and stories of those being photographed. Moreover, by employing a comic vision in the photographs and King's text, the project disarms readers and viewers even as it pointedly critiques a tradition of objectifying Natives through images and written commentaries. Staats's playful mockery of King's desire to pretend he is a photographer and King's love of joking, frame the essay itself, infusing the project with an ironic vision that takes pleasure in the subversive aspects of generic hybridity and celebrates the existence of these writers, while still acknowledging a history of photographic racism.

Masking the Subject

Shortly after completing this initial collection of twelve photographs, King and Staats decided to divide the labours of their joint project, named the 'Medicine River Photographic Expedition,' a title that pays tribute to King's first novel and the made-for-television version of the book. The two men first met on the set of the movie *Medicine River*, where Staats was photographing stills of the film and King was involved in the production of his screenplay. In 1994, King undertook his own journey, which he outlines as follows:

> The plan was simple. I would roam around North America visiting reserves and reservations, villages and towns, sprawling metropolises and large cities, searching out Native artists wherever they might be. And, in or around the year 2000, I would publish a very large and impressive book of portraits.
> Not one of my brighter ideas. ('Artist's Statement' 1)

In this statement, which appeared with six photographs in an exhibition at the Weisman Museum in Minneapolis, Minnesota, from October 1997 to the summer of 1998, King takes up a self-effacing stance that disarms the reader and provides a cautionary tale of where naïve ambition can lead. As with the previous project, King evokes the figure of Edward

Curtis as the model for his own expedition. But this time, again, the joke
is apparently played on Curtis and other non-Native photographers who
costumed their subjects to create a look of authenticity: 'Not to be out-
done by Curtis, I took along a few Lone Ranger masks' (1). King takes
his accessory from a scene in *Green Grass, Running Water,* where First
Woman, trapped in a canyon with several dead rangers and a group of
live rangers seeking revenge on their colleague's killer, dons a piece of
'black cloth' with holes for her eyes to protect herself from harm (58).
Once First Woman is wearing the improvised mask, the rangers immediately identify her as 'the Lone Ranger' and offer to shoot her Indian
companion, Ahdamn, dead (58). This disguise literally masks First
Woman's racial and sexual 'otherness,' ensuring her survival and granting her the authority to keep Ahdamn alive. It is this conceit of masking
that King borrows for his photographic shoot with the intention of
taking various pictures of Natives wearing a Lone Ranger–style mask,
including himself (see cover photo), an idea that he describes as simply
'a little Native humor. An Aboriginal joke' ('Artist's Statement' 1).

Prior to exhibiting the photographs in a museum setting, King published a selection of them and an accompanying essay, which provides
yet another account of his evolving collaboration with Staats. His photographs of Native American writers and artists and his text appear in a
1995 issue of the *Hungry Mind Review.* King includes portraits of Sherman Alexie, Lisa Mayo, Gloria Miguel, R.C. Gorman, Michael Kabotie,
and Paula Gunn Allen. In his essay, aptly titled 'Shooting the Lone
Ranger,' King recalls telling Staats why the Lone Ranger 'always wore
the mask in the first place and why he never took it off' (36):

> I knew Greg would be impressed with my revelation, so I called him.
> 'The Lone Ranger is a what?'
> 'An Indian,' I explained. 'That's why he wears a mask.'
> 'Is this a cultural thing?'
> 'He might even be a woman.' (36)

In all of the photographs published in the *Hungry Mind Review,* with one
exception, the artists and writers are masked. Notably, Paula Gunn
Allen, a Native-American feminist scholar and activist, whose photograph appears alone on the page – with text but no other pictures – has
her mask resting on her forehead to reveal her face and the fact that she
is an Indian woman.

Throughout the essay, King self-consciously reflects on the problems of a Native-identified photographer who uses the mask in his work to subvert the power of that icon: 'Within the frontier myth, Indians are most often villains and cowboys are most often heroes. An Indian in a Lone Ranger mask was a contradiction at best' (37). But, as King explains, the intellectual challenge that he wanted to pose to viewers of his photographs soon backfires on him. The photographs are designed to occupy a space of 'in-betweenness.' Indians play cowboys, Native women perform versions of masculinity, and the racialized villain becomes, temporarily, the White hero. Nonetheless, King's desire to show that the Lone Ranger has an identity other than the mask is obscured by the impact of the mask itself, which catches the attention of viewers and distracts them:

> Out of curiosity, I began showing some of the Lone Ranger photographs to magazine and newspaper people in New Mexico, Utah, and California. Everyone enjoyed the photographs ... They're clever, they all told me. It's the mask that does it.
> The comments were meant to be encouraging, I guess, but it would have been nice if the magazine and newspaper people had been able to look at the photographs and wonder, just for a moment, how an Indian had gotten behind the mask in the first place, or what, once there and looking out, an Indian might have seen from such a vantage point.
> I expected to be asked about the artists. Who was that masked ... person? A painter? A weaver? A writer? A dancer, perhaps, or a carver? Who were their people, their relations? Where were they from?
> I hadn't expected that all they would see was the mask. (37)

Apparently, the counter-movement of these deliberately inter-cultural images, which are designed to talk back to this dominant discourse, remain unrecognized by those who only see the photographs. In the context of the published article, however, King is able to use his essay to alert viewers to the images that are intended to rehearse alternative categories of meaning; the layering of the mask onto the faces of various Native writers and artists constitutes an ironic re-visioning of the Lone Ranger as a symbol of White male heroism. The details of the subject of each photograph (including the name, tribal affiliation, and occupation of the person) appear on the same page where King expresses surprise that viewers do not inquire about the identity of those behind the mask, thereby redirecting readers by putting text and image side by side in a dialogic fashion. Similarly, when King exhibited a selection of these photographs in Minneapolis, the same commentary was prominently placed beside the photographs themselves in the form of an artist's statement. By encouraging viewers to look again at the images and to examine the people *beneath* the mask instead of simply acknowledging the ironic placement of the masks themselves, King urges those who are in the museum setting, like those who read the article, to return to his photographs and contribute to the refashioning of their potential meanings.

Such generic hybridity reflects the collective and collaborative dimension of King's work. He juxtaposes his own comic vision, a perspective that is grounded in trickster aesthetics, with images of Indians, taken by Indians. By blurring the boundaries between generic classifications and presenting segments of this project in a range of contexts, whether in an art museum, as a published article (which places text and photographs side by side on the page), or as images circulated amongst audiences without an accompanying text, King defies the fixity imposed on Curtis's subjects and foregrounds the subjectivity of his experience as a photographer, writer, and co-creator of this project. King's writing/photography projects have continued to evolve in the last few years as he explores new subjects. For example, he exhibited another series of photographs at the Ansel Adams Gallery in San Francisco during the fall of 1998.[1] The series is titled 'New Voices / New Visions' and takes a different direction than his 'Medicine River' endeavour. The Lone Ranger mask is missing from these black and white photographs, which record a trip King took across America with his two mixed-blood children. King wanted to take his children to see various major historical sites in Native American history (such as Custer's Last Stand, in Montana), but the trip also included visits to various places across the country that still sell Native kitsch and perpetuate stereotypical images of Indianness. Because the main subjects portrayed in the photographs are his children, the series has a decidedly personal focus. The photographs typically juxtapose images of the children at a historical monument or in front of an example of Indian kitsch, in order to play with and contest the clichéd vision of Natives as a dying race (see fig. 3). Situated in a gallery adjacent to a more prominent display of late nineteenth-and early twentieth-century images taken by Curtis and other White photographers, the location of this exhibition can be read as ironically countering the notion of the vanishing Indian with King's photographs of Native youths, who are clearly alive and well at the end of the twentieth century.

King's interest in genre crossings extends beyond photography to encompass radio and television. The orality of the radio medium is particularly important to King, whose own writing comes out of the Native

Figure 3

oral storytelling tradition and reflects an acute awareness of how difficult it is to replicate the spoken word on the page. King is also conscious
of the accessibility of radio, which reaches a broader segment of the
population than books or photographic exhibitions, and recognizes the
close affinities between Native cultural practices (with their focus on the
power of the spoken word) and the medium of radio.

Oral/Audio Traditions

If the Native photograph is a collective artifact, it follows that the Native
text is an active agent. Like its 'Classical' Western counterpart, Native

storytelling was originally an oral mode, its content only written down recently. As such, it actively constructed an audience and was a communal endeavour. Oral telling, which requires speakers and listeners, differs from contemporary reading practices, which, in general, comprise a solitary practice – taking place, as they do, between reader and book. Oral storytelling is inherently performative, for it is an overtly interactive mode of production. That is, oral narratives involve a speaker addressing an audience, an audience that can, if it wishes, interrupt the speaker, influence the story through body language, and affect the shape the story will take.

To write down oral stories, as many Native theorists have argued, is to Westernize Native traditions, and to lose the nuance of the originary tales. Indeed, on one level, to write the stories is to shift them from a communal to a more individual experience. It should be noted that we are not trying to pit one mode against another here, but, rather, to establish the differences that exist between the oral and the written. Native literature, as primarily oral, was largely ignored since, as Krupat suggests in *The Voice in the Margin*, '... even the most recent and most complexly composed Native American works are still likely to have roots in or relations to oral traditions that differ considerably in their procedures from those of the dominant, text-based culture: if these works are indeed equivalently excellent, still it must be recognized that they are differently excellent' (55). King's texts attempt to cross the differences Krupat highlights, for they work to conflate the oral and written modes, and function, in effect, as 'hybrid' works. Their hybridity is apparent in the ways in which they imbue the written word with oral significance, in that many of the jokes they embody must be vocalized in order to be understood. The implication of characters with names like 'Ah-damn' or 'Jo Hovaugh' require an internal 'sounding' in order to catch the written joke. Since, if these appellations are not sounded, they do not signify, they manifest written/oral constructs.

Within King's works, the interactive nature of oral telling is part of the fiction. In various passages in *Green Grass, Running Water*, the problematics of orality are underscored. Ishmael's effort to tell a creation story is rendered in the following fashion:

All right.

In the beginning there was nothing. Just the water. Everywhere you looked, that's where the water was. It was pretty water, too.

'Was it like that wonderful, misty water in California,' says Coyote, 'with all those friendly bubbles and interesting stuff that falls to the bottom of your glass?'

'No,' I says, 'this water is clear.'

'Was it like that lovely red water in Oklahoma,' says Coyote, 'with all those friendly bubbles and interesting stuff that floats to the top of your glass?'

'No,' I says, 'this water is blue.'

'Was it like that water in Toronto ...'

'Pay attention,' I says, 'or we'll have to do this again.' (88)

Ishmael does get to tell his/her story, despite Coyote's interruptions, but other tellers in King's stories are not so fortunate. In 'One Good Story, That One,' the Native teller is stopped from telling the tales she wants to tell:

Okay, I says. Tell about Billy Frank and the dead-river pig. Funny story, that one, Billy Frank and the dead-river pig. Pretty big pig. Billy is real small, like Napiao my friend. Hurt his back, lost his truck.

Those ones like old stories, says my friend, maybe how the world was put together. Good Indian story like that ... (*One* 5)

Reminiscent of Lionel James in *Medicine River*, who must tell 'old' stories despite his own preferences, the narrator here must relate the tales her (White) listeners want to hear. What is lost, in the telling, therefore, is the contemporary Native tale, which is deferred and displaced through listener intervention. Concomitantly, however, King makes a political point through the silencing of his tellers, since he, as author, writes in the interruptions and demonstrates how traditional tellers have been silenced by their White audiences. Moreover, King frequently substitutes contemporary media for traditional venues.

It is not coincidental that King is a frequent figure on CBC radio programs, for radio provides a means of oral storytelling. Radio, while a 'new' medium, can be used to extend ancient traditions. Although contemporary audiences may not remember the days when radio reigned supreme, a time when social and familial groups huddled around their Victrola to thrill to the latest segment of *The Shadow*, or *Charlie McCarthy*, King's readings do, to some extent, recreate the effects of traditional Native orality, though radio listeners cannot interrupt or influence the speaker in the same way as can an audience to an oral performance. However, as the Canadian national broadcast network, CBC reaches audiences all over Canada, audiences that might otherwise be excluded from King's works. As a 'free' medium, requiring only access to a radio, oral broadcast provides a forum for including national audiences in a fashion that direct oral telling cannot replicate. It does, therefore, create a much broader audience for oral tales, and retains some of the flavour of the originary venue.

Dead Dog Café

King has taken his radio readings a step further – in 1995, he began to write and star in a half-hour CBC radio program, entitled *The Dead Dog Café Comedy Hour*. Initially relegated to a regional program by CBC management, who 'found the scripts too slow,' *Dead Dog* soon found a large and vocal audience whose letters of support ensured the show a place on national radio (Stackhouse A10). Named after Latisha Morningstar's restaurant in *Green Grass, Running Water*, this on-air café serves up running gags and regular program segments through which it mocks and inverts virtually every aspect of dominant discourse, at the same time as it uses a dominant medium (CBC Radio) to do so. *The Dead Dog Café Comedy Hour* (the second half-hour 'just flies by') provides its listeners with a zany 'view' into alterna(rra)tives, as it contiguously offers a performative space wherein reverse discourse is enacted and personified.

Along with King, who stars as himself and performs as the program's 'straight man,' are Gracie Heavyhand (played by Edna Rain) and Jasper Friendly Bear (played by Floyd Favel Starr). Gracie and Jasper, as 'full-bloods,' continually 'sympathize' with Tom because he is only part-Native, and never cease to try to 'Indianize' him. Notably, the two parody Eurocentric and Native stereotypes, often speaking Cree or Cherokee on the air. In contrast, Tom serves as the program's anchor / straight man, always castigating them for their outrageousness, and providing a point of entry (if a conflicted one) for non-Native listeners. As Gracie's last name – Heavyhand – suggests, this is a show that deliberately highlights the ludicrousness of clinging to reductive racial stereotypes that don't allow for alternatives.

The Dead Dog Café Comedy Hour includes segments like 'Ten Reasons to Keep Indians in Canada,' 'Trust Tonto,' 'Aboriginal Decorating Tips,' 'Reserve Recipes,' 'Road Blockade Reports,' and 'What Do You Do?' which features interviews, conducted by Jasper and Gracie, with various Native celebrities and artists. Graham Greene, Tantoo Cardinal, Douglas Cardinal, Jane Ash Poitras, Tomson Highway, and Carol Miller are among the many who have appeared to date. Louis Riel is always scheduled to appear in the second half-hour. The questions posed to the guests complement and subvert those featured on TV shows like *Entertainment Tonight*; here, Jasper and Gracie focus on what the celebrities do when they're not being famous (e.g., some of the answers include 'I eat doughnuts,' and 'I renovate my house').

The regular segments generally provide challenges to engrained cultural stereotypes. In 'Ten Reasons to Keep Indians in Canada,' Jasper recites his rationale for the continuation of Aboriginal existence. His reasons include such barbed 'proofs' as Natives give law enforcement personnel live targets for practice; keep anthropologists from digging up White graveyards; and provide a reliable source of adoptions for non-Native couples. In 'Trust Tonto,' Jasper welcomes questions from listeners about Canadian culture, beseeching his audience to ask Tonto, who hails from the Six Nations Reserve, for he is a better source than some 'White guy in a mask' who shoots people with silver bullets and is '*an American*.' The 'Aboriginal Decorating Tips' portion of *Dead Dog Café* is particularly biting, inverting stereotypes by invoking 'Native wisdom' and thereby exposing the absurdities of racial superiority. One tip is to keep cars in your yard – lots of them – as a means of honouring the history of the automobile, a practice, Jasper explains, Whites don't understand. Gracie chimes in with her tip, which is to frame your pawn tickets and hang them on your living-room walls. These juxtaposed comments serve as reminders of the poor economic conditions of most Native communities, which are a direct result of colonization.

Interspersed throughout the regular segments are various jibes and running gags. At one point, Gracie and Jasper establish the Confederated Indian Bank of Canada, or the CIBC. When Tom hears of this, he argues: 'You can't do that, someone else had that name first – the Canadian Imperial Bank of Commerce.' But Gracie retorts, 'Who came first? Indians or Imperialists?' quickly forestalling any further objections. In the 'Authentic Indian Names' skit, Gracie and Jasper spin wheels and offer names to 'listeners' who request one, with the proviso that the recipient write in and offer a story recounting his/her most interesting encounter with an Indian. Such names include Barbara Floppy Tomahawk (for Jane Fonda – a reference to the Atlanta Braves hand-cheer), Gladstone Greasy Giggle, and Beulah Tardy Chicken. Jasper and Gracie continually try to entice Tom with a 'real' name, and Tom consistently refuses, but his 'Whiteness' is a comic mainstay of the comedy 'hour' and serves as a means of 'talking back' to those critics who have condemned him for not being 'Native enough.' Gracie and Jasper always laugh at Tom's 'White' accent, and make him play all the White characters. For example, the segment 'Band Councillor' stars Jasper as the title character – who has the ability, after dashing into a Petrocan washroom and repeating, 'How, How, How, and How,' to transform himself into 'Band Councillor' – a superhero ready to fight evil everywhere, with the aid of his trusty White assistant, Ottawa Bob (played, of course, by Tom), and his faithful 'administrative assistant,' Wilma Trueblue (Gracie).

Such moments of comic acknowledgment of King's mixed-blood status raise important questions about the subversive nature of the radio show and its complex messages regarding race and identity. As the comic straight man, the character of 'Tom' is always vulnerable to ridicule by the other Native characters, whose identity as Natives is never in doubt. Yet, as the writer of the show and a mixed-blood man who wants to resist rigid or fixed definitions of Natives that exclude a pan-Indian perspective, *Dead Dog* allows King to explore the dangers of categorizing race in a binary fashion. He manages to subvert this insider/outsider construct by both authoring the show and allowing his character's voice to represent that which is 'in-between' stereotypical notions of Whites and Natives.

In a similarly comic vein, the program forestalls potential objections to its content by constructing listener's letters that enable the cast to make fun of both Whites and Natives. In one, a 'letter-writer' asks if Natives are ever going to shut up, accept that they have lost, refuse government handouts, and stop whining? Jasper responds to this tirade with a terse 'No, No, No, and No.' To Tom's mock horror, Gracie and Jasper crack jokes (Question: Where in Canada do Indians outnumber Whites? Answer: In prisons). They also star in segments like 'Canadian Justice,' a play on NBC's *Law and Order*, in which a White man gets community service for unlawful confinement and sexual assault, and a Native gets two years and a $5,000 fine for hunting out of season on reserve land. Mid-season of the first year, Jasper decided to introduce 'Indians Anonymous,' a 'public service' feature through which Indians who have become White are 'helped from becoming Indians again.' Tom, of course, stars: 'Hi my name is Tom, and I'm an Indian. I've been an Indian for 54 years, but for the last six years, I've been White. For the last few years I've found myself making disparaging remarks about *Dances with Wolves, The Last of the Mohicans*, and *Pocahontas*.' Jasper and Gracie are quick to advise, and offer tips on how to 'save' Tom from himself.

In the program's second season, Jasper, ever the creative one, introduced a new segment, the 'intellectual' part of the program, called 'Fireside Friendly Bear,' in which he reads Great Canadian Literature. The catch is that his readings all derive from the *Royal Commission Report on Aboriginal Peoples*, which was released around that time. Jasper and Gracie are also the creative inspirations behind *The Dead Dog Café Comedy Hour*'s Christmas special – which was produced in the spring. In this, they are joined by the Dead Dog Café Chorus and Powwow Drum Team, and everyone sings the 'Twelve Days of Christmas.' But the lyrics differ from the standard version, and this carol includes such lines as 'On the first day of Christmas, the government gave to me: residential schooling, massive unemployment, cultural relocation, postage stamp reserves,' and so on. On *The Dead Dog Café*, wisecracks are alive and well.

While King sees *Dead Dog* as an important tool – giving non-Natives a window on Aboriginal culture and letting 'native people have a bit of a laugh at white people' – he is also aware of its limits (Stackhouse A10). As King explains when describing a recent theatrical performance of *The Dead Dog Café* to a predominantly White audience, 'We're a circus that comes to town and sets up next to the white community ... As long as you don't let the lions and tigers out the cage, it's okay' (A10). Describing the show as a travelling circus of caged wild animals provides an apt metaphor for King's frustrations with Canada's treatment of Aboriginal peoples and Canadian responses to accusations of racism. He is acutely aware that though humour is a 'survival strategy' for Native peoples, it can also be destructive; having accessed a mainstream medium for his 'socially relevant' humour requires a delicate balancing act and an ability to laugh at non-Natives and Natives alike (A10).

Floyd Favel Starr, the voice of Jasper, is especially ambivalent about the humour of *Dead Dog* precisely because of the show's content and audience. Born and raised on the Poundmaker Reserve, outside North Battleford, Saskatchewan, Starr acknowledges that laughter 'is the great leveller' in Native communities, but is uncertain about how such humour transfers to non-Native cultural contexts (A11). In particular, he is wary of how Native actors are often segregated into stereotypical Aboriginal roles, either as 'the noble, tragic, spiritual Indian' or a 'vaudeville' player (A11), and regards *Dead Dog* as the latter. After delivering a recent live performance of the show in Regina and retreating backstage, Starr entered the lobby, where he was greeted with accolades from the White audience, praise that makes him uncomfortable precisely because he feels it replicates Native/non-Native segregation. As an Aboriginal actor playing a Native role, Starr sees himself as a participant in what he calls a 'red man's "minstrel show"' (A11). To counter this, in the *Governor of the Dew*, a play he recently wrote and directed, Starr cast non-Natives in Native roles, in an effort to bridge the gap between the two populations and to highlight the constructedness of Aboriginal identity. Starr's critique of *Dead Dog* and his fear that 'Natives contribute 50 percent of their own ghettoization' certainly complicate King's show by pointing out the dangers of replicating reductive paradigms of Nativeness for mass consumption (A10). However, King is careful to foreground the multiplicity of his targets and to use the show as a form of education as well as entertainment that reaches audiences far beyond those who read his books. *The Dead Dog Café* may entertain White audiences. Yet, it also provokes many non-Natives to reflect on their own discomfort with Canadian racism and depicts Aboriginals who actively take pleasure in ironically reconfiguring stereotypes of themselves and others.[2]

Amazingly, on some levels, since the *Dead Dog Café*'s whiplash humour spares no one (Americans, Russians, Canadians, churches, courts, schools, TV, the Pope, Conrad Black, *and* Natives), the program continued on the air for six years – always anticipating Louis Riel's appearance in the second half-hour, and always signing off with the same words: 'Stay Calm, Be Brave, and Wait for the Signs.' And its popularity is clear: it went off the air in 2000, despite its sustained audience appeal. Since its final episode, the cast has also produced a *Dead Dog* musical and continues to occasionally give special live performances, such as a Victoria Day special in Regina in 2001. Moreover, the web page for the show remains active, with links to a variety of segments from the tape archives of *Dead Dog Café*, photos of the cast, and lists of listeners who have acquired an authentic Indian name. This site ensures continued interaction with fans, long after the end of the show. It offers another form of audience access that includes information on how to acquire tapes of *Dead Dog* episodes and souvenir t-shirts, a commercialization that ironically replicates, in real life, Latisha Morningstar's own successful commercialization of the food at the fictive Dead Dog Café.

Televising Nativeness

Television is another medium that has the ability to reach a wide spectrum of viewers, and, like radio, it too offers the potential of a participative space. Broadcast TV, located firmly in the realm of popular culture, is conventionally perceived as a 'low culture' venue; nonetheless, it is also a medium that allows for collective interaction. As Cawelti asserts, popular forums speak to a cultural demand and, despite 'a certain degree of inertia in the process,' are forums that are 'largely dependent on audience response' (34). Foregrounding the important role audiences play in the construction of popular texts, the critic counters the commonly held notion that popular viewers are simply passive consumers. In turn, Thomas Schatz highlights the cooperative nature of mass culture, when, quoting Henry Nash Smith on the western, he argues for the interactive nature of (a particularly White mode of) formula fiction:

> Smith's fundamental thesis is that these authors participated, with their publishers and audience, in the creative celebration of the values and ideals associated with westward expansion, thereby engendering and sustaining the Western myth. He contends that the public writer is not pandering to his market by lowering himself to the level of the mass audience, but rather that he or she is cooperating with it in formulating and reinforcing collective values and ideals. (11)

Schatz builds upon Smith's thesis and asserts that consumers often participate in the construction of these texts, and even set market trends:

> In underscoring the relationship of pulp Western novels to a mass audience and hence to American folklore, however, Smith's study adds an important dimension to our discussion. He suggests that these novels were written not only for the mass audience, but *by* them as well. Produced by depersonalized representatives of the collective, anonymous public and functioning to celebrate basic beliefs and values, their formulas might be regarded not only as popular or even elite art but also as *cultural ritual* – as a form of collective expression seemingly obsolete in an age of mass technology and a genuinely 'silent majority' ... The basis for this viewpoint is the level of *active but indirect audience participation* in the formulation of any popular commercial form. (11–12)

With a commercial genre, reader input (through demand and consumption) is important because, inevitably, the bottom line is sales. If consumers do not consume the advertised goods, the goods are quickly abandoned in favour of those more profitable. Hence, a simplistic condemnation of consumerism for its capitalist imbrications overlooks the ways in which it also affords a cooperative space that is accountable to its audience.

Although television is often constructed as a mediocre second cousin to film (the culturally dominant 'art' form), in many ways it is a more viewer-friendly medium. While media critics like John Ellis assert that TV is inherently 'conservative' because its 'mass audience' concentration relegates it to a 'middle ground' (224–8), it does not necessarily follow that the 'middle ground' TV inhabits is devoid of political agency. Television's 'mass appeal' may seem dangerously homogenizing, but, at the same time, it allows for subversion. Indeed, Jackie Byars argues that the medium has always pushed at cultural boundaries:

> The languages that we speak in turn speak in and through us ... A minority discourse – a feminine voice – has been engaged in a long-standing, active, though not always explicit, opposition to the dominant, masculine discourses in popular American film and television. Drawing on and expanding theories that acknowledge a long overshadowed minority discourse allows us to see a tradition of challenge in the contested narrative spaces not only at the margins, but at the very centre, of American culture. (128–9)

The possibilities television offers are a result, in part, of the viewing space in which it resides. That is, whereas film is watched in a public theatre, amidst a crowd of strangers (a venue that inhibits its audience [Ellis 26]), television is located in the home, historically replacing radio as the main form of domestic entertainment. Like radio, TV is often watched in groups and, given the comfort of its 'home' locus, generates viewer commentary and discussion. Further, television produces a wide range of images and portrayals that, normalized and conservative as they may be, are consequential since they reach into so many viewing spaces. Christine Gledhill points to how the depiction of disenfranchised or minority groups in mainstream narratives plays an important role in identity formulation:

> We need representations that take account of identities – representations that work with a degree of fluidity and contradiction – and we need to forge different identities – ones that help us make productive use of the contradictions of our lives. This means entering socio-economic, cultural and linguistic struggle to define and establish them in the media, which function as centres for the production and circulation of identity. (72)

Gledhill's observations, here, highlight the representational potential of popular culture, and her work, in general, illustrates the complicated weave of conflicting and even paradoxical components manifested by broadcast television. Indeed, an exemplar of that weave can be located in visual media portrayals of Natives.

Despite cultural contentions to the contrary, television has been more open to Native re-visions than the medium of film. Certainly, recent films have attempted to mitigate the traditional Hollywood offerings of 'cowboy and Indian' sagas (sagas that King lampoons and rewrites in passages like those in *Green Grass, Running Water* where the Native elders alter the endings of westerns); however, the medium continues to maintain a White focus. For all the critical attention afforded cinematic productions like *Dances with Wolves*, this film (and those like it) still retains a strong White male focus and offers messages to the effect that 'Natives are people too.' There have been few mainstream films, to date, that document Native experiences from Native perspectives. But television does.

Like film, televisual productions during the 1960s and '70s were permeated with cowboy and Indian series. Since that time, however, different forms of 'westerns' have appeared. American programs like *Northern Exposure* and Canadian series like *North of 60* offer a re-vision of the Native stereotypes that once dominated the airwaves. Indeed, *North of 60* is performed and sometimes written by Native artists – artists who include Thomas King. The program was produced by CBC, the network that, in 1992, televised a TV movie based on King's novel *Medicine River.*

Medicine River, adapted for the screen by King, is a very different work from the novel of the same name and to which it bears little resemblance. Altered and revamped for television, the tele-film inhabits a different medium than the written work, and evidences how diverse forms must be judged on their own terms, and in the context of their own venues. Within its own milieu, *Medicine River* is a highly subversive endeavour. One of the first mainstream adaptations of a Native text, it features a predominantly Native cast, starring Graham Greene, of *Dances with Wolves* fame, and Tom Jackson, of *North of 60.*

The tele-film opens by dramatizing Will Horse Capture's (mis)adventure in Africa. A photojournalist, Will is imprisoned by a rebel leader, and his camera offers him an avenue of escape when the rebel leader requests a portrait. Despite Will's protests that he doesn't 'do portraits,' he does agree to snap the photograph and is released. The camera then cuts to Will's home in Toronto, and his relationship with his partner/agent, Ellen, a blonde White woman. This interlude, in turn, is broken by a summons for Will to attend his mother's funeral at his childhood home in Medicine River.

At the Medicine River airport, Will is greeted by Harlen Bigbear, who embarks on various efforts to keep Will in the West. One of Harlen's schemes involves the production of a Native calendar. As Harlen explains, the Natives needed a van to transport their basketball team, but could only secure government funds for a calendar. Thus, they used the calendar money to buy the van, secured a bank loan to purchase the photography equipment necessary for the calendar, and now need to produce the calendar to repay the bank loan and to fulfil their government obligation. Will, who reiterates his plea that he doesn't 'do portraits,' is recruited as calendar photographer. The calendar structures the format of the movie and becomes a commemoration of the Native peoples of Alberta (rather than the flower calendar the government desired). Through it, Harlen introduces Will to various local Native characters, and involves him in the daily life of Medicine River. When Will meets Louise Heavyman, the pregnant accountant for the Native group, his interest is piqued, and she becomes one of the primary reasons he extends his stay in Medicine River. Despite Ellen's efforts to lure him back to Toronto – a city whose name Harlen can never remember ('Ahhhh, Montreal?') – Will ultimately decides that his place is in the West. The tele-film, consequently, pushes at various boundaries: through Will's relationship with Ellen; through his involvement with the independent Louise, who does not want a husband or a live-in partner; and through the inversion of the East/West binary (by conflating Toronto and Montreal, the major Eastern cities, Medicine River is posited as the site that is different and compelling).

Medicine River also crosses genres through the incorporation of photography into its televisual frames. Photographs of Native elders are interspersed throughout the program, which then push at the boundaries of the frames, culminating in the concluding scene wherein all the Natives gather for the collective photograph. As in the novel, Will is included within this photo, over which the closing credits run. As it highlights the familial venture of content and production through the credits, this shot also encompasses viewers, who, as audience, make the tele-film possible. In so doing, *Medicine River* offers a culmination of the interstices of genre crossings, as it itself intersects the media of photography, television, and film, and exemplifies the possibility of re-visionary material in a mainstream 'low culture' venue.

King's works, therefore, comprise an eclectic blend of genres, media, and disciplines, foregrounding their interactive potential. This Native author utilizes and exploits the political possibilities of the formats available to him, and blends them into a cooperative and collective multimedia aggregate. Such an endeavour testifies both to the flexibility of alternative venues, as well as to their diverse capacities, and, in the process, renders each an interactive forum for discursive reconstruction. And with the new addition of the cable channel Aboriginal Peoples Television, the medium is opened to further altern(arr)atives. However, since, at time of writing, the cable channel has only been offered for a short time, viewers must stay tuned – for future developments.

CHAPTER FIVE

Humouring Race and Nationality

Border crossings and re-crossings of various kinds are central to King's
work. As a writer, photographer, and even an actor (King makes a
cameo appearance in the television movie of *Medicine River* as a member
of a local basketball team, who comically taunts Will's initial clumsiness
on the court), his creative endeavours blend different genres and blur
the boundaries that typically separate disciplinary categories. By playing
with audience expectations and posing provocative questions about how
we define texts and their contexts, King cultivates a vision of hybridity
and diversity that highlights the complex political and cultural double
bind faced by a writer who produces genre-crossing texts that also straddle the forty-ninth parallel. This artistic and political mélange, however,
is not merely an attempt to erase categorical distinctions altogether.
Even though King's texts can be read as contesting the primacy of the
Canadian-U.S. border and standard Western divisions between literary
forms, he also works to establish and maintain certain distinct political
identities and the boundaries that support those positions in his texts.

Specifically, King's representations of the Canadian-U.S. border in
short stories like 'Borders,' and his depiction of race relations on both
sides of and across the forty-ninth parallel, demonstrate the permeability of 'race' and 'nation' as definitive categories. Conjoining in himself
the two partly collapsed dichotomies of Native and non-Native, Canadian and U.S., King regularly portrays how racial and national dividing
lines work – and do not work. In 'Borders,' the determination of a
Blackfoot woman to retain her tribal identity becomes a paradigmatic
parable about how borders enforce certain definitions and practices;
about how they sometimes function differently under scrutiny; and
about how little present political divisions have to do with other social

realities that predated and survived the carving up of the North American continent. The last point is especially important and reminds us that the 'borders' of King's title are plural. The Native is denied entry at a national boundary precisely because she insists she is Native. Refusing to be pushed across one border, she is refused permission to cross another.

In 'Borders,' King uses comedy as a strategy to highlight the ironies of a political situation in which competing notions of 'nation' and 'race' vie for domination. By refusing to locate herself within the discourse of 'nation,' as defined by Canada and the United States, King's female protagonist offers a third term that predates the creation of these two political entities. Her insistence that there is a 'Blackfoot side' destabilizes the precision of the forty-ninth parallel (136). Not surprisingly, then, the border guards quickly 'lose their sense of humor' when confronted with this alternative vision of nation (136), a conceptualization that incongruously revises the terms of the debate over national identity. In King's short story, the border guards repeatedly try to erase the protagonist's 'side' because, if they do not, they have to acknowledge the prior existence of the Blackfoot on both sides of the border. Such an act would displace the primacy of the forty-ninth parallel (and presumably undermine the guards' authority to demand that citizens declare their nationality as either Canadian or American). Hence, the humour of this scenario, achieved at the border guards' expense, derives, in part, from the juxtaposition of differing perspectives on what constitutes a nation and who has the last word on this concept.

'Borders' also explores a legacy of racial hierarchies that King's protagonist is attempting to reconfigure. Historically, Utah and Alberta provided places of settlement for Mormons. This influx of Mormons is reflected in the narrator's sister's vivid description of Salt Lake City, with its temples and 'good skiing,' amenities that her mother dismisses because they are also readily available in Alberta (137). The existence of Mormon temples in Utah and Alberta both suggests the pervasiveness of Mormon theology and symbolizes how racism has shaped land occupancy throughout the region. The Native as racial Other is a central tenet of Mormon theology. According to the *Book of Mormon*, God brought the Nephites from Israel to the New World as his chosen people. Those who strayed from true Christianity were eventually punished: God turned them into a dark and loathsome people. Natives in the New World were, for Mormons, the marked-as-sinners descendants of the Nephites, and one mission of the Church was to bring them back to the Truth again. By converting Natives, Mormons presumed that they would be transformed into a 'fair' people.[1] Such racism is playfully but also pointedly fore-grounded in King's narrative. One reason that may well have prompted Laetitia (the narrator's sister) to move to Utah would be to dispute her former boyfriend's teasing description: "'It's a great place,' Lester would say. 'Nothing but blondes in the whole state'" (137).

The racial implications of Mormon settlements in southern Alberta, on what should have been Blackfoot lands, are more directly invoked in 'Borders' through the young narrator's references to the names of local towns and nearby cities in Alberta, including Coutts and Cardston. Cardston, for instance, derives not just from Ora Card's leading a band of Mormons into southern Alberta at the end of the nineteenth cen-tury,[2] but also from the decision of Commissioner Steele of the North West Mounted Police to impose a 'cordon sanitaire' on the Blackfoot. The Canadian Blackfoot, he concluded, would be more manageable if they could not mingle freely with their American confederates, and so a strip of land on the southern side of the promised reserve (which was originally to be bounded by the international border) was confiscated and made available for non-Native settlement. For years, Indians were prohibited from crossing this land, even though it cut the Alberta Black-foot off from their promised timber reserves, which were supposed to supply the population with the lodge poles and firewood they otherwise lacked. The border was thus shaped by both national and racial differ-ences, differences that impeded the free flow of the Blackfoot. Ironi-cally, the Mormons were invited into Canada to settle on Blackfoot lands for the precise purpose of keeping the Blackfoot out – the 'Canadian' Blackfoot out of the United States, and the 'American' Blackfoot out of Canada.

'Borders' offers its own counter-discourse to the dominant definitions of nation and race, inducing cultural resistance to the fixity of these terms, and opening up possible alternatives. Here, the performative becomes a mode of intervention that generates subversive spaces by facilitating the re-creation of 'race' and 'nation' as discursive concepts. Laetitia's determination to move to Salt Lake City, a border crossing that challenges the racial make-up of the state, and the narrator's mother's desire to have her own national affiliation acknowledged by the border guards on both sides of the forty-ninth parallel, can be read as political acts that are intended to reverse (even if only temporarily) dominant paradigms. Re-figuring the forms that constitute a subject's identity, these characters encourage readers to re-vision how discourse has relegated Natives living in North America to the status of national and racial 'otherness.'

Border Colours

Individual and collective imagination play a central role in the construction of nation and race and, thus, have an equally important role in King's comic inversions of these concepts. As Benedict Anderson argues, the nation is 'an *imagined* political community' that is both 'inherently limited and sovereign' (15, our emphasis). Anderson's definition conveys the symbolic power of national identity for those who reside within its borders and acknowledge its significance. Although the residents of a nation may never 'know most of their fellow-members, meet them, or even hear of them ... the image of their communion' powerfully binds the population together, creating a sense of belonging and purpose (15). Hence, the writing of a nation's history – the narration of its existence through rhetorical forms – becomes an important political and cultural act. Such records are a tangible reflection of the power of the imagination to create and sustain a distinct national identity. But this notion of the unity of a nation and its population via rhetorical forms poses its own set of problems because nations are based on the premise of unity. According to Anderson, 'regardless of the inequality and exploitation that may prevail ... the nation is always conceived as a deep, horizontal comradeship' (16). But the unity of nation is always 'ultimately impossible precisely because it can be represented as such only through a suppression and repression, symbolic or otherwise, of difference' (Stratton and Ang 135). The sovereignty that a nation claims to assert as a universal ideal is always reliant on the existence of an 'other,' without whom the nation could not claim its dominant position. Clearly, ambivalence is an integral part of this concept.

King takes this ambivalence and uses it to explore the humorous incongruities that underlie the formation of borders and the stories that these dividing lines generate. More specifically, King's discourse reflects Native frustrations with the forty-ninth parallel and how these frustrations are played out to comic ends. In an interview with Constance Rooke, King describes the impact of a politically based national identity on Natives living on both sides of the border:

Well, I guess I'm supposed to say that I believe in the line that exists between the US and Canada, but for me it's an imaginary line. It's a line from somebody else's imagination; it's not my imagination. It divides people like the Mohawk into Canadian Mohawks and US Mohawks. They're the same people. It divides the Blackfoot who live in Browning from the Blackfoot who live at Standoff, for example. So the line is a political line, that border line ... that kind of border and that kind of nationalism create centres that I don't think do Indian people any good. It suggests things to us that we should become, things I'm not much interested in becoming. (72)

King points out that the priority given to the forty-ninth parallel means that tribal conceptions of nation are ignored or dismissed altogether. As Cheryl Walker notes, in her study of nineteenth-century Native American literature and nationalism, 'Native Americans had not traditionally understood nations as the West came to define them. Nor did race play much of a role in their thinking. In Indian oral traditions the nation originally meant simply the people and the environment they inhabited, an environment without legislated boundaries' (4–5). In fact, the notion of an Indian 'nation' may be described as 'prenational, reflecting a worldview more akin to the unself-consciously coherent sacralized communities that preceded modern political arrangements' (6). Yet, tribal imaginations remain a vital part of Native self-conception and provide a starting point for Indians to reconceptualize themselves and their identities, beyond the confines of non-Native political lines. King shows how ludicrous the Canadian-U.S. border appears – from a Native perspective – when he notes that it separates populations who are 'the same people,' who have the same traditions and belief systems, and even share the same tribal language. Moreover, the horizontal comradeship that Anderson describes as part of the construction of a nation only applies to those who are located at the centre and see that border as a primary source of self-definition.

Policing Race and Nation

Part of the process of establishing and sustaining standard definitions of nation and race involves the policing of those who challenge or deviate from the norm, situations that take on a special resonance when King's texts revise these formulations by re-enacting the legacy of western movies and the history of colonization on both sides of the border. For instance, in 'Borders,' the initial stand-off between the narrator's mother and the border guards has a 'western' subtext. When the first border guard and his reinforcement come out of the customs building to approach the car, they walk 'swaying back and forth like two cowboys headed for a bar or a gunfight' (135). They are headed for a confrontation with an Indian that continues a five-hundred-year-old debate over just where the dividing lines between Whites and Natives should be drawn in both racial and national terms. The fact that these lines have been, for the most part, forcibly inflicted on Native peoples is also suggested in the story by the number of customs officers – particularly Americans – who carry guns. Ironically, although the Blackfoot mother is not allowed to carry firearms across the border, she is repeatedly questioned on that score.

King imaginatively reworks the forcible violence that underlies this border-crossing scenario in a somewhat different context, in *Green Grass, Running Water*, when the four Native runaways alter the outcome of a videotaped John Wayne movie, as discussed previously. This movie is owned by Bill Bursum, the White proprietor of an electronics shop near the reserve, and a fan of cowboy westerns. Notably, Bursum is also involved in the land dispute over the site of the dam and the construction of lakefront vacation properties on reserve lands. As the owner of a section of the lakefront, who cannot build until Eli's cabin is removed, Bursum repeatedly urges Eli to move it. Eli's insistence that he will stay there 'as long as the grass is green and the waters run' seems ridiculous to Bursum, who sees Native treaties between the federal government and local tribes as merely 'contracts, and no one signed a contract for eternity. No one. Even the E-Z Pay contracts Bursum offered to his customers ... never ran much past five or ten years' (224). Midway through the novel, Bursum creates a massive visual display, called 'The Map,' in the window of his store, depicting Canada and the United States in the form of a digitized screen image (108). The store owner revels in the power of the window display, which is intended to convey a 'unifying metaphor' of identity (108). But when asked by a Native employee to locate Blossom on the screens, Bursum gestures vaguely at the televisions. He takes pride in the map precisely because it 'was like having the universe there on the wall, being able to see everything, being in control' (109). By asserting his vision on the television screens, however, Bursum erases distinctive tribal identities altogether.

Bursum's visual demonstration of his commitment to transnational capitalism, even at the expense of his local and primarily Native customer base, is intimately connected to his interest in cowboy westerns, films that use visual markers of race both in defining who belongs to the community and who is different or 'other.' Lionel observes Bursum as he watches his favourite John Wayne film with the four Native runaways: 'How Bursum loved his Westerns ... Every one was the same as each other. Predictable. Cowboys looked like cowboys. Indians looked like Indians' (264). The concept of race relies on these visible distinctions, as Peter Li explains in *Race and Ethnic Relations in Canada*: 'Superficial physical traits are regarded as ... grounds for classifying people into racial groups; skin colour in particular is ... held to be the most salient characteristic in differentiating between "white" and "coloured" people' (3). Moreover, the biological and genetic factors that are used to identify distinctive racial groups are 'also held to determine people's mental, social, and cultural capabilities' (3). Bursum, not surprisingly, is often dismissive of his Native employees' abilities. When building 'The Map,' for instance, he is sure that Lionel will never understand it: 'Power and control – the essences of effective advertising – were, Bursum had decided years before, outside the range of the Indian imagination' (109). Thus, the Native runaways' alterations to Bursum's treasured John Wayne film take on an added resonance because they manage to do precisely what Bursum has presumed to be beyond the capacity of Native peoples: imaginatively to seize power and control from people, like Bursum, who see themselves as superior.

The Natives in Bursum's store take great delight in the Native elders' reworking of the cowboy western. Nor is their manipulation of a technology that has been used to relegate Indians to 'otherness' confined to the single videotape of the film. The four mythic figures also appear in a television version of the same movie that is watched by various members of the community – Latisha, Lionel, and Charlie – as well as Dr Hovaugh and Babo. Hovaugh and Babo, however, are the only ones to notice that the escaped patients have inserted themselves into the movie. While Hovaugh panics, (the African-American) Babo relishes the trickery of these Native figures who transgress the distinction between art and life in order to (or, at least, to try to) alter the formulaic outcome of this movie for the television-watching population. Bursum assumes that the Native population lacks the ability to understand the power of the media, a presumption that is clearly faulty given the changes that these mythic figures make to the western 'classic.' In fact, Bursum becomes the butt of the joke in this case precisely because he blames technology, rather than the Native community, for what he perceives as an erroneous outcome in the movie's plot: 'Well, something sure as hell got screwed up ... Damn. You put your faith in good equipment and look what happens' (268).

Bursum's comfort with the formulaic qualities of the western as a genre, in which advancing (White) civilization displaces (Indian) savagery through violence and domination, reflects his unquestioning acceptance of racial hierarchies that are determined by visible markers, like the exaggerated nose and the long black hair of the Indian chief in the John Wayne film. But, as King's novel repeatedly demonstrates, these physical traits are often little more than social constructs. Charlie Looking Bear, who watches the movie in Bursum's store, realizes that the Native chief in the film is his father, Portland Looking Bear, who changed his name to Iron Eyes Screeching Eagle and donned a rubber nose to land starring Native roles in various Hollywood westerns. As we have mentioned, Portland initially expressed contempt for the nose and nailed it to the wall of his bathroom. But, after six months without a job, Portland's wife entered the bathroom one morning and discovered that the nose was gone. Paradoxically, once Portland agreed to wear the nose on-screen, he was able to revive his career and win parts that he could not otherwise get. Yet the rubber nose also impedes his breathing and changes the sound of his voice. In time, it becomes a rotting and smelly appendage that dominates his face and makes 'people ... measure their distance' (130).

Portland's nose symbolizes the close links between what Peggy Phelan calls 'representational visibility and political power' (1). The visibility of racial difference in the western helps to reinforce distinctions that have been established at the level of discourse. As Phelan goes on to explain, 'Seeing the other is a social form of self-reproduction. For in looking at/ for the other, we seek to re-present ourselves to ourselves' (21). In this John Wayne movie, the physical markers of race, which include Portland's obscenely large nose, provide non-Native audience members (such as Bursum) with a visible justification for the cowboy's attempts to destroy the Indians. Though Portland initially rejects the nose as a clown-like appendage that mocks his racial identity, the film – and his appearance in it with the nose – offers White and Native viewers alike an opportunity to take pleasure in the voyeuristic aspects of seeing what constitutes the Native 'other.' The movie, when untouched by the Native runaways, gives Bursum the chance temporarily to overturn Eli's defiant refusal to move his cabin from the dam's spillway by watching White cowboys handily defeat their Indian enemies. Once altered, however, the film inverts the powerlessness of the Indians' visibility and encourages readers to recognize the constructedness of race as a category that is then used to justify the destruction of one population by another.

De-linking Race and Nation

Although the concept of race cuts across national borders, including the forty-ninth parallel, 'discrimination, classification and the organization of social relations between "races" takes place within nation-states,' where the regulation of specific policies about citizenship and access to resources can be enforced (Guibernau 86). The terms 'nation' and 'race' are closely linked by their mutual reliance on power relations and the existence of a minority group that may be used to justify the supremacy of the majority. Minority groups are not necessarily numerically smaller. Yet they are perceived as inferior and usually face 'prejudice and unequal treatment' (87). In this context, race 'becomes a political category fixing a well-defined distinction between various groups' that is reinforced by the minority population's limited access to education, employment, and housing (88).

The dispossession of a colonized people (or minority group), such as Native North Americans, is typically facilitated by their misrepresentation. By portraying a minority population as deserving of what is done to them, those in the majority legitimize their own superiority and give themselves licence to regulate the concept of race via the enforcement of national borders. This point is made effectively by King in another of his short stories, one that turns on the policing of race through the policing of representation of race *and* nation. Simply put, 'Joe the Painter and the Deer Island Massacre' tells the story of a White man, in a small California coastal town, who sets out to win the large cash prize that is offered for the best pageant commemorating the town's centennial. Three entries compete for the prize. The first portrays how a prostitute enlisted some of her associates and clients to put out a New Year's Eve fire that might have destroyed the town because 'most of the firemen were at a party and pretty drunk' (111). The second is 'real dull' and consists of some businessmen who act out 'the founding of the first city council' (111). The third, and the focus of the story, is the pageant produced by Joe, who decides that he will portray the actual founding of the town, which involved a massacre of local Natives who were in the way of the first White settlers.

To this end, he recruits one Native friend to find 'thirty or forty Indians. All kinds ... you know, men, women, and kids' willing to act in the pageant (103). As 'the Native Son Players,' the Indians act out the arrival of European settlers. The play traces the initially peaceful relationship between the different peoples, the growth of the non-Native settlement and its increasing encroachment onto Indian land, and the resolution of that problem by – the climax of the pageant – a surprise attack on the Indians camped on Deer Island, the one place they insisted they wouldn't share, but which the new settlers have nonetheless claimed. At the end of the performance, Joe, as Matthew Larson, the founder of the town, reveals that his is a mission of colonization at any cost: 'I abhor the taking of a human life but civilization needs a strong arm to open the frontier. Farewell, Redman. Know that from your bones will spring a new and stronger community forever' (116). Not surprisingly, this pageant does not win the award, which goes to the businessmen's 'real dull' play.

Although Joe is an unlikely candidate to precipitate a comic inversion of White-authored history, that is exactly what he does in King's narrative. Part of his success in doing so depends upon his race: Joe is not even asked to submit a script for the pageant, when it is initially presented, and his idea is repeatedly praised by the mayor and a selection jury. The fact that Joe is White leads the jury to presume he will reinforce the reigning narrative of nation, and police the concept of race in an 'appropriate' fashion. Joe is expected to present an account of the massacre that legitimates Matthew Larson's elimination of the Native residents on the island. But Joe is both respectful of American nationalism and appreciative of other kinds of civic pride, whether it involves standing for the Canadian anthem when it is being played on television or attending political rallies of all the different parties.

Nevertheless, Joe is not immune from stereotyping, himself. The Natives who are called upon to perform Indian roles are partly in disguise, as a result of Joe's attempts to replicate the racial 'authenticity' of what he identifies as uniquely Indian. Shortly after rehearsals start, Joe tells the narrator: 'Your Indians don't look like Indians' (110). In his brutally honest fashion, Joe insists that, to be historically accurate, the Native participants in the pageant need to have 'long hair with braids': 'They all got crew cuts! Hell, we can't have Indians with crew cuts. No one's going to believe that Indians in 1863 had crew cuts ... We got to find them some wigs' (110). As with the John Wayne movie in which Portland Looking Bear has to don a rubber nose to attain a more Indian appearance, Joe's desire to put wigs on his actors reflects the non-Native population's need to construct a particular vision of what constitutes Indianness, a manageable and easily recognized representation of the 'other.' Yet, despite Joe's tendency to rely on clichéd notions of what is authentically 'Indian,' including his assumption that all of the Native actors for the pageant own and live in tents and thus would be happiest with camping accommodations during rehearsals, he still manages to turn these same stereotypes inside out.

Joe is attentive to the historical record, as the narrator explains, even when it favours Natives by depicting them as eloquent rather than uncivilized:

> Halfway through the act, I came out to complain that Larson and his people were encroaching on my people's land. I thought it sounded strange for an Indian in 1863 to complain about whites 'encroaching' on their land but Joe swore that it was a direct quote from the historical record. Redbird had a better vocabulary than I did. (113)

Further, Joe does not hesitate to include a graphic confrontation between the Indians and Larson's men that depicts the deliberate genocide of Natives by the settlers. Rather than shying away from enacting the raid itself, Joe devotes an entire act of the pageant to this task. Aided by various props, this final portion of the pageant parodies the massacre. The Indians wear 'jeans and jackets 'cause we couldn't find any good costumes for all of them'; various guns, knives, and an old sword borrowed from a local resident constitute the White settlers' collection of weapons; the noise of the gunshots is generated by the players, who are unable to locate any blanks for the guns themselves; and the blood wounds inflicted on the sleeping Natives are represented by plastic bags of ketchup that prove a challenge to burst (115). The weapons, costumes, and special effects highlight the comic subtext of this pageant, which both invokes history, and then reveals some of the incongruities in the event itself. One of the most striking is that the pageant, which commemorates the passing of the Indians, takes place only because there are still Natives to play almost all of the roles. Preparing to perform, on Deer Island, how they were exterminated on Deer Island, these Natives also partly re-enact the life their ancestors led there before the massacre, which includes drumming, dancing, 'singing a few social songs,' telling traditional stories, and hearing 'the frogs in the distance and the water pushing at the edges of the island' (108). Again, not surprisingly, only the Native actors 'enjoyed ... [the] pageant,' and tell Joe that should he ever 'need Indians again to just give them a call' (117).

Racial Crossings

In *Green Grass, Running Water*, the story of Babo Jones, a cleaner at the American mental hospital that housed the runaway Natives, exemplifies how race continues to be policed by the nation-state, and conversely, what strategies minority characters, and authors like King, use to challenge these stereotypes. Jones, an African-American woman, is questioned by two White police officers, named Sergeant Cereno, and Jimmy Delano, who come to the hospital to investigate the patients' disappearance. Cereno, when he does not receive the answers he wants to hear from Babo, turns her questioning over to his junior officer, Jimmy, with the following line: 'Enough of this dog and pony show ... You finish up with Aunt Jemima' (45).

Although some readers may not know Melville's *Benito Cereno*, the Aunt Jemima reference establishes a framework for recognizing and mocking Cereno's racism. Those who do know Melville's text will recognize that, within it, Babo is the leader of a shipboard rebellion by African slaves against their Spanish master, Benito Cereno. Most of *Benito Cereno* is relayed through the voice of Captain Amasa Delano, a Yankee, who encounters Cereno's ship after the slave takeover. Delano boards Cereno's ship when he spots it lingering dangerously close to land. Babo successfully masks the slave rebellion, and Delano remains unaware of Cereno's desperate desire to escape with his life, until he leaves the ship. A crucial scene in the novella depicts Babo brandishing a razor and shaving Benito Cereno as the ship's captain proceeds to tell Delano about the history of his voyage. This ritual paradoxically ensures the African's control over what Cereno reveals, even though his actions appear to show deference to the ship's master. Cereno shakes with fear throughout the ordeal, and Babo eventually draws blood with his straight razor. This threat to Cereno's life keeps him from talking honestly to Delano.

The Babo who appears in *Green Grass, Running Water* is a female descendant and namesake of this Black rebel, who, at the end of *Benito Cereno*, is put in irons and burned for his transgressive actions. Babo alludes to him when she tells Jimmy Delano: 'My great-great grandfather was a barber on a ship. Sailed all over the place, cutting hair, shaving people ... Now, my great-great-grandfather could handle a blade. Have I got stories – ' (75–6). With this intertext, the Indians' escape from the mental hospital becomes a parodic repetition of an earlier rebellion, facilitated once again by Babo, who tells the officers that 'someone could have forgotten to lock the door ... Someone could have helped them escape' (44). Cereno, however, misses Babo's clues precisely because he cannot fathom how she may have succeeded in undermining Whiteness as a mark of superiority.

On her trip to Canada with Dr Hovaugh to find the Native runaways, Babo, like the escapees, who recognize the world needs fixing, notices that both the Canadian and American flagpoles at the forty-ninth parallel need straightening. Her attentiveness signals the need to pay attention and look more closely at the situation to perceive all of its subtleties, including those that might not fit the conventions of a Eurocentric linear narrative. Throughout, King's novel repeatedly emphasizes the need to acknowledge a variety of perspectives, including those expressed by Native North Americans. The narrator even admonishes Coyote several times with instructions to 'pay attention' (31) and to 'forget being helpful ... Sit down and listen' (191). As Fee and Flick point out, borders and the tendency to dwell on them can 'make us stupid and allow us to remain so if we let them' (Fee and Flick 132). They also contend that King's work demands 'cross-border thinking' from readers (138). That is, rather than perceiving borderlines as a way to define and regulate populations, King's writing encourages 'lateral (or bilateral or trilateral)' movement by readers across American, Canadian, and Native lines (138); in addition to 'the disciplinary borders between English literature, Native Studies, and Anthropology, [as well as] the literary border between Canadian and American literature.' Fee and Flick note, however, that the most important border 'is between white ignorance and red knowledge' (132). To 'pay attention,' therefore, requires patience and a closer examination of stories and perspectives presented in *Green Grass, Running Water* by characters who are usually relegated to the margins, like Babo.

Locating Oneself

Part of the challenge posed by the policing of race and nation is the sense of alienation that many of King's Native characters experience because they are continually negotiating the borders between their tribal reserves and the world beyond, which is typically dominated by Eurocentric values. The struggle to create alterna(rra)tives that both encompass and subvert the dominance of the political nation-state over the tribal nation adds a poignant and often tragically ironic dimension to King's overtly comic texts. This internal conflict complicates those readings of race and nation that focus on the forty-ninth parallel by exploring the policing that takes place within the nation-state. 'Joe the Painter and the Deer Island Massacre,' for example, demonstrates how most non-Native citizens, with the exception of Joe, try to hide or forget a North American history of Indian genocide. But the desire of some Natives to pass as White, and to be accepted as part of the establishment in the context of the Canadian nation-state, also becomes an issue in King's fiction.

In particular, King's texts explore the tensions between race and nation for Natives living in Canada, a country with its own uncertainties about its national identity. As a country with a legacy of colonization under the British monarch, a recently signed constitution (1982), and no single act of revolution to mark the end of this colonial relationship, Canada's self-image differs substantially from that of the United States. Canada is embroiled in its own set of contradictions, especially regarding Native peoples. As Terry Goldie explains in *Fear and Temptation: The Image of the Indigene in Canadian, Australian, and New Zealand Literatures*, non-Native Canadians have one of two choices. They may attempt to incorporate 'the Other,' or 'white culture may reject the indigene' altogether, a decision – though increasingly unpopular – that has created a legacy of New World history that begins with the arrival of European settlers (13). More typically, Goldie suggests non-Natives choose the former, and 'in their need to become "native," to belong here, whites in Canada ... have adopted a process ... termed "indigenization" ... which suggests the impossible necessity of becoming indigenous' (13). For White writers, in particular, 'the only chance for indigenization seems to be through writing about the humans who are truly indigenous, [such as] the Indians' (13). In other words, these non-Natives view their textual portraits of Natives as an opportunity to negotiate for and gain a sense of national belonging that is otherwise inaccessible or illegitimate.

In her study of how Indians are depicted by White English-Canadian authors, Margery Fee stresses the important roles that Natives living in Canada play in the construction and maintenance of a Canadian notion of romantic nationalism. Native characters, paradoxically, strengthen Canadians' conceptions of their own, unique cultural identity. Fee explains that

it is difficult to kill off the literary Indian for good ... One explanation for his stubborn immortality here may be that many of the techniques that might kill him off ... come from cultures where nationalism is not an issue ... Marginal cultures can rarely afford to be cynical about nationalism: we are afraid that if we don't believe in Indians, we will have to become Americans. (29–30)

The fear of Manifest Destiny, in Fee's opinion, is one reason why Natives remain an especially important and complex 'other' for Canadians. Daniel Francis makes a similar point in *The Imaginary Indian* by noting that 'sometimes we thought it was simply a matter of conquering the Indians, taking their territory, and absorbing them out of existence. Then America would be ours. Sometimes we thought just the opposite, that we had to become Indians in order to be at home' (222–3). For Francis, 'this myth of transformation lies at the heart of Canadian culture: Canadians need to transform themselves into Indians' (223). Natives provide access to something that is indigenous to that place, which ties them to the land in a manner that colonial settlement never can. White Americans historically have treated Blacks as a reflection of everything they were not by institutionalizing slavery. Although Natives were also seen as representing a lower, corrupted nature, their fate in the United States primarily involved relocation and extermination rather than mass enslavement. Canada has also been involved in the marginalization of racial minorities. But, in English Canada's case, 'the Other has been located in the native, who has been used to solidify the White-English Canadian identity' (Walton 78).

Rather than relay another White version of Native otherness, King's texts take this familiar trajectory and redirect it, in order to explore how various Indian characters attempt to construct themselves as White Canadians and end up transgressing standard notions of race and nation to assert their own Native-centred perspectives of these concepts. In his interview with Rooke, King expresses his frustration that nationalism is based on superiority/inferiority relationships: 'Canadians may not feel superior to the British, but they damn well feel superior to Indians' (72). Such power relations are especially difficult for Natives who have been raised on the reserve: if success is measured in a traditionally Eurocentric fashion (through individual achievement of wealth and power), leaving the reserve and integrating oneself into the mainstream becomes an obvious strategy. In *Green Grass, Running Water*, King examines the difficulties with this tactic in a bitterly comic fashion that inverts hierarchical presumptions of White superiority and criticizes the ways in which Natives perpetuate their own sense of inferiority by focusing on standard definitions of nation and race. Eli Stands Alone, for example, in his youth, embodies a desire to become White, a decision that changes when he returns to the reserve in later life. *Green Grass, Running Water* provides a retrospective reading of Eli's life through his experiences on and off the reserve. Eli becomes a model of the struggle to locate racial and national identity outside of Eurocentric frameworks and to find a sense of satisfaction in 'in-betweenness.' At the same time, Eli demonstrates how helpful knowing the dominant discourse can be for those who want to reverse the subordination of Native peoples.

At the beginning of *Green Grass, Running Water*, Norma tells Lionel, a television salesman who is going through his own rejection of his tribal heritage, that 'your uncle [Eli] wanted to be a white man. Just like you ... A white man ... As if they were something special. As if there weren't enough of them in the world already' (30). Eli, we learn, has left the reserve as a young man and followed what he later recognizes to be an all too familiar path:

> It was a common enough theme in novels and movies. Indian leaves the traditional world of the reserve, goes to the city, and is destroyed. Indian leaves the traditional world of the reserve, is exposed to White culture, and becomes trapped between two worlds. Indian leaves the traditional world of the reserve, gets an education, and is shunned by his tribe ... The Indian who couldn't go home. (239)

Eli's life duplicates this formulaic narrative. He remains estranged from his family and the reserve for decades, making his home in Toronto and rarely returning to visit his relations. He performatively disassociates himself from his Indianness through silence. With Eli, racial and national affiliations within a tribal context are displaced by a commitment to the nation-state of Canada and an acknowledgment of its colonial ties.

Eli's relationship with Karen, a wealthy White woman, whom he meets in Toronto, adds another aspect to his attempts at racial passing. She is attracted to 'the idea that Eli was Indian' (137). Frantz Fanon, in *Black Skins, White Masks*, describes the role that White women play in validating the Whiteness of Black (or Native) men in strikingly personal terms: 'I wish to be acknowledged not as *black* but as *white* ... [W]ho but a white woman can do this for me? By loving me she proves that I am worthy of white love. I am loved like a white man. I am a white man' (63). This process of 'deracialization' works in two ways in *Green Grass, Running*

Water (71). Eli's desire to pass as White is facilitated by a partnership that validates his choice. Concomitantly, Eli offers Karen access to the culture of the indigenous other, whose ties to the land precede the claims of colonial settlers; through this association, she can play at being Indian.

Shortly after they strike up a friendship, Karen begins to lend Eli books on Indians. What primarily characterizes the books she offers him is that they are '*about* Indians. Histories, autobiographies, memoirs of writers who had gone west or who had lived with a particular tribe, romances of one sort or another' (136, our emphasis). Through these texts, Eli learns – and makes fun of – the formulas that have been used to construct and represent Natives as a racial 'other.' He also becomes acquainted with rules that govern interracial relationships between White women and Native men: 'There would be a conflict of some sort between the whites and the Indians. And Iron Eyes would be forced to choose between Annabelle and his people. In the end he would choose his people ... because Western writers seldom let Indians sleep with whites' (166). The erotic tensions between the exotic Native other and the White captive are replayed in Eli's own life when he goes to bed with Karen. She straddles him and pins him down before telling Eli that he is her 'Mystic Warrior' (138), a name that parodically invokes the legacy of White domination over Natives in a sexualized context. Here, Karen fetishizes Eli's 'Indianness' by rhetorically 'transforming the "unknown" (and potentially anxiety-inducing "other") into the "known" (the reassuring familiar)' (Phelan 94). His racial visibility is reframed and contained within well-known formulations, which, in turn, make Eli increasingly uneasy about his admiration of 'Whiteness' as a category he aspires to join.

When Karen becomes seriously ill with cancer, she asks Eli if they can visit his family and see the Sun Dance, a ceremony that she has persuaded him to attend in the past, despite his reluctance to 'go home,' especially with her (239). During the one previous journey they made back to the reserve, Karen is awestruck by the beauty of the Sun Dance setting, with the teepees, lodges, horses, and children: 'It's like it's right out of a movie ... It's like going back in time, Eli' (169). Karen reads the ceremony through her previous knowledge of westerns and commercialized representations of Indian traditions. Although she is respectful of the Sun Dance and eagerly shares the experience with others, once back in Toronto, Karen's 'ways of working the Sun Dance into the conversation' also make Eli feel estranged from his heritage, as he realizes that 'he didn't have the answers to the questions people wanted to ask' (220). Her mother and stepfather decide that they too want to join Eli and Karen at the Sun Dance. For Karen's parents, the ceremony offers 'one hell of a vacation' (221). Their well-meaning but naive interpretation of the Sun Dance replicates Karen's fetishistic treatment of Eli's race and threatens to turn what is supposed to be a private tribal ceremony into an opportunity to commodify Native culture.

Eli avoids subsequent visits to the reserve, feeling unsure himself about where he belongs because he has so thoroughly absorbed White conceptions of Natives. Nonetheless, he has become an expert in reading White texts of all kinds and playing these narratives out in his own life. This knowledge, which can be destructive, becomes useful when Eli does go home, after Karen's death, and actively begins to subvert White formulations of what constitutes 'Indianness.'

Although he returns to the reserve a few times to attend the Sun Dance ceremonies, Eli does not actually move back to the Blossom area until his mother dies and he learns that her hand-built house now blocks the proposed spillway for the dam and is in danger of being torn down. As we have argued, once he is back at the house, Eli immediately decides to block the construction of the dam and fight for the preservation of his mother's legacy, an act that subverts the generic White-authored narratives about Natives who leave the reserve never to return again. He articulates his own resistance to such stereotypes, which are based on the presumption that Natives actually want to become like Whites and be recognized as part of the nation-state, by taking these tired and familiar plots in another direction. Eli ironically notes that 'in the end, he had become what he had always been. An Indian ... An Indian back on the reserve' (219). Thus, when the dam-builder, Sifton, arrives for one of his daily visits to Eli's home, Eli is in an excellent position to argue against the notion that Natives are a dying breed whose tribal rights as individual nations are non-existent:

> Sifton stayed in the chair. 'You know what the problem is? This country doesn't have an Indian policy. Nobody knows what the hell anybody else is doing.'
>
> 'Got the treaties.'
>
> 'Hell, Eli, those treaties aren't worth a damn. Government only makes them for convenience. Who'd of guessed that there would still be Indians kicking around in the twentieth century.'
>
> 'One of life's little embarrassments.'

'Besides, you guys aren't real Indians anyway. I mean, you drive cars, watch television, go to hockey games. Look at you. You're a university professor.'

'That's my profession. Being an Indian isn't a profession.' (119)

Eli recognizes the absurdity of Sifton's claims and deliberately undercuts the White dam manager's desire to relegate the Indians to the distant past or see them as 'inauthentic' for having participated in a program of forced assimilation. Nor is he willing to let Sifton insist that White-governed progress is the only answer for the reserve.

Moreover, when Sifton invokes Melville's Bartleby the Scrivener' as an example of a man who, like Eli, 'didn't want to do anything to improve his life' (119), Eli uses his intimate knowledge of Eurocentric constructions of Indian stereotypes to expose the comic dimensions of this comparison. Eli names the Melville story, providing the title and author, both of which Sifton has forgotten, and then proceeds to undercut the dam manager's reading of Bartleby's demise:

'"Bartleby the Scrivener." One of Herman Melville's short stories.'

'I guess. The point is that this guy had lost touch with reality. And you know what happens to him at the end of the story?'

'It's fiction, Cliff.'

'He dies. That's what happens. Suggest anything to you?'

'We all die, Cliff.' (120)

Like the blood Babo draws from Cereno's neck, Eli's point that all human beings will eventually die blurs the boundaries between racial difference, a distinction that Sifton is relying on to eliminate those Natives who are impeding the progress of his dam. Eli's rhetorical skill, his sharp sense of irony, and his willingness to deconstruct Sifton's assumptions make for a series of entertaining verbal exchanges between the two. When Sifton gives up in frustration at the end of the conversation, Eli warns him about the dangers of assuming that Whites can control Indians or, for that matter, the natural world as they are trying to do with the dam: 'You can't hold water back forever' (120). Sifton may see the dam 'as part of the natural landscape,' but Eli knows better (121). His perceptiveness also demonstrates the need for non-Native readers to 'pay attention' and look beyond the visible markers of race, a task that is facilitated by learning to read differently and to negotiate incongruities, contradictions, and spaces of liminality rather than relying on White-authored definitions of identity, which reinforce static and hierarchical notions of nation and race.

Border Studies: Reconfiguring the Mexican-American Focus

King's explorations of race and nation can be read as expanding and reconfiguring the field of border studies, an area of scholarly inquiry that has gained prominence because of the national and racial tensions that exist at the Mexican-U.S. border. Border studies is a field that moves across genres and disciplinary borders, but also specifically examines the ways in which race and nation are constructed and reinforced via policing. As Renée Hulan reminds readers, '... the division of the continent into nation-states does not reflect the ancient relationship with the land shared by Aboriginal peoples of the Americas' (17). King's narratives add another important dimension to border studies by depicting the mutability of race and nation for Native peoples in a specifically Canadian-U.S. context. If, as we have argued, King uses Native humour to undermine Eurocentric expectations and to offer alternative definitions of identity and community, how does his writing re-imagine the realm of border studies? What do King's comic inversions of racial and national hierarchies contribute to this rapidly expanding field, and how might his textual focus on the forty-ninth parallel challenge or alter directions for future inquiry?[3]

King's most recent novel, *Truth and Bright Water*, addresses and reworks some of the central debates within border studies regarding race and nation in a typically subversive and comic fashion. The title of the novel couples the Canadian town of Bright Water with the American town of Truth, ironically locating the source of 'truth' south of the Canadian border, and thus reminding readers of the colonial perceptions that still circulate in Canada regarding American superiority. This wordplay also invokes long-standing Canadian fears of Manifest Destiny: the possibility that American troops will invade Canada and claim it for themselves. Although such a military operation may seem ludicrous today, the imperial relations between Canada and the United States are reflected in the United States' current economic and cultural involvement in Canada. Foreign trade, the ownership of businesses, and the circulation of television, film, and printed materials produced in 'America' and exported north of the border all have an impact on constructions of Canadian national identity.

Unlike 'Borders,' the stretch of the forty-ninth parallel depicted in

Truth and Bright Water is not governmentally patrolled. As becomes clear, however, it remains plagued by imperial practices *and* the desire of non-Natives living on both sides of the border to exploit Native populations at their convenience, and for their own profit. The young Aboriginal narrator of the novel begins by describing the towns, relative to one another:

> At a distance, the bridge between Truth and Bright Water looks whole and complete, a pale thin line, delicate and precise, bending over the Shield and slipping back into the land like a knife. But if you walk down into the coulees and stand in the shadow of the deserted columns and the concrete arches, you can look up through the open planking and the rusting webs of iron mesh, and see the sky. (1)

The porousness of the bridge is not a deliberate feature of the structure, for it has been abandoned midway through construction, despite the promise that it will bring prosperity to this predominantly Native-populated area by boosting tourism.

Many members of the Native community express their disappointment with the bridge, which they see as a lost opportunity, particularly once construction comes to a halt. As local real estate agent Miles Deardorf ironically notes during a discussion about the bridge's demise, 'Franklin bet on the bridge ... and look what happened' (165). Designed to reroute tourists into the area, the bridge is intended to connect the reserve in Bright Water to the town itself and create a direct link between Truth, on the American side, with its Canadian counterpart. But those who have watched the promised bridge appear and then – literally – begin to disintegrate take a more ambivalent but also ironic view of the subject. For example, Gabriel Tucker initially points out that a 'bridge like that would have kicked the economy in the ass and got it jumping' (166). However, this regretful tone is soon undercut by humour, when Miles suggests that Gabriel think about investing in Parliament Lake, yet another development that is intended to revitalize the economy:

> Skee takes out a paper towel and blows his nose into it. 'You talking about Parliament Lake?'
>
> 'It's lakefront property.'
>
> 'It's a mud flat,' says Gabriel.
>
> Miles takes out a ten and drops it on the counter. 'Soon as they fill the

lake again, you won't be able to buy property like that for love nor money.'

'You believe that,' says Gabriel, 'and I've got a bridge I can sell you.' (167)

Meta-fictively, Parliament Lake is the name of the land development scheme in *Green Grass, Running Water* that is sabotaged by the four Native mythic figures. Thus, when Gabriel compares Parliament Lake to the unfinished bridge, what he is mocking is the assumption that these government-funded projects – on both sides of the border – are intended to benefit Natives. In this context, the bridge becomes a monument to non-Native conceptions of the differences between the Canadian and U.S. sides, a dividing line that, paradoxically, seems ridiculously artificial to the local Native community.

For the narrator and his mother, the act of crossing the Canadian-U.S. border is not what counts. In fact, when the young boy goes with his mother to visit his grandmother, who lives in Bright Water, and they travel across the river on the aging ferry, the mother takes a moment to note that the river predates the bridge, as well as the construction of those borders and boundaries that divide Canada from the United States:

My mother stops pulling for a moment and looks over the edge of the bucket. 'It's been here since the beginning of time,' she says. 'Did you know that?'

'The ferry?'

'No,' she says. 'The river.' (52)

Much like the narrator's insistence in *Green Grass, Running Water* that Coyote 'pay attention,' the mother, here, presents a subversive reading of the border that favours the natural world and notions of mutability over the fixity of the nation-state, which depends upon the construction and reinforcement of various kinds of boundaries for its existence. The boy adds yet another youthfully irreverent and revealing perspective to conceptions of borders when he takes a cruise around a local lake, as part of a family holiday. During the boat ride, the narrator is surprised to learn that 'the Canadian / United States border ran right through the middle of the lake' (78). As he explains, 'When the guy driving the boat told us that, I expected to see a floating fence or inner tubes with barbed wire and lights, something to keep people from straying from

one country into the other' (78). His imaginary rendering of the border emphasizes the presumption that the border is always policed, an
image more appropriate to the Mexican-U.S. border than the forty-
ninth parallel. Yet, ironically, the boy and his mother performatively
undermine the solidity of this dividing line every time they journey
across the river by ferry, and, literally, stray across the border at their
own discretion.

Even King's choice of name for his young narrator becomes an ironic
comment on the fluidity of borders. The boy is called Tecumseh, a
name that alludes to the Shawnee war-chief and pan-tribal political
leader who fought for Native ownership of lands in what would become
Canada and already was the United States, during the late-eighteenth
and early nineteenth centuries.[4] Tecumseh urged specific tribes, among
them the Cherokee, Muscogee, Choctaws, Chickasaws, and Seminoles,
to join together and form a political confederacy that would be independent from the American government and British colonialism. His
attempts at centralizing the political leadership of Native tribes, both
within the United States and the British colonies, were regarded with
scepticism by many Native peoples. Tecumseh's desire to hold onto
Native lands through tribal confederation alludes to the struggles faced
by King's narrator, who must negotiate a world in which borders and
boundaries are typically defined by non-Natives, and, conversely, undermined by the activities of Natives (including himself) who make regular
trips across the river.

The levity directed at the border, and Eurocentric presumptions that
the border must be maintained, is most clearly expressed in *Truth and
Bright Water* by Monroe Swimmer, a Native artist who employs Tecumseh
as an assistant for the summer. As part of Swimmer's project to reclaim
the Prairies for the Native community and wildlife, he builds a series of
iron buffalo silhouettes that he takes out to the horizon and scatters in a
symbolic gesture, which is intended to comment on the increasing confinement of Native peoples to reserves, and animals (like the buffalo) to
pens, where they become tourist attractions designed to draw non-
Natives to the area. After unloading a dozen of the buffalo, Monroe
insists that he and Tecumseh, who has helped with the move, hold a
Native ceremony to acknowledge these animal statues and their significance. But neither one possesses the requisite sweetgrass or tobacco. As
a result, the artist joins Tecumseh in creating their own tribute to the
buffalo and life before the border:

'There's Canada,' he says. Then he turns and spreads his arms. 'And this is the United States.' He spins around in a full circle, stumbles, and goes down in a heap. 'Ridiculous, isn't it?' ...

Monroe beats his hand on the hood of the truck, and we stand on the prairies and sing the part of the honour song I know, and then Monroe insists that we sing the title song from *Oklahoma!* Monroe leaves his wig on for the honour song, but takes it off for 'Oklahoma!' Soldier joins in, and when we finish, Monroe turns away and wipes his eyes. (131–2)

This ritual suggests the inanity of treating the two sides of the river as different, and pointedly recalls how the primarily non-Native ranchers and cowboys who settled the Prairies were not, in fact, alone on these lands, despite such depictions of the West in musicals such as *Oklahoma!*[5] By mentioning *Oklahoma!* King alludes to a Cherokee dramatist, Lynn Riggs, who authored *Green Grow the Lilacs* in 1931, a play that became the basis of that Broadway hit. However, Monroe's invocation of the musical and the state of Oklahoma also recalls a specific moment in Native American history and a particularly brutal legacy of colonization. Here, comedy is tempered by the tragic fact of removal, and humour takes on an ironic 'bite.'

Oklahoma was the final destination for those Native Americans who were evicted from their ancient homelands in the mid-nineteenth century by the American government. The same tribes that Tecumseh tried to gather together to form a political confederacy were displaced and forced to undertake the long journey to Oklahoma, a trip that killed many members of the community. The route to Oklahoma was called 'Nunna daul Isunyi,' or the 'Trail Where We Cried,' to reflect the pain and suffering that tribal populations endured as a result of the American government's mandate. The route later became known in English as the 'Trail of Tears.' As Russell Thornton explains, in his study of the demographics of the trail, poor 'weather,' abuse by soldiers, starvation, exposure, accidents, exhaustion en-route, 'bereavement and [the] loss of homes' meant that many who began the journey never reached their final destination (77).

In particular, Rebecca Neugin's magic realist–infused appearance in *Truth and Bright Water* underlines the gravity of this historical legacy. As King has explained, Neugin is a Cherokee woman who actually travelled the Trail of Tears from Georgia to Oklahoma and relayed her childhood experience of displacement to an interviewer later in life (Andrews

180).[6] Her most vivid memory of the trip involved her pet duck, an animal that the young girl apparently squeezed so tightly during the journey that the duck died. In *Truth and Bright Water*, Neugin reappears as a child who stays at Happy Trails during 'Indian Days' and befriends Tecumseh (101). She is accompanied by John Ross (the name of the principal chief of the Cherokee during the military removal in 1838, who led his people to Oklahoma after a long struggle to keep ownership of their tribal lands in Georgia). In King's novel, this historical reference is pointedly updated: Ross lives in a big red trailer and travels with the rest of the community as nomads, still without a homeland. Wearing 'a long dress that is torn and frayed at the hem and at the sleeves, as if the material has been ripped rather than cut,' Rebecca spends much of the novel searching for her missing duck, a symbolic representation of the trauma that the Trail of Tears has inflicted on Native Americans of all ages (101). Tecumseh even notes, when he visits Rebecca at the campground, that 'she looks tired, as if she's walked a long ways today and still has a long ways to go' (197). His description becomes a reminder of the physical toll that the trip across the United States took on those Natives who were so abruptly displaced from their lands. Further, Rebecca's dress, with its torn hem, recalls the ingenuity of the Native women who underwent this journey and had to create clothing for themselves and their families on the trail without any tools: they tore the fabric and tried to hide the ragged seams by pinning it. Here, however, Rebecca's dress with its frayed edges becomes a visible reminder of that legacy of racism and colonialism that intersects with and undercuts the aspects of levity associated with *Oklahoma!* King's text, with its invocation of both the Cherokee-authored play that became a hit musical, and the story of Rebecca Neugin, layers the comic and tragic dimensions of history to expose the brutality of the concepts of nation and race when imposed on Native communities.

Monroe juxtaposes aspects of tribal culture that have been passed on through generations to Tecumseh, the young narrator, whose namesake fought for Native self-government and the retention of tribal lands, with a sanitized musical version of White settlement in the Prairies. This ironic invocation and rereading of the significance of *Oklahoma!* – a formulaic love story that presents a vision of the West virtually devoid of Natives – reminds non-Native audiences of how limited their visions of the Prairies really are. The imposition of borders and boundaries is also perceived as ludicrous by Monroe, because he sees the randomness of separating one side of the river from the other, an act that, like the Trail of Tears, forcibly removes and redefines individual and community identities according to non-Native values. By removing his wig for the musical number rather than the honour song, and choosing to include references to *Oklahoma!* in a ceremony designed to undermine White control over the border and those who occupy both sides of it, Swimmer comically reconfigures the politics of the forty-ninth parallel to accommodate his own mandate: to emphasize the absurdity of those individuals who assume that they can either own or control the Prairies, and to reclaim this land for its prior occupants – the Aboriginal tribes and the buffalo herds that once roamed the area. Certainly, the buffalo who have left the Prairies, the 'smart ones,' in the words of Tecumseh's father, who 'got a good look at the Whites ... [and] took off,' cannot be resurrected literally (91). But the iron buffalo that Monroe and Tecumseh scatter before and after the ceremony – sixty in all – add another dimension to Monroe's commentary on the constructed nature of the border.

At the end of the day, the artist quizzes the boy about the buffalo statues, and takes special delight in Tecumseh's observation: 'They look *sort of* real' (135, our emphasis). Read through Homi Bhabha's concept of the 'in-between,' Monroe offers an artistic vision that subverts the stability of the border; the buffalo statues are a reminder that the reality of the forty-ninth parallel is little more than a constructed line, designed to suit the agenda of the nation-state. By highlighting the impossibility of conveying a singular reality, Monroe also foregrounds the limits of his own art; in other words, he cannot turn back the clock and repair the historical eradication of the buffalo. Instead, Monroe's statues – and Tecumseh's response to them – suggest the need to cultivate multiple, self-reflexive visions of the border that project a diverse array of realities, rather than replacing one hegemonic perspective with another. Moreover, through this discussion of Monroe's artistry, King can reflect critically on his own position as a Native writer who is himself located 'in-between' the forty-ninth parallel and uses the border as a site of alternative significations, without claiming to offer a definitive or utopian alternative.

These moments vividly demonstrate how non-Native interests are irrelevant to the Indian community, a community that has always seen the border as mutable. In his study of borderlands, New contends that the border is 'a process – a set of names, distances, and durations. It is also a set of questions' (28). Rather than seeing the border as a stable entity, Tecumseh's mother and Monroe Swimmer offer different ways of viewing this dividing line and contest its dominance. They refuse to accept the primacy of the border and insist that the young narrator look more critically at the construction of nation-states. Part of Monroe's strategy is to make jokes and ironic comments that redirect the narrator's attention to the river, discursively disempower 'whatever appears to be a larger or more dominant force,' namely the border, and pass on a tradition of self-preservation via humour and irony (New 47). Here, reading and interpreting the border within a Native context – especially when done with the tools of humour and irony – becomes a powerful symbol of resistance.

Dividing Walls

Not surprisingly, King's treatment of the forty-ninth parallel varies substantially from those writers who challenge that other major North American border: the line that divides the United States from Mexico. The Canadian-U.S. border is not characterized by the daily life-and-death horrors of the Mexican-U.S. border, which is marked by dividing walls, armed guards, and searchlights that are designed to prevent unauthorized crossings. The forty-ninth parallel exemplifies what Scott Michaelsen and David E. Johnson call a '"soft"' border, because it lacks the overtly militaristic aspects of the American/Mexican border (1). As noted, in *Truth and Bright Water*, when the narrator and his mother decide to visit family members who live on the Canadian side, they simply take the ferry, 'an old iron bucket suspended on a cable ... [with] enough room in it for four people' (42). The mother pulls the bucket across by grabbing the cable with her hands and sliding it along. There are no border guards at the other end. This benign image of the forty-ninth parallel contrasts vividly with the violence of the Mexican-U.S. border, an 'unnatural boundary' where hierarchies of race and nation are constantly being enforced (Anzaldúa 3).

The Mexican-U.S. border has become the focal point of border studies, a new interdisciplinary field that explores the figurative and literal significance of the border for those who live at the centre and on the margins. Johnson and Michaelsen describe the visual impact of this particular border, noting that 'along the Rio Grande are miles upon miles of cement trenches, chain-link fences, light-green paddy wagons, uniforms, binoculars, and soon, perhaps, steel walls, as well as multiple paranoid discourses of national and racial contagion'(1). The physical existence of the Mexican-U.S. border offers a tangible and powerful site of departure for border writing, as it is called, which challenges the totalizing boundaries of nation and disturbs 'those ideological maneuvers through which "imagined communities" are given essentialist identities' (Bhabha, *Location* 149). These narratives articulate a project of de-territorialization or fragmentation that operates by exposing the 'differences in reference codes between two or more cultures' (Hicks xxiii–xxv). Gloria Anzaldúa, for example, focuses on the border at the Rio Grande, which separates Mexico from the United States. This border, as she explains, is 'where the Third World grates against the first and bleeds' (3). The political line also legitimates the often violent policing of race and nation:

> Gringos in the U.S. Southwest consider the inhabitants of the borderlands transgressors, aliens – whether they possess documents or not, whether they're Chicanos, Indians, or Blacks. Do not enter, trespassers will be raped, maimed, strangled, gassed, shot. The only 'legitimate' inhabitants are those in power, the whites and those who align themselves with whites. (Anzaldúa 3–4)

The border forcibly prevents the free flow of individuals between these two nation-states by limiting the movement of Mexicans into the United States. As Hicks explains, 'In the Mexican-U.S. border region, Latinos are stopped routinely by the *migra* [U.S. immigration officers] and asked for identification. Thousands are deported every month and even more live in fear of deportation' (114). Moreover, Anzaldúa notes that this regulation works both ways: the border may keep Mexicans from coming northward, but conversely, a darker skin colour and the inability to speak English may be used as justification for expelling an individual from the United States and sending the person southward, even if he or she is (Native) American-born and raised.[7]

A central part of the historical legacy of the Mexican-U.S. border is the separation of Indians from their tribal lands. Indians originally occupied the Southwestern United States, migrated into Mexico and Central America, and became the ancestors of the Aztecs. As Leslie Marmon Silko explains, the survival of the Uto-Aztecan languages attests to this cross-border heritage: 'The Uto-Aztecan languages are spoken as far north as Taos Pueblo near the Colorado border, all the way south to Mexico City. Before the arrival of the Europeans, the indigenous communities throughout this region not only conducted commerce; the people shared cosmologies and oral narratives' (122–3). From the sixteenth century onward, Spanish, Indian, and Mestizo (people of mixed Spanish and Indian blood) populations began exploring and settling in the Southwest again. According to Anzaldúa, 'for the Indians, this constituted a return to the place of origin' (5). But by the mid-1800s, with the westward movement of American settlers and troops, native Texans of Mexican descent and various Indian tribes were divided from each other as Texas became a republic and the border was moved south one hundred miles to the Rio Grande. What followed was the gradual annexation of lands from the Indians living north of the border, a process of dispossession and fragmentation that is still taking place today.[8]

While the visibility of the Mexican-U.S. border and the militaristic aspects of policing that dividing line make it the obvious focus of border studies, recent critiques of this rapidly growing field caution against the tendency to retreat into the image of the Indian for a romanticized version of identity that transcends border marginality. Many of the pioneering border theorists (including Anzaldúa and Hicks) avoid borders altogether by creating narratives that read 'like a story of classic heroism: a text overcomes the impediments of being marginal to two or more cultures' by transforming the divisions between races, sexualities, languages, and political geographies (Castronovo 195). Subjects do not have to make choices between these labels 'in order to live in the world' (196). The danger of treating the border in this manner is that border writing and border studies become utopian spaces where 'in-betweeness' has no political impact or relevance.

King's work, and his focus on the Canadian-U.S. border, provide a useful alterna(rra)tive to the current concerns of border studies by exploring the relevance of the forty-ninth parallel for Native peoples. Certainly what is at stake at the forty-ninth parallel is considerably different from the overt and often deadly policing of the border at the Rio Grande. The economic disparity between Mexicans and Americans also creates a tension that is much less apparent in the case of Canada and the United States, where levels of poverty are quite similar, and basic amenities are often identical. As Clark Blaise describes it, the forty-ninth parallel is more concerned with 'psychic death,' especially for those who go south of the border (4). Nationalism, in this context, operates on the level of ideological and emotional commitment. But for Native peoples, the Canadian-U.S. border is a tangible dividing line between tribes that has far broader implications; the creation of nations has led to the separation of communities, the dislocation of populations, and the loss of land and economic self-reliance for Native peoples. Such fragmentation yields a wide array of narratives that negotiate the conflict between claims of nationhood and tribal priority.

A central part of border studies is the recognition that borders are places of reading and interpretation, subject to revision: how we read borders, and who is included and excluded by them are ongoing questions. King's works adapt and reconfigure these concerns without treating the border as a space of utopian alterity. His characters actively try to reverse the discursive norms that have been used to entrench Western versions of nationalism and disempower Native peoples. At the same time, however, King's texts also suggest an awareness of the limits of this approach.

In his work on border studies, Russ Castronovo outlines the need for 'cautionary tales about the border,' which do not simply celebrate the potential inherent in the contact zone but also acknowledge 'the ineradicable trappings of power that patrol the boundaries of any area of culture' (203). Castronovo argues that the same discursive acts that 'undermine the nation are also susceptible to recontainment and suppression' (203). King's works reflect this doubled vision, which is both informed by a postmodern desire to move beyond the confines of nation and national borders, and critical of the limitations of a utopian vision. The female protagonist of 'Borders' may finally succeed in visiting her daughter without having to declare her citizenship as Canadian; however, there is no promise that such exceptions will be permitted in the future. In fact, border guards continue to harass Native peoples in subsequent texts, including *Green Grass, Running Water*, where Alberta's family's traditional costumes are destroyed. When the narrator of *Truth and Bright Water* crosses into Canada with his father for a day trip, King's characters take aim at this border racism, even as they acknowledge its power:

'Border's coming up,' he says. 'Time to get rid of it.'
　'What?'
　'The grass.'
　'Marijuana?'
　'Canadian guards find even a little bit of seed, and they go ape-shit,' says my father. 'Better lose the booze too.'
　'You're kidding, right?'
　'Canadian jails are worse than the Mexican ones.'
　'But you're kidding, right?'
　'You know why?' My father gears down. We slide through the American border and roll to a stop at a log office with a Canadian flag on the pole. 'Mexican jails are full of Mexicans,' says my father, 'but Canadian jails are full of Indians.'

A couple of guards come out to the truck and ask us all about liquor and cigarettes, and my father shakes his head and smiles and talks like the Indians you seen in the westerns on television. We have to stop by the side of the building so the guards can look in the back of the truck, but there's nothing there, so it's okay.

'Welcome to Canada,' the guard tells us. 'Have a nice day.'

As we clear the border, my father looks at me. 'They love that dumb Indian routine. You see how friendly those assholes were.' (85–6)

The narrator's father is clearly annoyed that he has to play the part of a stereotypical 'Indian' to cross the border with ease. He also warns his son of the power of racism, which has relegated those who are deemed undesirable (namely, Aboriginals) to jail cells. Nevertheless, Tecumseh's father knows that he must find a way to work within the system to achieve his goals: in this case, his economic survival, for he is on his way to collect televisions from an Alberta dealer that he will resell for profit. King's depictions of border crossings may offer a subversive vision of how Natives performatively can revise stereotypes to achieve their own goals, but they are also cognizant that such victories are always temporary and subject to national retrenchment. Indeed, since to erase all borders is to threaten the viability of Native claims to land and natural resources, King's narratives constantly seek a balance between extremes, without losing the forcefulness of Native political messages.

The challenges inherent in creatively reconfiguring the border and addressing Native concerns, far more immediate than those of nation, are graphically highlighted at the end of *Truth and Bright Water*, when Lum, Tecumseh's cousin and friend, commits suicide, jumping from the unfinished bridge that straddles the forty-ninth parallel. Lum, who is haunted by memories of a dead mother who abandoned the family, and who is the victim of paternal physical abuse, is eager to leave his home town, telling Tecumseh that nobody 'comes back to Truth and Bright Water, unless they are crazy or dying' (67). But Lum is a young boy who lacks the practical means to come or go as he wishes; still searching for a summer job, and, in the meantime, without money, he relies on his father for food and shelter. Over the course of the novel, he is severely beaten and thrown out of the house by his father. Although Tecumseh notices the bruises and asks him about them, Lum remains silent, retreating instead to a fantasy world in which he wrestles with the legacy of his mother, asking himself repeatedly: 'Did you really think she was going to come back?' (176).

Once ejected from his house, Lum sets up camp on the bluff, cuts his hair off, bears his chest, and paints his face and body with red and black designs. When Tecumseh comes to visit his young friend, he realizes that Lum has resurrected the stereotypical notion of the cinematic Native: 'He looks like the Indians you see at the Saturday matinee' (225). But rather than treating this exercise as an artistic endeavour – as Monroe Swimmer does via cross-dressing – Lum uses his costume and his rhetoric to articulate the futility he feels, as a boy caught between the desire to reclaim his mother and the reality of his father's brutality. In addition, Lum offers a pointedly parodic reworking of Monroe's observation that 'what's wrong with this world' is that 'nobody has a sense of humour' (199). He informs Tecumseh that the world needs 'bullets ... There aren't enough bullets.' The young boy's quiet desperation surfaces yet again when he encounters a bewigged Monroe and Tecumseh on the bluff performing another ceremony and mistakenly thinks that the artist is his mother (227). Once Lum discovers that Swimmer and his friend are returning a Native skull (which the artist has recovered from a museum drawer) to tribal grounds by sacrificing it to the river, he takes it upon himself to enact his own ceremony of reburial – with a difference. Lum climbs the bridge that links Truth and Bright Water, carrying a skull with him, and ventures out onto the rusting webs, from which he proceeds to drop it. As he tells Tecumseh, 'All you have to do is let go,' a comment that resonates when Lum shortly after plunges to his death from the bridge, following the skull into the water (257). For Lum, the bridge that crosses the forty-ninth parallel symbolizes the despair of a Native boy who cannot find escape from feelings of insecurity and situations of abuse even within his own tribal community. Through Lum's death, King pointedly subverts the concept of the border – and the site of 'in-betweenness' that it offers – reminding readers that such utopian ideals ignore its lasting effects on the local populations,[9] and the daily realities of Native people whose identities have been fractured by colonialism.

By showing the Canadian-U.S. border as a site in process, constantly being reconfigured, King's work revises and subverts the heroism and linear teleology of many border narratives. His focus on the forty-ninth parallel shifts the terms of debates over border studies by moving discussions to a border that has its own legacy of differences. In particular, King exploits uncertainties about Canada's relationship to America in order to develop a sophisticated and ironic treatment of the border, and then uses this frame of ambivalence, at the same time avoiding an assimilation of Native tribal customs and traditions into a discourse of Euro-centric nationhood. His works refashion border studies by looking both within and beyond national borders to consider the legitimacy of inter-nal claims of solidarity. Borders may have protected Native Americans who crossed the forty-ninth parallel to escape the wrath of the U.S. mili-tary, but who do these lines protect now? Why is it not possible to under-stand borders as overlapping and intersecting lines that can also account for the prior existence of Indian tribes, like those of the Black-foot, who are neither Canadian nor American but both/and because of their location, which bestrides the forty-ninth parallel? Although per-haps not as overtly confrontational as many writers who depict life at the Mexican-U.S. border, especially those who write from a Mestizo/a per-spective, King's representations of the border reflect an awareness of the complexities of the forty-ninth parallel and a desire to use a 'trick-ster discourse' to explore this subject in a manner that recognizes and celebrates the tragic and comic aspects of the situation.

Ironically, the humour that infuses King's Native-centred depictions of the border has led many critics to see his work as non-confronta-tional. In a review of *One Good Story, That One*, Oakland Ross insists that what is 'most surprising' about King's stories is 'their complete freedom from bitterness' (C27). When discussing King's text, however, Ross describes his writing as 'taut, sharp-edged and very funny' (C27). Simi-larly, in his consideration of *Green Grass, Running Water*, Eric McCor-mack deems King's humour 'vital for a book that deals with some very heavy stuff,' but notes that it is tinged with kindness, which makes the humour not only 'palatable but persuasive' (41). Such readings of King's works serve specific purposes: King may be seen as a proponent of Native solidarity, and, yet, by treating his work as a benevolent and readily recuperated critique of Canada and the United States, critics are able to claim his texts as part of a body of national literature. In essence, King's works become 'a hostage to nationalism,' the very position King himself resists ('Godzilla' 12).

As we have argued in previous chapters, comedy is a tactic used by many ethnic minority writers to engage readers who might otherwise be resistant to the messages of a text, since humour disarms readers and can be used to bring otherwise disparate groups of people together. At the same time, the 'biting' aspects of King's comedy continue to take aim at the dominance of Eurocentric paradigms in a subversively comic fashion that rejects the confines of the nation-state and racial hierarchies as they are enforced at the border. For example, in the middle of *Truth and Bright Water*, the narrator's father quizzes his son about his knowledge of Canada:

> 'You know what's wrong with the world?' My father reaches under the seat and comes up with a bottle. The label says 'Wiser's.'
> 'Is that whisky?' I say.
> 'Whites,' he says. 'It's as simple as that.' My father passes me the bottle. I take a sniff. It's iced tea, and it's pretty good.
> 'That's because they took our land, right?'
> 'Nope.'
> 'Because they broke the treaties?'
> 'Double nope.'
> 'Because they're prejudiced ... ?'
> 'That what they teach you in school?' My father takes the bottle and has another drink. 'Listen up. It's because they got no sense of humour.'
> 'Skee tells some pretty good jokes.'
> 'Telling a joke and having a sense of humour,' says my father, 'are two different things.' (86–7)

As this passage points out, the survival of Native peoples has depended upon having a sense of humour, and on being able to see things in more than one way. Evidently, joke-telling does not make one a humour expert, especially when the jokes being told use Natives as the butt of their ridicule. Hence, rather than using humour to outwit others, King suggests here that a comic attitude can bring individuals together and provide a way to understand situations that might otherwise simply destroy tribal populations and their attempts to retain unique cultural identities; the fact that tribal cultures are inherently comic becomes a useful strategy for ensuring the community's survival and for undermining those who attempt to oppress Native peoples. By learning to read the border and recognize the comic dimensions of what is otherwise a destructive line for many Native tribes, the forty-ninth parallel becomes a space of negotiation *and* potential play; it may not offer the promise of a utopian escape, but it can be a place where Natives present their own imaginative readings of race, nation, and identity.

With this approach, King brings another perspective to the field of border studies and shifts scholarly eyes northward to a different border, a border that may lack the overt tensions of the Mexican-U.S. border, yet remains a site of ambivalence and negotiation, not only for Canadians (who may be fearful of Manifest Destiny), but also for Native North Americans, whose tribal communities are divided by the forty-ninth parallel. Contiguously, King's focus on the Canadian-U.S. border raises yet another set of questions about nationalism, imperialism, and racism. His texts implicate both Canada and the United States in the destruction of the Native North American population, a reading of these nations that is often ignored or buried in representations of the two countries. Canada, in particular, has tended to position itself as historically vulnerable to the controlling whims of Britain and the United States, reinforcing the perception that Canada is not responsible for its own imperializing actions, a notion that is deconstructed in King's texts, especially through depictions of the border. King's works offer a set of narratives that counter predominant notions of nation and race, and highlight how the pairing of these two concepts has obscured the stories of other people, particularly those people who are Native, and thus exist 'in-between' the borders that divide countries and (particular) nation-states.

CHAPTER SIX

The Comic Dimensions of Gender, Race, and Nation: King's Contestatory Narratives

In his introduction to *Imagined Communities*, Benedict Anderson argues for the formal universality of gender and nationality as 'socio-cultural' concepts (14). Anderson contends that 'in the modern world everyone can, should, will "have" a nationality, as he or she "has" a gender' (14). Although Anderson notes the contradictions inherent in such gross generalities, especially 'the irremediable particularity of ... [the] concrete manifestations' of nationality, which varies from country to country, apparently gender remains a stable measurement of one's identity: individuals are either male or female (14). What Anderson's formulation demonstrates is that gender and nationality both depend upon the existence of an other. As 'relational' terms, the meaningfulness of gender, like that of nation, derives from 'its inherence in a system of differences' (Parker et al. 5). Thus, identity is determined not only by the intrinsic properties of gender and nation but also by 'what it (presumably) is not' (5). Moreover, the assumption that everyone has a gender and a nationality does not necessarily imply that everyone 'has' a gender or nationality in the same way. Eve Kosofsky Sedgwick, in her critique of Anderson, contends that '"having" a gender is' not necessarily 'the same kind of act, process, or possession for every person or for every gender' (240). Rather than treating gender as a fixed entity, how one acquires a gender identity and what constitutes gender become topics of debate. This set of contradictions is the platform upon which King explores the complex intersections of nation and gender from a distinctly Native perspective. In King's texts, the idea of gender, like that of nation, is repeatedly deconstructed through a trickster discourse that takes aim at the hierarchical constructions of gender, race, and nation when based on conventional paradigms.

The following chapter examines the strategies King employs to create his own counter-narratives about gender, stories that expand and redefine the status of various Native characters by refusing to relegate these individuals to positions of alterity. In particular, King uses humour to blur the boundaries between male- and femaleness and to explore alternative constructions of gender identity. Additionally, his texts assess the impact of traditional notions of gender and nation on members of fictional Native communities, who must negotiate the traditionally matrilineal Indian world and the patriarchal formulations that underlie Eurocentric societies. King's work suggests that, for Natives, 'having' a gender is complicated by and interwoven with the topics of race and nation and the acquisition of an easily recognized national identity, especially when trying to cross the forty-ninth parallel. The manipulation and reconfiguration of gender becomes a survival tactic that gets King's characters out of tricky situations, protects them from being killed, and confounds the linear expectations of many of his non-Native characters. In King's narratives, the borders between race and nation are conceived as permeable and mutable. Likewise, traditional sex/gender systems, a phrase coined by Gayle Rubin that acknowledges the sustained interaction of chromosomal sex and social gender in the construction of an individual's gendered identity, are vulnerable to transgression and reconstitution. King's texts repeatedly disrupt normal subject positions, including those of sex and gender, in an effort to undermine dominant discursive representations of Native and to re-present these individuals as occupying other spaces and forms of identity.

King's narratives include a wide array of female characters who are in the process of negotiating an array of conflicting subject positions. These women have multiple, overlapping identities: they are citizens of the nation-state, members of a tribal population, entrepreneurs, elders of the community, mothers, daughters, and workers in various career fields. Some, like the narrator's grandmother in *Truth and Bright Water*, even possess the powers of a trickster. One of the central contradictions that these female characters face is that, although Native cultures were historically matrilineal and structured by 'egalitarian, gynecentric systems' (Allen 41), the arrival of European settlers several centuries ago meant the introduction of hierarchical, patriarchal systems of organization. The result was the 'replacing of a peaceful, nonpunitive, nonauthoritarian social system wherein women wield power' with 'one based on child terrorization, male dominance, and submission of women to male authority' (40–1). Nationalism replaced community, and with it followed policies of relocation and the attempted annihilation of various Native populations on both sides of the Canadian-U.S. border.

This process of colonization was followed by the creation of nations, a movement that furthered the assertion of a Eurocentric patriarchal vision of the land and its inhabitants. The tendency to equate the female body with the national body became a powerful but also destructive trope for non-Native and Native women alike. Traditionally, the sentimental attachment a national population expresses toward its homeland is figured as a female body 'whose violation by foreigners requires its citizens and allies to rush to her defense' (Parker et al. 6). The effectiveness of this gendered trope – woman as nation – depends upon a specific image of femaleness; the woman who figuratively embodies a homeland must be 'chaste, dutiful, daughterly or maternal' (6). Paradoxically, such iconography reflects the actual experiences of the female population within the context of nation. As the editors of *Nationalisms and Sexualities* point out, 'No nationalism in the world has ever granted women and men the same privileged access to the resources of the nation-state' (6). Women's claims to nationhood often depend upon marriage to a male citizen. Hence, women mark the limits of nation, even as they supposedly epitomize its symbolic virtues. With females relegated to the sidelines in the role of nurturing mothers, nationalism becomes the site for cultivating a 'distinctly homosocial form of male bonding' (6). Anderson's description of nationalism as 'a deep, horizontal comradeship' or '*fraternity*' exemplifies the male bias inherent in the construction of national power relations (16). Women may represent the nation, but their actual authority within this structure is minimal. Moreover, only when nationalist fervour recedes do women get the opportunity to fight for solidarity. In the case of colonialist situations, women's concerns are often sacrificed to the good of the anti-colonialist movement; conflict within a minority population is perceived as destructive to the cause of liberation and self-governance, and, thus, women's desires are either ignored altogether or relegated to consideration sometime in the future.

Generating Identities: Reconfiguring Marilyn Monroe

Several of King's texts explore the issue of self-sacrifice and subservience to a greater cause. In a deliberately comic but also ironic fashion, his works interrogate how female members of the Native community find ways of generating their own subversive spaces by re-performing the concepts of nation, race, and sex/gender. At the same time, King's narratives depict the potentially debilitating effects of race and gender hierarchies for Native women, such as in the case of Lucy Rabbit, a character in *Truth and Bright Water*, who aspires to look like Marilyn Monroe. Lucy carries a laminated picture of Monroe in her purse, dyes her hair blonde in order to look more like the Hollywood sex goddess, and even tells the novel's narrator that 'Marilyn Monroe was really Indian and that she was adopted out when she was a baby' (19). She stares at the photo of Monroe longingly and speculates on the star's tribal affiliation, which, Lucy insists, had to be hidden in order for her career to succeed. But when Lucy alters her hair colour, as the narrator explains, the results are disastrous: 'Lucy has been coming to my mother for several years, trying to get her hair to turn blonde, but the closest my mother has been able to get to the kind of baby-soft, yellow-white, dandelion hair that Marilyn has is flaming orange' (19). Incongruously, the dye job does make Lucy into a local celebrity because 'no one else in Truth or Bright Water [has] ... hair anywhere near that particular shade' (20). By visibly altering herself, Lucy stands out, a status that matches her brash and forthright personality. Nonetheless, Lucy's decision to become as near to blonde as she can is interpreted by some members of the community as her aspiration to embody the White conceptions of beauty and sexuality circulated by the mass media. Lum, one of the young male friends of the narrator, explains: 'Lucy wants to be Marilyn Monroe because no one gives a damn about Indians but everyone likes blondes. Even Indians' (21–2).

King's literary depiction of Lucy Rabbit closely resembles the work of Native-Canadian artist Shelley Niro, who has produced her own series of overtly tricksterish self-portraits, including one completed in 1992 in which she is dressed as Monroe. In the photograph, Niro dons a 1950s blonde wig and a white dress to reprise the famous scene from *The Seven Year Itch* where Monroe's dress rises over a subway grate, pushed up by the wind from below. Niro's rendition of this sexy scene caricatures the Monroe photograph in several ways: an electric fan is visible in the picture, revealing the prop that is used to achieve her flying skirt; Niro holds onto a device that allows her to take the self-portrait from afar; and she puts this picture side by side with two other self-portraits in the final composition, which she titles the '500 Year Itch,' invoking the colonial legacy of White settlement in North America (Ryan 77). The humour of this parodic self-representation as Monroe, when put beside candid pictures of Niro, allows the artist to contrast 'idealized notions of

(White) femininity with familial images of Native reality' (77). Allan Ryan examines some of the implications of Native women's desire to be White (as parodied by Niro), and focuses on its repercussions in relation to identity and self-esteem: 'Marilyn Monroe is no less a symbol of male fantasy within the Native community than without. Likewise Monroe and her bevy of latter-day clones are deemed no less worthy of admiration and emulation by Native women than they are by non-Native. What, then, are the consequences ...?' (80). Niro's awareness of the appeal of such women to the Native community and her desire to address the 'discord they create for both sexes' are taken in a slightly different direction in *Truth and Bright Water* (77).

In King's text, the visibly parodic intent of Niro's photograph is replaced by the development of Lucy's character throughout the novel as she gradually explains, in her own words, why she has repeatedly dyed her hair. Lum's assessment that Lucy wants to become White presumes that she is rejecting her Native heritage. Lucy, however, sees her hair as a means of celebrating her Indianness. She contends that Monroe dyed her locks because she was 'ashamed' of her Native blood, but that her own orange hair, which will never be blonde or cotton-candy soft, is a visible symbol of the impossibility of escaping the physical traits of one's racial or ethnic identity (201). When asked why she continues to dye her locks, Lucy bluntly explains: 'So Marilyn can see that bleaching your hair doesn't change a thing' (201). In this context, Lucy creates a counter-discourse of Native identity that, rather than merely pandering to Eurocentric definitions of beauty and perfection, mocks the inability of celebrities like Monroe to seize and celebrate their Indian heritage. By imagining Monroe as a tragic figure because she has missed a key part of her identity, Lucy reconfigures the typical vision of the White, blonde star to emphasize her constructedness, both in terms of race and sexuality.[1] Additionally, Lucy uses her reading of Monroe to show how the borders between race are, in fact, permeable, though often disguised by the wonders of a dye job, make-up, cosmetic surgery, a change in speech, or clothing. She tells her hairdresser, 'It's a small world ... It's a lot smaller than you think ... Everybody's related ... The trouble with this world is that you wouldn't know it from the way we behave' (202). Through this comment, Lucy conveys the centrality of community to Native identity, a community that extends far beyond the confines of the nuclear family or the limits of a particular racial group to include all members of society and the natural world. Lucy's inclusive and expansive vision of the connectedness of different races short-circuits the logic used to justify racial hierarchies. In this case, Monroe becomes the object of pity because she has not embraced her Native identity.

Like Eli in *Green Grass*, Lucy Rabbit demonstrates how helpful knowing and reconfiguring dominant discourse can be, especially for Natives who do not perceive themselves as inferior but may be seen that way in a White Western contextual framework. Lucy's reading of Monroe subverts the assumptions of those who assume that this Native woman's repeated dye jobs are merely an attempt to make herself into an icon of White beauty. For Lucy, Monroe may be a Hollywood star worthy of worship, but she is also an example of the danger of being perceived as something you are not. Monroe's larger-than-life image, the marketing of her perceived helplessness and sexy innocence, and her tragic suicide parallel the Hollywood construction of the Indian as a cinematic vision of 'Otherness,' destined to die out.

Lucy's actions also can be compared with those of Madonna, who defies her working-class American-Italian roots and challenges sexual stereotypes by parodying the figure of Marilyn Monroe. In contrast with Monroe, Madonna refuses to be perceived as a victim of the media, or to capitalize on the cliché of female vulnerability. As Karlene Faith points out, 'whereas Marilyn Monroe strategically achieved icon status in part by letting her breasts extend softly from a body that promised easy comfort,' Madonna – even when obviously imitating Monroe in her video 'Material Girl' (1985), which is based on the star's 'diamond-seeking 1950s sexpot in *Gentlemen Prefer Blondes*' – 'brings armour to the enterprise' with her aggressively fit body and witty revisioning of this Hollywood feature (43). Moreover, Faith notes that Madonna's version of Monroe stresses irreverent assertiveness and her sexualized personae 'seldom suggest a tragic ending,' a performative strategy that avoids replicating Monroe's own tragic death (47). Likewise, in King's novel, by giving her treatment of Monroe an explicitly racialized twist, Lucy is able to expose the narrow images of the Hollywood star – as well as those of Indians – and assert the tangible strength of her own identity as a woman who is very much alive and proud to be Native. King expands and reworks Shelley Niro's pointed portrait of herself as Monroe by emphasizing alternative ways of reading the star's status within Native communities. Monroe may be an object of desire for Native men and a potentially destructive model of Eurocentric femininity for Indian women, but Lucy's bold assessment of the star's discomfort with her own identity reiterates this Native female's comfort with herself and who she is – both within the local Indian community and beyond.

Humouring Race, Nation, and Gender

The intersections of race, gender, and nation further complicate the lives of Native women who are relegated to marginality in multiple categories. Creative rereadings and reinterpretations of these women's positions within the community and their ability to respond to often negative treatment by other people, especially men, become necessary in order to ensure their survival and independence. Humour and irony are crucial tactics for these female characters, who often need to reverse well-established hierarchies, deconstruct old biases, and contest popular assumptions in order to take control of their lives, on a variety of levels. Latisha, for example, a central character in *Green Grass, Running Water,* embodies a range of the conflicts that Native women face. She is a citizen of Canada, a prominent member of the Blackfoot tribe, the owner of the Dead Dog Café, and the mother of three children, fathered by a White American, named George Morningstar, who literally plays at being Native.

Latisha's relationship with George invokes and reworks an important intertext and familiar image in nineteenth-century Canadian political humour – the cartoon depiction of the encounter between Cousin Jonathan, the well-dressed American figure otherwise known as Uncle Sam, and the youthful maiden, Miss Canada, who is closely watched by her married guardian, Mrs Britannia. J.W. Bengough's cartoon entitled 'The Pertinent Question,' first published in 1869, is an example of this humorous representation of Canada's relationship with its southern neighbour. More specifically, Bengough's drawing conveys the gendered clichés associated with each country in a perceptive and succinct manner. In Bengough's cartoon, Mrs Britannia sits on a park bench with Miss Canada, holding the younger woman's hand and physically protecting her from Cousin Jonathan. Miss Canada looks toward her guardian, as if waiting for advice on how to proceed. Cousin Jonathan stands to the right of the two women, in dapper attire, which includes striped pants, a star-spangled vest, and a top hat; he casually slouches and picks his teeth with a pocket-knife, qualities that give his character a sinister edge. The dialogue that appears underneath the cartoon involves a telling exchange between the two female characters. Mrs Britannia asks if Miss Canada has 'ever given your cousin Jonathan any encouragement,' to which the young Miss Canada replies, 'Encouragement! Certainly not, Mama. I have told him we can *never* be united' (101). This emphatic response to Mrs Britannia's queries echoes the sustained

Canadian resistance to an American political takeover. But Bengough creates a sexual subtext for this political battle: the American desire to take control of Canada is depicted as a flirtation between an aggressive and crass male who doggedly pursues the virginal country in the hopes of bedding her.

Such figurative embodiments of national identity were used to articulate the tensions between Canada and the United States before and after the Canadian Confederation of 1867. The threat of American Manifest Destiny and Canada's desire to see itself as independent from its colonial progenitor were complicated by Britain's protective hold over the colony. The cartoon characters thus offered a way to succinctly summarize the conflicts and convey underlying messages of support or protest regarding alliances with Uncle Sam. *Green Grass, Running Water* recalls and revises this aspect of the Canadian humour tradition to include the perspectives of Native peoples, particularly women; the text also ironically suggests that the same kind of aggressive colonization that nineteenth-century Canadians feared from Americans was, in fact, being perpetrated by Canadian settlers' treatment of Natives. Throughout the novel, the personification of Canada as a shy female victim is mocked in order to remind readers that cartoons, like those of Bengough, disguise the historically prejudicial nature of White-authored Canadian political commentaries. Focusing readers' attention on *Green Grass* provides a counter-discourse to this cartoon narrative of nation, and acknowledges the links among gender, race, and nation that shape the lives of Native women such as Latisha.

Latisha's desire to escape the limitations of the local reserve community is what first leads her to notice George Morningstar. George differs from Latisha's formulaic vision of the local Native men 'with no butts in blue jeans, pearl-button shirts, worn-at-the-heel cowboy boots, straw hats with sweat lines, driving pickups or stacked against the shady sides of buildings like logs' (111). His attire is sophisticated and expensive-looking, and leaves a lasting impression on Latisha: 'tan cotton slacks and a billowy white cotton shirt that was loose in the body and tight at the cuffs. He had on oxblood loafers and patterned socks, and he had stood at the back of the gawking crowd and watched' (112). She is attracted to George precisely because he does 'not look like a cowboy or an Indian' and presumably fits neither of these roles (111). Latisha's desire to avoid these familiar stereotypes is part of her larger effort to find a place for herself beyond the local Native community, which she perceives as stifling. Although Latisha thinks that George defies the narrow cliché of cowboy or Indian, she soon discovers that, despite his apparent worldliness, he embodies the same oppressively racist (and sexist) ideas that she has been trying to escape. Foreshadowing the demise of the relationship that has not yet begun, the text interweaves Latisha's recollections of George with discussions at the Dead Dog Café; these discussions revolve around relationships and the authenticity of the so-called dog meat Latisha serves. In particular, the words of Jeanette, an older, bossy woman, who quizzes Latisha about her marital status, provide an ironic frame for the story that follows:

'Are you married?' asked Jeanette.

'No.'

'Very wise,' said Jeanette, leaning her head in Nelson's direction.

Then again, Latisha reflected, she wasn't single, exactly. But she definitely wasn't married.

Nelson had lifted the top piece of bread off his sandwich and was examining the meat with his fork. 'Looks like beef to me.' And he reached out to pat Latisha's butt. 'You were kidding, right?'

'Black Labrador,' said Latisha, avoiding Nelson's hand. 'You get more meat off black Labs.'

'Jesus!'

'But you have been married,' said Jeanette. 'Every woman makes that mistake at least once.' (111)

Latisha's mistake lies in choosing a man who, although he appears to be different, is intent on civilizing and colonizing her.

During their first evening together, George expresses pleasure that Latisha is 'a real Indian' (112). Shortly after, he nicknames her 'Country,' a term of endearment that underlines his perception of her as the embodiment of a land mass that needs to be dominated (112). He may delight in the fact that she is authentically 'other,' but this same assertion provides George with the tools to justify his desire to control her. George introduces Latisha to the local library, a place she has never visited, exposes her to classical music, and presents her with 'his copy of Kahil Gibran's *The Prophet*' on their three-month anniversary (113). Yet, once married, George's attempts to teach her his version of culture disappear and are replaced by sociological lectures about the differences between the United States and Canada, in which Canada is always regarded as the lesser nation. When Latisha tries to undermine George's 'generalizations,' she is dismissed as lacking the knowledge to make such judgments and retreats to the comfort of her children, whom she insists are 'Canadian' (132). Latisha's insistence on the 'Canadianness' of her children, as we have argued, asserts the distinctness of a unique Canadian identity against the global pervasiveness of Americans. In turn, it also represents one of the challenges faced by disenfranchised groups within the context of nation. For instance, women of ethnic and racial minorities are forced to appeal to national values in order 'to register their claims as political' (Parker et al. 8). Latisha's recourse to her status as a Canadian, rather than as a member of an Indian tribe, also recalls the national government's installation of a gender-biased law (as part of the 'Indian Act'), which from 1868 to 1985 ensured that Native women who married non-Natives lost their tribal rights.[2] Such paternalism was designed, in part, to regulate the 'breeding' of these women and to ensure that they became primarily aligned with the nation-state rather than their tribe. It is not surprising, then, that Latisha immediately turns to her Canadian identity as a source of self-definition. Certainly, by situating her children within the recognized framework of the nation-state, Latisha may be in a better position to argue with George, but in doing so, she also systematically ignores a legitimate (although only recently legal) alternative: aligning herself and her children with a tribal community.

The comic and tragic dimensions of George and his relationship with Latisha emerge through not only his rash analyses of American supremacy but also his sexist assertions and eventual abandonment of his family altogether. George's numerous affairs, which he describes as 'lapses in judgement,' his constant job switching, and his insistence, once he decides to stay home and be a full-time house-husband, that 'all the best cooks in the world are men' (159, 206), emphasize his sexist and racist ideologies. He even mocks Latisha and her brother for holding down steady jobs with the words 'Things that stand still, die' (159), an oblique reference to the reserve's desire to preserve traditions despite a lengthy history of colonization.

George, as a husband and father, is certainly an example of dubious manhood. And, as George Morningstar, he is a version of George Armstrong Custer. Like Custer, George was born in Ohio, lived in Michigan, and came west for adventure. Since Son of Morningstar was supposedly an Indian name for Custer, George's beatings of Latisha replace his namesake's Indian wars. George beats Latisha when she does not appreciate the fringed buckskin jacket he has inherited from a 'famous ancestor,' indicating that he is presumably a descendant of Custer as well as a re-embodiment of him. In fact, when George later reappears at the Sun Dance, after having been absent for several years, he sarcastically responds to the four Native runaways, who introduce themselves as the Lone Ranger, Ishmael, Robinson Crusoe, and Hawkeye: 'Right ... And I'm General Custer' (319). He has returned to take pictures of the Dance, an act that directly violates the no-camera policy at sacred ceremonies. In the course of trying to take pictures, which he wants to sell for profit, George also discovers that Lionel has acquired the fringed buckskin jacket and demands its return. The jacket, temporarily in the runaways' possession, has been passed on to Lionel to make him 'look a little like John Wayne' (252). As we have suggested, Lionel soon finds the jacket with its iron-hold and stale smell too confining, and he hands it back to George.

Possession of the jacket – a symbol of American attempts to control and destroy Native populations through military aggression – does not necessarily guarantee George's success in recolonizing Latisha. When he appears at the Sun Dance, George resurrects his old nickname for her, 'Country,' as a term of endearment. However, this time Latisha refuses to submit to his attempts to dominate her, which she recognizes as little more than an attempt to colonize and exploit Native peoples (especially women): 'Even before she turned, Latisha's arms instinctively came up and she stepped back, setting a distance between herself and the man behind her' (309). George initially claims the status of a 'family' member to justify taking pictures of the sacred dance, a ploy that Latisha immediately undercuts by reminding him that the no photography rule is 'for everybody, George' (316). Once his insider status is thwarted, George then rereads the ceremony itself in his own terms, describing the Sun Dance as 'more like a campout or picnic' than a private community ritual and, thus, a legitimate part of the public domain (316). But Latisha remembers how George's letters presented his familial abandonment in terms of a necessary adventure in self-exploration:

They were long letters, longer than the first one, but filled with the same enthusiasms and plans and dreams. There were poems, too, all about love and the moon and the stars and the seasons. They came at regular intervals, and for a while Latisha looked forward to them.

· Then she began to laugh.

And then she began to take them to work ...

The letters continued to come, and Latisha became bolder and bolder in her readings ...

And finally they became boring. Just like George. Even the poetry dulled. After Elizabeth was born, Latisha stopped reading them altogether ... (209–10)

Like Eli Stands Alone, Latisha becomes an expert in reading non-Native texts, a skill she has already begun to hone through the Dead Dog Café, a restaurant that profits from Eurocentric clichés about Natives. Once intimately familiar with George's self-serving sexist and racist rhetoric, Latisha refuses to listen to his excuses anymore or to find a place for him in her life.

Latisha also discovers alternative models of cultural identification that move beyond the national paradigms in which George situates her and her children. As noted earlier, Latisha is visited at her restaurant by a group of tourists, including E. Pauline Johnson, a mixed-blood (Mohawk and English) writer and performer, who openly celebrates her mixed heritage. As part of Latisha's tip, she receives a copy of a Johnson text, *The Shagganappi*, which calls for Native peoples to acknowledge and take pride in their Indian identity. Johnson's appearance at the café frames Latisha's memories of George's constant comparisons between Canada and the United States, and ironically undercuts the primacy of his perspective. George's assertions that Americans are better than Canadians are deemed to be gross 'generalizations' (132), and he ignores the concept of tribal nationality altogether. Instead of asserting the Canadianness of her children, in opposition to George's extreme vision of American superiority, Johnson's presence, and the book she leaves behind, remind Latisha that she needs to account for the tribal roots that she and her children share, rather than simply defining her family through the context of the nation-state. Polly's appearance at the café, therefore, motivates Latisha to reconfigure George's binary construction of nationhood. When she encounters her husband again at the Sun Dance, a site of community renewal and healing, she has engendered new thresholds of meaning that acknowledge and celebrate the 'in-betweenness' of her own identity as well as those of her children.

Reproducing the Nation

Latisha provides a model for another female family member, Alberta, who has also been subjected to, and broken free from, the strictures of dominant discourse. Much like George's nickname for Latisha – 'Country' – Alberta's name invokes the notion of provincial lands waiting to be colonized by non-Native settlers (although already occupied by Native peoples). This figurative colonization is actually what initially happens to Alberta. She follows what she perceives to be the 'driving expectations' of gender and social convention, despite her fear of 'being lost in someone else' (70), and marries a young man she meets at university. But Alberta soon discovers that Bob, her new husband, wants 'a wife,' not 'a woman' (71). He expects her to postpone her degree, get a job, and bear children, while he completes his education. Bob assumes that she will comply with an obedient and subservient model of womanhood, in which her identity derives from her husband's achievements. Yet he also expects her to labour on their behalf, without gaining the education that would allow her to be independent and command a higher salary. In Bob's terms, Alberta's earning power is a temporary measure that will improve their standard of living in the short term and allow him to gain the signs of material success that he desires. When Alberta refuses to comply, Bob makes a racist joke that reveals his conception of her: 'Nobody needs those things. But everyone wants them. You want them. I want them. You don't want to spend the rest of your life in a teepee, do you?' (71). For Bob, Alberta's unwillingness to submit to his demands reflects a racial and cultural backwardness that parallels the commitment of Native tribes to preserving cultural traditions and ways of life. By reading the teepee as a clichéd image of Native primitivism, Bob suggests that Alberta is resisting civilization and the material symbols of this conversion to Eurocentric paradigms. Not surprisingly, Alberta and Bob are divorced shortly after. When Alberta reflects on the failed marriage, she is baffled by Bob's expectations: '... she couldn't remember ever saying or even hinting that she wanted to stay at home, and she didn't think that she had ever suggested that she would be willing to put him through university' (71).

Alberta is frustrated by male perceptions of femaleness that relegate women, especially minority women, to the role of dutiful, submissive wife and mother. However, she realizes that this construction of ideal womanhood is not limited to relationships between White men and Native women. In *Green Grass, Running Water*, Alberta's description of Bob anticipates the story of Amos, Alberta's father, a man who abuses and berates his wife. Alberta recalls a night she witnessed as a child, when a drunken Amos drove his pick-up into the outhouse and then proceeded to curse and throw bottles at his wife before finally passing out on the porch. When the family checked on him in the morning, Amos was gone; he never returned, and Alberta is surprised that her mother 'never seemed to wonder where he had gone' (74). With these memories fresh in her mind, Alberta concludes that men – Native or not – are all the same: 'They all demanded something, insisted on privileges, special favors' (74). Alberta chooses to enjoy male company on her own terms, while still refusing to be the passive object of a man's desires and control.

To avoid making a commitment, Alberta decides to have two men in her life at all times, a strategy that allows her to circumvent the 'well-defined' stages of a typical male-female relationship:

> [H]aving both Lionel and Charlie relieved her of the anxiety of a single relationship in which events were supposed to rumble along progressively ... First dates, long talks, simple passion, necking, petting, sex, serious conversations, commitment, the brief stops along the line to marriage and beyond. Alberta had just gotten beyond sex with both men before derailing the social locomotive on a grassy shoulder of pleasant companionship and periodic intercourse. (37)

One man defuses the other. With Charlie and Lionel, Alberta subverts the notion of conventional heterosexual pairing and installs her own agenda: a rigorous teleology is transformed into liberating periodicity, and she can switch from one man to the other whenever and as often as she chooses. And what she chooses is to continue switch-hitting: 'When Charlie started talking commitment, Alberta phoned Lionel. When Lionel started hinting about spending more time together, Alberta would fly to Edmonton [and Charlie] for two or three weekends in a row' (37). Financially secure, well-educated, and living in Calgary, Alberta uses the distance between the two men to maintain her own independence and home-base.

Alberta inverts the notion of domestic, dependent womanhood in a deliberately comic fashion by playing one man off against the other. However, this switching of partners does not eventually lead (as it would in a traditional comedy) to resolution, marriage, and eternal happiness. Instead, the standard notion that men desire freedom and women want commitment is reversed, and Alberta decides that her story will have a quite different ending. She adapts and reconfigures key elements of the formulaic seduction plot to achieve her desire for independence. Hence, rather than emphasizing the crucial importance of making the right choice in assessing the proper qualities of the would-be husband over the dubious morality of the seducer, the romantic triangle Alberta creates is designed to ensure that she will *not* be seduced into marriage, a fate to be avoided at all costs. Whereas the two men, within the conventions of a seduction plot, are differentiated (one is clearly right for the female protagonist and the other wrong), Lionel and Charlie are treated as essentially equivalent. Despite their obvious differences, they are, for Alberta, much the same in that, 'like all men,' they want to get married. Alberta thus performatively enacts her own concept of self-sufficient womanhood in order to retain her freedom.

The men in Alberta's life fail to see what she is doing and repeatedly try to insert her into conventional notions of the docile, domesticated woman, no matter how far-fetched such notions are. When Lionel envisions putting his life in order, he imagines a conversation with Alberta that places her in the role of a submissive bride. Although he tells himself that he will see what Alberta thinks of his plans and consider 'how her ideas fit in with his' (233), the dialogue he creates is predicated on Alberta's unwavering devotion to him, even if it means sacrificing her career:

'I'm going back to university. I expect to be a lawyer. Are you interested in coming along?'
   'I just want to be where you are.'
   'What about your career?'
   'It can wait. I can always pick it up later.'
   'And children?'
   'Lionel, I'd love to have your children.' (233)

Lionel's resurrection of the conventional romantic comedy becomes ridiculous when framed by Alberta's memories of her father and her steadfast determination to avoid a second attempt at wedded bliss. In addition, the 'conversation' he creates recapitulates, point for point, another one in which she did not participate, since Lionel imagines her 'saying' the same things she never said to Bob, her first husband.

Alberta actively inverts yet another feature of the seduction plot through her desire to bear a child alone. In its prototypical form, the epitome of a fallen woman's disgrace was the illegitimate child she bore, a shameful legacy that regularly proved fatal. Alberta, after she has established herself as a successful university professor of Native Studies, decides that she wants to have a child without marrying the father. When she considers her options, Alberta contemplates an accidental pregnancy, but realizes that doing so would create 'a masculine muscle-flexing contest' because each 'would want to know who the father was,' and, as soon as she revealed that information, 'the winner would insist that he marry her on the spot and the loser would disappear' (54). To avoid a virility competition between Charlie and Lionel, Alberta considers two other routes: sex with a stranger (with which she cannot go through), and artificial insemination.

The latter proves particularly frustrating because of the patriarchal, heterosexual, and nationalistic values that underlie the process of approval for insemination. In her study of gender and nation, Nira Yuval-Davis explains that, as the 'biological "producers" of children/ people,' women ensure that the population is sustained and replenished; without new citizens, a country has a very short lifespan. Because 'the myth (or reality) of "common origin" plays' a central role 'in the construction of most ... national collectivities, one usually joins the collectivity by being born into it' (26). Yuval-Davis notes that in the case of settler societies, including Canada, '"common destiny"' may have been the crucial factor in the constitution of the nation. However, in order to build the population, 'an implicit, if not explicit, hierarchy of desirability of "origin" and culture' becomes central to immigration and natal policies (27). Knowing one's true 'origin' is considered to be essential to an 'individual's identity and identification with specific ethnic and national collectivities' (28). Further, such Western modes of identity construction stress that the 'conception of a child is the outcome of a single sexual act' involving a man and a woman. Lesbianism and androgyny are deemed 'abhorrent' because those categories threaten the reproductive roles of women as keepers of the nation (Mosse 90).

Accordingly, when Alberta tries to take the process of reproduction into her own hands, she soon discovers that the pretext of a heterosexual coupling, one legally sanctified by church and state, is a necessary prerequisite for acceptance into the clinic's program. The clinic's receptionist warns Alberta that when she comes to the psychological interview she must bring her husband: 'We can't begin the interview process unless both the husband and the wife are here ... A lot of people make that mistake' (150). Despite the clinic's insistence that it does accept single women, Alberta realizes that its claim of equity is superficial. Evidently she needs a husband even if he cannot father a baby. She must perform her role as prescribed by patriarchy to get past the bureaucracy of the clinic, or be denied the opportunity to conceive.

The concept of the nuclear family that sustains the nation is contrasted with Alberta's Native-inflected notion of what family and nation mean. As a professor of Native studies, she is well aware of the history of genocide that has shaped the experiences of Native North American tribes. Her university lectures suggest that knowing the history of Natives living on one side of the border, whether north or south of the forty-ninth parallel, is not enough – nation is little more than an arbitrary designation. What counts for Native North Americans are tribal affiliations and relations with the world in general. This collective and broad definition of family, which does not depend on the heterosexual and legally binding union of a single man and woman, offers a communal alternative to Alberta, through which she can maintain her independence and still be part of a 'family.' By re-performing these formulaic constructions, Alberta creates a space for her own version of motherhood, one that is not tied to marriage or the perpetuation of a national citizenry.

King adds a trickster twist to Alberta's story when Coyote decides to impregnate her. This method of conception parodies the miracle of the Virgin Mary, who marries Joseph after being impregnated by the Holy Spirit. In this case, however, Coyote is unconcerned about Alberta's marital status. Rather than impregnating her in order to create a saviour of humanity, Coyote is simply fooling around, under the guise of trying to be 'helpful' (348). At the end of the novel, when the four Native runaways discover what Coyote has been up to, they repeatedly admonish the trickster's actions:

'The last time you fooled around like this,' said Robinson Crusoe, 'the world got very wet.'

'And we had to start all over again,' said Hawkeye.

'I didn't do anything,' says Coyote. 'I just sang a little.'

'Oh, boy,' said the Lone Ranger.

'I just danced a little, too,' says Coyote.

'Oh, boy' said Ishmael.

'But I was helpful, too,' says Coyote. 'That woman who wanted a baby. Now, that was helpful.'

'Helpful!' said Robinson Crusoe. 'You remember the last time you did that?'

'I'm quite sure I was in Kamloops,' says Coyote.

'We haven't straightened out *that* mess yet,' said Hawkeye.

'Hee-hee,' says Coyote. 'Hee-hee.' (348)

Coyote's irreverent willingness to invert, reverse, and undermine the limits imposed by the runaways as they repair the world, parallels Alberta's desire to bypass the rules and regulations that govern artificial insemination. As a figure who is never explicitly gendered in the novel, and seems to operate beyond the scope of a simple sexual polarity, Coyote's impregnation of Alberta challenges normative subject positions. Coyote offers a site of 'in-betweenness,' which thrives on ambiguity and transgression.

By giving Alberta the opportunity to have a child without having to succumb to marriage, Coyote helps her successfully to enact her own counter-definitions of identity and community. Once pregnant, Alberta is free to explore relationships with whomever she wants, male or female. As the story of Moby-Jane and Changing Woman illustrates, lesbian pairings can contest the dominance of patriarchy and the imposition of national obligations by facilitating sexual and emotional partnerships that subvert an agenda of coupling and reproduction for the sake of population increases. Alberta's interactions with Connie, a police officer who handles her stolen-car report, suggests that, for women, there are viable alternatives to a man who, as Connie wryly notes, is 'a nice thing to have around but so's a dishwasher' (255). Their coded conversation in Connie's car, in which the women reveal to each other that they are 'women's libber[s],' and then sit talking 'until the windows fogged up,' may be read as a parody of the clichéd teenage backseat sexual encounter; the difference here is that the two women talk, reflecting on the frustrations of a male-dominated system, in which Connie, despite her badge, is little more than 'a secretary' (257). When Connie eventually drops Alberta off, Alberta asks her into the Dead Dog Café for coffee, and though Connie has to postpone accepting the invitation, it's implied that the two women plan to meet again. Moreover, when Alberta enters the Café, having gotten wet after Connie leaves, Latisha offers her a hairdryer, which not only rids Alberta of her hypothermia but also takes on a sexual dimension: 'In fact, working the nozzle of the hair dryer in particular directions felt slightly erotic' (295). When Latisha returns to the table, she lightly mocks Alberta, asking: 'Besides wanting to play with my hair dryer, what brings you to town?' She then jokingly offers herself up as an alternative to her brother, Lionel. As Latisha clearly understands, given her own experiences with George, Alberta wants pregnancy without the baggage that goes along with it or even the physical interaction that is required to get pregnant in the first place. The personal ad that Latisha teasingly creates for Alberta reflects this desire to escape the need for sex with men:

Successful university professor seeking employment as a single parent desires discrete short-term relationship with attractive, considerate person. Men need not apply. Intercourse not required. Willing to drive great distances. Own car essential. (296)

Not only does Alberta concede that the advertisement is, indeed, accurate, but she decides that she will accompany Latisha to the Sun Dance, rather than waiting around for Lionel. Through her conversations with Connie and Latisha, Alberta explores alternatives to the tired heterosexual paradigm to which she has become hostage in her quest for a baby, and begins to act on other possibilities. Sexuality, for Alberta, becomes an increasingly flexible range of options that are not constrained by the pressures of national duty.

Alberta's pregnancy also demonstrates – in a comic fashion – the total irrelevancy and expendability of men even when it comes to conception, a fact that Lionel, for one, fails to realize. At the conclusion of the novel, Alberta gathers with the rest of her family at the site of Eli's cabin to decide whether they will rebuild it. She arrives in Charlie's car, which Lionel takes as a sign that she has chosen a mate. After Charlie announces that he has lost his job and is off to visit his father in Los Angeles, Lionel says, 'So ... I guess you're going with Charlie,' a comment that prompts Norma to hit him on the shoulder and laughingly ask: 'Why on earth would she do something like that?' (353). As Alberta points out, 'I haven't got time to be running after lawyers in Los Angeles. I work for a living' (353). Her response deflates the myth of female dependency that Lionel has rehearsed in his own mind, an ideal he seems unwilling to abandon. Even after Charlie leaves the site, Lionel tries to arrange for a weekend with Alberta, an attempt that fails because the women gathered there – Latisha, Norma, and Alberta – have already decided that their first priority is to rebuild the cabin, with or without his help.

Nor do the women acquiesce to Lionel's patriarchal assumptions when he offers to participate in this process of reconstruction. He may want to think that he can simply follow in the steps of his uncle, Eli, and live in the cabin once it is finished, but Norma undercuts his attempts to claim the property for himself: 'Not your turn ... It's my turn. Your turn will come soon enough' (354). This matriarchal reordering of priority tests Lionel's patience and reconfigures power relations within the family by returning the cabin to the next, rightful inheritor, regardless of gender. Just as the dam has been reclaimed via the actions of Coyote

and the four Native runaways and returned to its natural state, so must
Lionel re-evaluate the masculinist paradigms he has used to define what
constitutes success and to determine how he thinks others should act.

The Tricks of Gender Identities

The trickster figure, Coyote, enables an exploration of the mutability of
sex/gender systems in an explicitly humorous manner. Because tricksters are characterized by a lack of boundaries and the ability to transform themselves at will, they represent and enact ambiguity, especially
sexual ambiguity. Although many tricksters are identified as male,
because of an 'ambient phallus,' Babcock and Cox explain that tricksters also 'frequently transform themselves into women and are sometimes represented as hermaphrodites. Moreover, female coyotes are not
unknown in either traditional or contemporary Native [North] American literatures' (100). That the trickster is typically described with male
pronouns and 'characterized by exaggerated phallicism' is arguably the
result of a male bias in the collection and interpretation of trickster
stories, along with the Eurocentric presumption that Indian women
embody stability and passivity (100). Discomfort and uncertainty about
sex/gender distinctions are easily rectified if the trickster can be
deemed either male or female.

The functional essence of the trickster is a rejection of established
rules and a continual revision of what constitutes 'in-betweenness.' Part
of the trickster's purpose is to release individual and communal repression and redirect this anxiety into pleasure, a Freudian mechanism that
allows those who listen to stories of the trickster's antics to enjoy themselves and still retain a sense of cultural order. The trickster indulges the
fantasies of those listening and exemplifies how anything is possible; this
same figure also educates children on what is appropriate conduct. Not
surprisingly, then, Babcock-Abrahams identifies the trickster with 'the
comic modality or marginality where violation is the general precondi-
tion for laughter and communitas, and there tends to be an incorporation of the outsider, a levelling of hierarchy, a reversal of statuses' (153).
King's trickster in *Green Grass, Running Water* fits this formulation. Coyote attacks Eurocentric, and specifically patriarchal, conceptions of
identity and community by remaining an ambiguous character, who
wants to meddle with the world, copulate, sing, dance, and eat copious
amounts of food, but who is unconstrained by the singularity of one sex
or another. In turn, this trickster crosses the divide between humans

and animals by rejecting Noah's ban on bestiality,[3] as s/he thwarts racial difference by assuming both Native and non-Native characteristics.

Evidently, 'having' a gender, or any kind of rigidly fixed identity, proves a tricky business for Coyote. Throughout King's texts, Coyote remains, for the most part, an ambiguously gendered figure, who is apt to make mistakes and cause trouble rather than successfully repair what has gone wrong in the world. When Coyote does take on a gendered identity, the trickster is usually female, as is evidenced by *A Coyote Columbus Story* and 'The One about Coyote Going West.'[4] The deliberate gendering of Coyote in these particular stories undercuts the dominance of the White patriarchal God of Judeo-Christian culture, celebrates the matriarchal roots of Native tribal societies, and posits diversity rather than the system of centrality and hierarchy so often favoured by Western societies. By allowing for and respecting differences, Coyote's actions and identities undercut hegemonic systems that typically relegate Native North Americans to the margins. Moreover, Coyote's crass irreverence, self-absorption, and characteristic imperfections offer an alternative vision of the world that does not simply rest on clear binary oppositions between the omnipotence of God and the errors of humankind.

As Bhabha argues, we 'need to think beyond narratives of originary and initial subjectivities and to focus on those moments or processes that are produced in the articulation of cultural differences' (*Location* 1). Coyote's presence in King's works, particularly in *Green Grass, Running Water,* may be an expression of cultural difference, yet it offers a comic twist to these narratives by exploring Native-centred notions of identity and selfhood. Indeed, the chaos Coyote provokes by refusing to listen and choosing to play creates spaces in which various characters can begin to articulate their own definitions of selfhood – both individually and communally – and undercut the imposition of Western cultural paradigms. Coyote's impregnation of Alberta, the trickster's realization that George is taking illegal photos of the Sun Dance, and the instigation of the earthquake, which destroys the dam and returns the water to its natural path, also contest the logic of non-contradiction by which one (usually Eurocentrically imposed) identification or definition of selfhood is always more important than others. Alberta is able to defy the assumption that she needs a husband to have a child; George's claim to be an insider to the Blackfoot community, from which he intends to profit, is revealed as exploitative; and the tribe is able to stop colonial acts of appropriation. Moreover, the waters that have been confined and controlled by national and provincial regulation finally again run free.

Coyote's actions may bring about solutions, but the trickster may also, in doing so, destroy lives (including Eli Stands Alone's), make mistakes, and create a whole new set of problems. By sustaining this ambivalence through the trickster Coyote, King avoids presenting a reductive counter-narrative to that of Judeo-Christian patriarchy. Instead, readers are encouraged to heed the ironically charged multiple visions of identity and community, which remain in flux through to the last page of the novel, where the story begins yet again.

Coyote is one part of the effort, in *Green Grass, Running Water,* to expose and undermine 'the binary logic upon which authoritarian power structures are founded' (Lamont-Stewart 128). Linda Lamont-Stewart argues that Coyote's ambivalently gendered identity may not precipitate the complete collapse of the 'power structures' within which these 'gender crossings' are performed, but the trickster does offer 'the possibility of constructing a more inclusive and equitable cultural configuration' (128). King's depiction of Coyote may not appear overtly to dismantle the concepts of gender, race, and nation. However, his presence, especially as a figure of ambivalence, in narratives that redefine and contest the limits of Native identity, precipitates a fundamental shift in how one thinks about and defines these concepts. For many Native tribes (e.g., the Navajo), 'the telling of a story amounts to the actual creation or re-creation of a reality' (Ramsey 34). Thus, by including an ambiguously gendered Coyote, who delights in transgressing the rules that regulate sexual reproduction and ensure the maintenance of national and racial differences, King's text articulates another kind of reality in which alternatives to these dominant paradigms not only exist, but symbolically interrupt and displace them. Yet, this reality remains provisional and open to change as Coyote repeatedly returns to mess with the world after failing to listen to the narrator's advice. Those who have the power, in King's novel, are the figures who understand the 'reality' that many non-Natives desire and want to perpetuate, and also possess the ability creatively to re-perform the binary concepts of gender, race, and nation (based on self/other) to suit their own purposes.

The tribal traditions of many Native North American communities provide another relevant context for analysing King's playfully subversive revisions to conventional sex/gender systems in *Green Grass, Running Water.* Native conceptions of gender identity can and often do vary substantially from those of dominant discourse, in which anything that does not fit the construction of a male/female opposition is perceived as deviant. In particular, Sabine Lang's insightful essay on gender variance in Native American tribes offers a rationale for why King includes ambiguously gendered figures (such as the trickster) in his novel:

> Regardless of the specific differences in the construction of gender and gender roles, a majority of Native American cultures define gender in a way that allows for the cultural construction of more than two genders, which has come to be termed *gender variance* in recent anthropological writings. Gender variance is defined by Jacobs and Cromwell (1992: 63) as 'cultural constructions of multiple genders (i.e., more than two) and the opportunity for individuals to change gender roles and identities over the course of their lifetime.' (103)

Several Native American groups have recently coined the phrase 'two-spirit' to describe 'alternatively gendered people of either sex' (100). As the introduction to *Two-Spirit People* outlines, 'two-spirit' displaces 'berdache,' the term that anthropologists historically used to label what they considered to be special gender roles in Aboriginal cultures, including 'ceremonial tranvestism, institutionalized homosexuality, and gender variance / multiple genders' (4). By creating their own terminology, the First Nations hope to halt the tendency among some anthropologists simply to conflate Eurocentric conceptions of homosexuality with the figure of the 'berdache' and to romanticize this phenomenon repeatedly. Lang explains that, in many Native American cultures, three or four genders exist, including 'women, men, two-spirit/womanly-males, and ... two-spirit/womanly-females' (103). But these labels do not refer to 'sexual behaviour even though certain kinds of sexual behaviour may be considered culturally appropriate for an individual belonging to any gender category' (103). The integration of this two-spirit status into most First Nations tribal cultures is in accordance with the worldviews presented by these groups, 'which appreciate and recognize ambivalence and change both in individuals and in the world at large' (103). It is not surprising, therefore, that the trickster in King's text, Coyote, possesses a shape-shifting physical form, expresses uncertainty about the outcome of various tricks, and is willing to interfere with conventional methods of impregnation, and yet cannot be reduced to a single gender identity.

During the last century, the American and Canadian governments repeatedly tried to eradicate 'two-spirit' members of Native North American tribes, in order to civilize the community and to find a place for everyone within normative (meaning heterosexual) conceptions of gender identity. For example, there are records of American bureaucrats who, in 1915, saw the sexually explicit ceremonial dances among the Hopi Indians and insisted that such conduct be suppressed. What was deemed most deviant by the officials 'were the antics of the clown dancers, who used both homosexual and heterosexual humor as a way of providing relief in the otherwise serious ceremonies' (Williams 177). Walter Williams speculates that 'since the Hopi did not see sex as dirty or antireligious, and did not separate humor from ceremony, they must have been confounded by the white's suppression' of these explicitly sexualized antics (177). Such governmental pressures were intended to ensure the existence of clearly delineated roles that left no room for experimentation with sex/gender systems. But the imposition of these paradigms simply meant that Native North Americans had to find creative strategies to undermine the constraints, ploys that have typically included comic parodies.

King's novel offers an ironic commentary on the limits of Judeo-Christian religions and alters the rigidity of the sex/gender systems that underpin them through the presence of a trickster and the introduction of four Native runaways. The runaways, who change gender identities several times over the course of the novel to protect themselves, travel with Coyote and try to keep the trickster out of trouble. These figures' names represent the life cycle of humans from a matriarchal and distinctly Native perspective: First Woman, Changing Woman, Thought Woman, and Old Woman. They began their earthly mission in the water and resisted being incorporated into a Judeo-Christian scheme, in which specific religious rules, as voiced by male figures including God, Noah, the Archangel Gabriel, and Young Man Walking on Water, dominate. These four runaways repeatedly invert or alter Christian frameworks, despite the efforts of several White male characters to wield the Word over the world and its inhabitants. They also become the catalysts for various colonial confrontations, in which dominant conceptions of nation, race, and gender are explicitly revised through comic means.

After First Woman and Ahdamn are expelled from First Woman's garden by GOD, they discover a bunch of 'dead rangers.' Their concerns about what do with the bodies are quickly displaced by the arrival of a group of 'live rangers,' who are armed and immediately assume that the bodies they find are 'the work of Indians' (58). Although they are unarmed, First Woman and Ahdamn are conveniently available for punishment. In order to halt this process of false accusation and murder, First Woman employs a little cross-racial cross-dressing. As we have discussed, she quickly prepares and dons a black mask and proclaims herself to be the Lone Ranger, a recognizably White male hero. The success of her deception, however far-fetched, is reflected by First Woman's ability to protect Ahdamn from harm. Although the rangers are tempted to kill Ahdamn because he looks Indian, First Woman manages to talk them out of shooting him:

> No, no, says First Woman. That's my Indian friend. He helped save me from the rangers.
>
>   You mean the Indians, don't you? says those rangers.
>
>   That's right, says First Woman with the mask on. His name is Tonto.
>
>   That's a stupid name, says those rangers. Maybe we should call him Little Beaver or Chingachgook or Blue Duck.
>
>   No, says First Woman, his name is Tonto.
>
>   Yes, says Ahdamn, who is holding his knees from banging together, my name is Tonto.
>
>   Okay, says those rangers, but don't say we didn't try to help. And they gallop off, looking for Indians and buffalo and poor people and other good things to kill. (58–9)

The rangers' dismissive treatment of Tonto – whose '"Indian-sounding" name means "numbskull," "fool," or "stupid" in Spanish' – demonstrates their inability to see beyond the visible markers of gender and racial difference (Flick 141). In fact, the name 'Tonto' invokes another legacy of Indian colonization and dispossession in North and South America – that of the Spanish conquistadors. Rather than reading 'in-between' the lines, the rangers look for what is familiar and normal to them and end up duped, at least temporarily. The danger of such narrow readings of identity, however, is that once First Woman takes off the mask, as she does after the rangers leave, she immediately returns to the position of Native other and is vulnerable to persecution. Before she can don her mask again, soldiers appear, grab First Woman and Ahdamn, and arrest them for 'being Indian' (59).

By continuing to use fantasy and the possibilities of performance to outwit Whites who would like to confine her, First Woman creatively resists the fixity of gender and racial identity. As with Eli, knowing the dominant discourse and how to subvert it becomes crucial for First Woman and her various Native female partners. Unlike Ahdamn, who asks her, '... who is Tonto?' after having assumed the persona to save his life (59), First Woman is well versed in what rangers and soldiers want to hear and regularly uses these familiar cultural symbols to redirect the colonial narrative of Native dispossession and annihilation. With these tactics, First Woman can actually walk out of prison as the Lone Ranger and continue to fix up the world in opposition to the other kinds of fixing that are going on (including the imprisonment of the Indians at Fort Marion and the dam being built on reserve lands in Alberta).

The Lone Ranger is accompanied on these later missions, not by Tonto, but by the three other mythic Native women, who work under similar false names. And with all four – the Lone Ranger, Ishmael, Robinson Crusoe, and Hawkeye – the significance of the name change is the same. The colonial pairing of a typically White male master and subordinate Native servant or sidekick (Tonto, Queequeg, Friday, and Chingachgook) is doubly reversed. The Native female (posing as male) occupies the dominant position, despite having been erased entirely from the 'later' constructions of these relationships.

Not surprisingly, the four Native runaways find a multitude of strategies to undermine Judeo-Christian male figures. First Woman refuses to play Eve in the Garden of Eden because there are many other 'nice places to live' (57). Similarly, Changing Woman declines the opportunity to procreate with a crass and belligerent Noah, who blames Eve for his shit-filled canoe, and insists that Changing Woman must be his new wife (a replacement for the woman he has thrown overboard in a fit of rage). Noah's desire to assert a hierarchical relationship between man and animals, and his presumption that women are subordinate to him, suggest an obsession with categorical distinctions that will ensure he remains on top. Changing Woman, however, recognizes other more appealing sexual possibilities, including a lesbian affair with Moby-Jane, the Great Black Whale. Likewise, Thought Woman refuses the Annunciation and turns down the Archangel Gabriel's invitation to be the mother of Jesus; Old Woman directs Young Man Walking on Water to his lost boat and his disciples, and saves the group by quelling the waves, despite his insistence that it is against the rules for anyone but him to work a miracle – a miracle that he, incidentally, could not work himself. These refusals to play the expected part in a particular set of raced and gendered configurations constitute a sustained refutation of the Christian story and the distinctly White, patriarchal, heterosexual crux of that narrative, which involves the working out of God's plan for humanity through the mission of his son.

By continually inverting the presumed outcomes of Judeo-Christian stories, and favouring the perspectives of the four Native runaways, who refuse to be contained by such rules, King creates a narrative in which boundary crossings and re-crossings of various kinds become standard practice. Noah may claim that bestiality is against the rules, but this does not stop Changing Woman from engaging in a sensual and sexually pleasurable swim with Moby-Jane.

The four mythic Native women also invert the concept of nation as the site of male homosocial bonding by refusing merely to act as passive, female vessels for the purpose of procreation. They are unwilling to purchase one identity at the expense of another, especially when the surrender involves submission to a national agenda that disregards Native claims altogether. As a result, these women travel and work together, creating a female-centred community that continually eludes containment within traditional paradigms. They slip across the border between Canada and the United States unnoticed by border guards, and don and discard various gendered and raced identities as needed to protect themselves. This group of women, therefore, take the mythic underpinnings of the creation of nation, a framework in which gender and racial differences are regulated, and alter the notion of self-invention to suit their own purposes. In doing so, the female figures expose the limitations of such binary constructs as gender and nation, as they also demonstrate how these conceptualizations are socially maintained and politically motivated. If boundaries are, as we have argued, the site where things begin their '*presencing*,' then the boundaries between fixed notions of nation, race, and gender also can become generative 'in-between' spaces for King's mythic characters (Bhabha, *Location* 5). Additionally, these figures help various characters within the novel to realize that there may not be a single, standard way in which one 'has' a national or a gendered identity (Sedgwick 239), nor can individuals always be defined adequately by these terms.

Reading Monroe Swimmer

In *Truth and Bright Water*, King extends and reconfigures his discussion of gender, race, and nation through the figure of Monroe Swimmer, a Native artist who returns to his tribal community, purchases an abandoned church located on the American side of the river, and proceeds to paint it out of existence. As the narrator explains, the church Swimmer occupies represents a long history of racial oppression and dispossession:

> The church sits on a rise above Truth, overlooking the river and the bridge. Built at the turn of the century, it is a plain, squarish building with a raised porch, high windows, and a dark steeple ... with a set and angle that make it look as if a thick spike has been driven through the church itself and hammered into the prairies.
>
> The church was built by the Methodists as a mission to the Indians. The Baptists owned it for a while in the forties. They sold it to the Nazarenes, who sold it to the First Assembly of God, who sold it to the Sacred Word Gospel, who left the church standing empty and moved down the river to Prairie View just after construction on the bridge stopped ...
>
> [O]n days when the sky surges out of the mountains, gun-metal and wild, and the wind turns the grass into a tide, if you stand on the river bottom looking up at the bluff, you might imagine that what you see is not a church gone to hell but a ship leaned at the keel, sparkling in the light, pitching over the horizon in search of a new world. (1–2).

Here, Columbus's voyage to the New World and the subsequent attempts to Christianize Native North Americans are parodically reinterpreted through the church's history and its dilapidated state. While the church may be deteriorating, it also remains a visible symbol of Eurocentric attempts to impose religious order on the land and its inhabitants. Appropriately, this image of colonization remains active and visible to those who recognize the ironic aspects of the church and its location. The narrator's description of the church's strategic setting demonstrates its potentially ominous presence: 'When the Methodists built the church, they built it on the highest point of land they could find, so no matter where you stood, on either side of the river, you could always see it' (42). But the growth of Truth, the local town, has led to the virtual disappearance of the church on the horizon, blocked from sight by a variety of modern conveniences, including a motel, a bank, and an oil tower, which are sources of profit for the Native and non-Native business owners.

Monroe's return adds another dimension to this narrative because, rather than buying the property to commercially exploit the reservation and attract tourists, he purchases the church in order to present his own artistic counter-memories of Native life on the Plains. A famous painter

who has worked all over the world, Monroe employs his talents to play a
joke on the legacy of North American missionaries, and to reclaim the
land on which the church was constructed for the local Native community. In doing so, he undermines the nationalistic claims made on both
sides of the river by the Canadian and American governments. He uses
paints to dramatize the gradual consumption of the church by the land,
and thus erases one symbol of colonization that has led to the division of
the Blackfoot territory. When Tecumseh visits the church shortly after
Swimmer's arrival, he is surprised to discover that the artist has managed to make part of the church disappear: 'The entire east side of the
church is gone. Or at least it looks gone. I don't know how Monroe has
done it, but he's painted this side so that it blends in with the prairies
and the sky, and he's done such a good job that it looks as if part of the
church has been chewed off' (43).

As with Eli Stands Alone and Lucy Rabbit, the character of Monroe
Swimmer demonstrates how Native characters can revise standard conceptions of Indian 'otherness' by offering their own Native-centred perceptions of identity. Notably, Swimmer has returned to the community
after having spent years travelling 'around the world fixing paintings,' a
task that involves restoring works of art – primarily nineteenth-century
landscapes by European and White American artists – to their original
grandeur (129). Renowned for his 'magic brushes,' Monroe garners
wealth and fame until he is called in by the Smithsonian to repair a
'painting of a lake at dawn' (129). He discovers that every time he
attempts to fix the painting, 'images that weren't in the original' begin
to bleed through; no matter how much Swimmer tries to obfuscate
these images, he cannot disguise what lies beneath the untouched landscape (130). The comic and tragic aspects of Monroe's craft emerge as
he describes to the young narrator how 'Indians' keep emerging
through the layers of paint: 'There was an Indian village on the lake,
slowly coming up through the layers of paint. Clear as day' (130).
Although Tecumseh initially dismisses Swimmer's description of this
multi-layered painting as 'crazy,' the ironic juxtaposition between the
tranquil emptiness depicted in the standard nineteenth-century landscapes and the advent of a functioning Native community offers the narrator a useful model for reading the ambivalence of White-authored
texts (130). Monroe's acute awareness of how certain Eurocentric
images – like the 'primeval paradise' depicted in landscape paintings –
have been used to cover up the existence of Native peoples, leads him to
create his own artistic counter-images (129). These images contest the

idea that North America was an uninhabited Eden, waiting to be colonized and civilized. In turn, Swimmer's capacity to refashion his racial and gender identity, a series of cross-dressings that challenge the young narrator to look again, becomes part of his comic reconfiguration of Native history, which has been literally erased from view.

As mentioned previously, part of Monroe's creative attempt to 'save the world' involves creating a collection of sculptures in the shape of buffalo that he scatters across the Prairie horizon with the narrator's help (131). For the Blackfoot tribe, the buffalo was recognized as a sacred animal. According to several versions of Blackfoot creation narratives, in order to survive the attacks of buffalo, who hooked and ate the first humans, these people were taught by Napi (also known as Old Man, a creator / culture hero / trickster figure) 'how to construct and use bows and arrows' (Harrod 44). With this knowledge, the first humans could kill and eat the buffalo, rather than be destroyed by them. Despite the power reversal in the relationship between humans and animals, the Blackfoot continued to recognize the sacredness of the buffalo, and paid tribute to the power and beauty of the animal through various ceremonies that ensured the survival of both parties, as it solidified good relations between them. For instance, part of the Sun Dance involves the creation of a sweat lodge with a decorated buffalo skull resting at its apex. The reverence shown for the buffalo attests to the tribe's respect for the Sun, which, according to various oral narratives, chose this animal 'above all creatures' to provide food and shelter for the community (130). Consequently, the gathering and preparation of buffalo tongues (a sacred delicacy) at the Sun Dance was intended to reconcile 'the moral tensions engendered by the killing and eating of this animal' (133). Because of the close relations between humans and animals in Native cosmology, such expressions of respect were a necessary part of the ceremony and achieved a transcendence that was otherwise unavailable.

Moreover, vision experiences – which consisted of imaginative interactions with animals and objects (that often transmuted into a person) – were considered an integral part of life for the Blackfoot. Access to such visions was not limited by a person's station in life. These 'dream-visions' and 'waking-visions' involved a 'powerful burst of imaginal content which displaces the sense of everyday experience' and enabled individuals to journey into other worlds (Harrod 27–8). In the case of King's novel, the visions themselves are less important than the acceptance of alternative ways of seeing. The tribal tradition of acknowledging and respecting the interrelatedness of humans and animals, and the ability to see and interpret other viewpoints, provide an important framework for understanding the humorous aspects of Swimmer's creative restoration of the buffalo, especially when the artist has Tecumseh, newly hired as his assistant, unveil them:

'You see that tarp?' Monroe walks towards the back corner. I follow him. It's dark there, and at first I don't see a thing. 'Take it off.'

The tarp is about the same colour as the shadows. And it's heavy. Lifting one edge is easy enough, but pulling it off is real work. Underneath is a long line of iron figures stacked against each other like folding chairs. Even up close, I can't tell what they are supposed to be.

'Bring one out here,' says Monroe. 'Let's take a look at it.'

The figure is heavier than the tarp. I'm afraid of scratching the wood floor and I'm hoping that Monroe will take the wig off and help. But he doesn't.

'What do you think?'

It's a buffalo. Or at least, it's the outline of a buffalo. Flat iron wire bent into the shape of a buffalo. I look back at the stack. There must be at least two hundred pieces.

'Three hundred and sixty,' says Monroe, reading my mind. 'I had them made up before I left Toronto. It's my new restoration project.' (130)

Monroe's buffalo sculptures can be read as a comic response to the existence and survival of the church property. Rather than allowing the church to dominate the natural world, he creates a scene where the church building blends into and is swallowed by the natural landscape. The buffalo sculptures, which come in all 'different shapes and sizes,' are then able to occupy the plains, invoking and recalling an era when these animals lived without the threat of extinction, before the arrival of Europeans (131). These sculptures, in particular, counter the local tribe's attempts to resurrect the buffalo as a vehicle for commercial profit and exploitation during 'Indian Days.' Just across the river, in Bright Water, a herd of buffalo has been brought in to entertain the tourists, who pay for the privilege of watching local Natives try to shoot the animals with paint pellets as they ride motorcycles around the fenced enclosure. The buffalo instinctively follow the moving vehicles and try to charge them, creating a showdown that dramatizes the conflict between people and animals, and providing opportunities for tourists to take pictures and revel in the thrill of such confrontations. As Lum, the narrator's best friend, aptly explains, this exhibition is best described as a 'white man's wet dream' (151). It gives selected tourists, who watch or even pay to ride the motorcycles, a chance to 'go Native,' without having to reflect on the circumstances that have created such spectacles.

The live buffalo used for this performance are confined to a paddock, in an ironic replication of the circumstances imposed on the local Native population, who have also, over time, been confined to their reservations, with little possibility of reclaiming the vast lands they once occupied. Like the buffalo, Indians too were expected to die out, and, thus, many of the tourists who visit the reservation and attend the 'Indian Days' celebration see their trip to Truth and Bright Water as a form of entertainment. One non-Native family, from Kingston, Ontario, inform the narrator's father that they 'normally spend their summers on Prince Edward Island but decided to come west this year to find the real Indians' (234). Conversely, the local Native population is often compelled to take on these performative stereotypes in order to ensure their economic survival. For example, Happy Trails, an aptly named recreation vehicle park built by the band, is designed to target visitors who will pay for the opportunity to 'camp on a Native reserve' (100). As the narrator's father explains, 'Franklin figured that a herd of buffalo would bring in the tourists and help fill up Happy Trails' (89).

The symbolic significance of the analogy between the buffalo and the local tribe is a crucial part of Swimmer's own subversive agenda, and also informs his comic acts of cross-racial cross-dressing. When Monroe and the narrator begin to set up the iron buffalo sculptures, a process of 'restoration' that reverses the desire of galleries around the globe to cover up images of Natives, the narrator learns the merits of this imaginative process. Tecumseh may insist that there is 'a real herd of buffalo over in Bright Water,' but Swimmer's sculptures – outlines of buffalo with bodies that the narrator's dog can poke his nose through – become far more substantial precisely because they demand that the boy see and understand things that the White tourists at Happy Trails cannot, including counter-memories of a past without a church, when the buffalo (and the Native populations) roamed free (198). The narrator's father insists that the tactics of the buffalo, who 'took off' and never came back, are an example that the Indian population should have fol-

lowed: 'Soon as the smart ones got a good look at Whites, they took off
... That's the mistake we made ... We should have gone with them' (91).
Monroe's resurrected buffalo, however, provide a parodic recreation of
the past that depends upon creativity and humour, empowering the
local Native population by inverting some of the same strategies that
non-Native artists have used to paint over or erase the existence of Indians except as objects of consumption, or cultural artifacts of 'Otherness.' The buffalo offer a model that will help Tecumseh to understand
his tribal history, to find innovative ways to sustain that past in his imagination, and to bring the buffalo into the present. As the boy comments
at the end of the novel, shortly after the tragic death of his best friend, 'I
can see the buffalo on both sides of the coulees and on the bluff over-
looking the Shield. A few of them have wandered off and aren't where
they're supposed to be, but most of them have stayed put. Monroe says
they might move around a bit and that it isn't a worry ...' (262). Such
flexibility and freedom offer a subversive counter-narrative to the
restraint imposed on the buffalo that have been brought in for Indian
Days and remain behind the locked gates of the paddock, unable to
leave. But the sculptures also elude reductive or simplistic readings.
Instead, some of the buffalo remain in place while others figuratively
roam across the coulees; there is no one perfect spot for the animal
sculptures and the histories they conjure up. Similarly, Monroe himself
plays with the divide between us and them, Native and non-Native, male
and female, through his various costumes and disguises, outfits that, like
the buffalo sculptures, contest reductive formulations by making the
narrator look again.

When the narrator first officially meets Monroe at the church, he is
wearing jeans, a logo T-shirt that reads 'Monroe Shocks' (a playful reference to both the artist's style and a brand of car-shocks), and a long
black wig that conceals his short, grey hair (45). It is the wig that differ-
entiates Swimmer, making him look more like a Native movie star than a
'famous Indian artist,' a title that Monroe gives himself until he comes
'up with something better' (46). According to the narrator, 'aside from
the hair, which reminds me of Graham Greene's hair in *Dances With
Wolves,* he looks ordinary' (45). The artist's ability to alter his appearance becomes a ploy for commenting on the commodification of
Natives; for example, Monroe dresses up as a German tourist during
Indian Days, and reformulates sex/gender and racial categories by don-
ning a blond wig to perform a ritual burial. These performances chal-

lenge the narrator's assumptions about the stability of such categories, which, up to this point, he has accepted and perpetuated without much thought.

Monroe enacts several different racial and sexual identities – taking on White, Native, male, female, and transgendered personae – over the course of the novel. During a visit to the church where Swimmer lives, for instance, the narrator sees a silhouette in the doorway, which is not clearly male or female. Only when he hears Monroe's voice does he recognize the artist, who is wearing a long dark-haired wig, braided and tied with a red cloth, and has painted his face in ritual fashion to represent the Blackfoot belief in the power of the sun and the moon. These ceremonial preparations, adapted from the traditional Sun Dance, allow Monroe to complete the distribution of his iron buffalo sculptures, and to teach Tecumseh the importance of seeing beyond the surface. As Swimmer explains to the boy, 'Realism will only take you so far' (198), especially when its reality is shaped by a Eurocentric agenda of absolutes. The appropriation and cultivation of 'in-between' spaces become a necessary survival tool for Swimmer, a perspective that he attempts to pass on to the narrator by emphasizing the power of humour: 'You know what's wrong with this world? ... Nobody has a sense of humour' (199). As with the narrator's father, Monroe suggests that the ability to perceive unexpected juxtapositions and to enjoy the differences and similarities that emerge is one way for Natives to thrive, against all odds. Likewise, when Swimmer appears at Indian Days, carrying a camera and wearing a 'red Hawaiian shirt,' white cowboy boots, and giant sunglasses, and then snaps the narrator's picture, the artist parodically re-performs the tourist's desire to fix Native peoples, to reproduce them in a commodified form that can be distributed and circulated as a fetish object (in much the same fashion as the memories and photographs of dead celebrities like Elvis Presley and Marilyn Monroe) (216). In his tourist garb, Monroe plays at being White, blurring the boundaries between the Whites and Natives at this gathering. The artist has come to Indian Days, not to gawk at the Indians, but to admire his successful elimination of the church from the horizon, an act of erasure that may leave Swimmer unable to locate where he lives, and still give him a sense of great pride. This tourist does not take a picture of the church as it looms above the town; instead, Monroe snaps various photographs of 'Truth and the bluff where the church use to be,' recording another restoration, which this time involves his comic response to a history of dispossession and religious oppression (218).

Swimmer makes several attempts to disrupt the subject positions accorded to Natives. Perhaps his most successful guise is the one that frames the plot of *Truth and Bright Water,* a case of mistaken identity that encourages the narrator to use his imagination to create new notions of race, nation, and gender. The artist dons a blond wig, invoking the ghost of Marilyn Monroe and memories of Lum's mother, and undertakes a ritual reburial of the Native bones he has discovered in museums around the world. Swimmer's cross-racial cross-dressing, like Lucy Rabbit's dyed hair, becomes a performative strategy that disrupts 'conservative sex/gender scripts' (Faith 110). As Swimmer later tells the narrator, through his access to various museums, he has successfully reclaimed the skeletons of hundreds of Indian children. These skeletons have been relegated to 'drawers and boxes and stuck away on dusty shelves,' where they remain until 'some bright graduate student opens the drawer, takes a look, writes a paper, and shuts the drawer' (250–1). Using his 'famous Indian artist' status, Swimmer takes the opportunity not only to restore paintings, but also to recover the bodies of the Native children, whose bones have been removed from their communities and hidden from view. Here, King recalls the 1986 discovery by Northern Cheyenne leaders that the Smithsonian was in possession of 18,500 ancestral remains.[5] In order to address this conflict between physical anthropologists and Native Americans, the United States Congress passed the Native American Graves Protection and Repatriation Act in 1990. Nevertheless, the subject of Native North American bone reclamation remains a subject of debate in both the United States and Canada.

The artist's attempts to return the bones to the river, however, initially leads to a case of mistaken identity, as Lum and the narrator watch Monroe (disguised by his wig) complete a late night burial. What they see is a woman tossing the unknown contents of a suitcase into the waters below, an act that leads them to speculate about what the woman is doing and why she has come to such a deserted spot to unburden herself. When the figure plunges into the river a few minutes later, they go to investigate and find a single, finely polished human skull; the woman seems to have disappeared and may even be dead. For days afterward, the narrator tries 'to imagine what the woman was doing on the Horns' (63), and plays out a number of formulaic (primarily romance-driven) scenarios that reinforce heterosexual and racial norms:

My first theory is that she's angry about something. Maybe her boyfriend or her husband has left her. Maybe she stuffs his favourite clothes into a suitcase, drives out to the river in a fury, and throws everything into the water ...

This theory is simple and complete. The only problem is that there are better places to throw a suitcase into the river ...

My second theory is that the woman's boyfriend or husband has died or been killed. She packs his favourite clothes in his favourite suitcase and drives out to the Horns. When she gets there, she discovers that she can't bear simply to throw the suitcase into the river, so she jumps in with it and, as a gesture of love, floats along with the suitcase for a ways before she sets it free in the current ...

The third theory is more melodramatic, and suicide sounds too much like a movie for me to like it much.

But maybe someone the woman loves has left her or has died, and she's depressed ... she puts on her best dress and drives to the Horns. She waits on the cliff for the moon to rise, and just as it does, she clutches the suit-case to her chest and jumps off ...

It's an okay theory, but there are better ways to kill yourself. Everybody knows that putting a hose in a car's exhaust, or taking a lot of sleeping pills ... or cutting your wrists ... or jumping out the window of a tall building – and there are several tall buildings in Truth – would be quicker and more effective ...

The skull is the problem. Any one of these theories work out fine until I get to the skull. The easiest way to manage it is to forget it altogether. It probably has nothing to do with the woman. (63–4, 68–9)

Tecumseh's vision of a distressed woman, who comes to the river to end her life, mourn the loss of a loved one, or express her anger, becomes increasingly complex as Lum begins to believe that the mysterious female is his mother, returning from the dead. The discovery of the finely polished and preserved skull adds another twist to Tecumseh's otherwise fairly standard narratives of a romance gone wrong. The iden-tity of this so-called female figure does not become clear until Monroe completes his task of painting the church out of existence, a moment of revelation that challenges the narrator's presumptions that he has, in fact, seen a woman.

In his capacity as the artist's assistant, Tecumseh carries, and then drops, a mysterious box that contains both Swimmer's blond wig and another finely polished skull, two objects that reveal the identity of the mysterious female figure out on the Horns. After Monroe explains the origins of the bones and tells the narrator that it was, in fact, him at the river that night, they go together to bury the skull, an act of improvisation and revision that has both comic and tragic consequences. The young boy's discovery that the scorned or mourning White woman he imagined is a Native man, who has reclaimed the bones of his ancestors from institutional scrutiny, inverts the very basis of the romantic narratives he has conjured to explain what he saw. The discovery of the skull on the Horns after the woman disappears is the missing piece of the puzzle. It may not fit the heterosexual formulation of plots based on death, desire, and rejection; yet the skull provides an important symbol of how Natives have been constructed as an extinct species, worthy of scrutiny only when dead. In turn, by wearing a blond wig during the burial ceremony, Monroe can be read as revising conceptions of his White female namesake, Marilyn Monroe.

Through his re-presentation of Monroe, Swimmer redirects standard and often shopworn narratives about the life and demise of this actor; he offers a Native-inflected account of Monroe's significance by refashioning the meanings of her fair skin and dyed hair in a playful but also provocative manner. Appropriately enough, Marilyn Monroe has been described as an underrated comic actor, who was mistakenly reduced to the role of blonde bombshell by the press and the public. Ignoring other aspects of her performances, critics contained and commodified her. Similarly, as Monroe Swimmer notes, the lack of humour in the world today is what has created stratification and hierarchies amongst populations: 'We spend all our time looking for dragons to kill ... Even in the old days, they were never the problem' (199). Offering up his own version of Monroe in a ceremony that combines Native and non-Native traditions and symbols, Swimmer begins to reassert the importance of humour as a tactic for survival, and the cultivation of community across race and gender dividing lines. In Swimmer's version of events, Marilyn Monroe acknowledges her 'real' racial heritage by subverting the cinematic plots, tabloid stories, and photographs that have fixed her identity and frozen her in time. Like the Indian children who are left in drawers to be scrutinized at the convenience of museum officials and experts, Marilyn Monroe's memory is vulnerable to creative reconstructions that idealize White femininity and solidify racial hierarchies, without considering the possibility that she may not be the epitome of Whiteness. In this instance, Swimmer is able to appropriate the legacy of the blonde bombshell to complete a task (i.e., to return the

Native bones to their rightful resting place), which actively demonstrates how Marilyn and the skeletons of the Native children are, indeed, interrelated.

Even so, Monroe's attempt to 'fix' the world and restore counter-memories comes with its own price. Like the trickster Coyote and the four female Native mythic figures in *Green Grass, Running Water*, who manage to dismantle the dam and, in the process, must watch Eli die, Swimmer's repetition of his ceremonial burial of the bones of Native children has a tragic consequence. When Lum discovers Monroe – wearing the blond wig – and the narrator about to throw another skull in the river, he mistakenly assumes that the artist is, in fact, the ghost of his dead mother, and prepares to shoot her. Even though the narrator snatches tne wig off Swimmer's head and tells Lum, 'We thought it was a woman, but it wasn't' (252), the memory of Lum's mother and the boy's sense of betrayal lead him onto the deteriorating bridge that joins Truth and Bright Water, and eventually he plunges to his death, as the narrator watches in vain. Lum's death, and his fall into the river, which embodies both national separation by dividing Canada from the United States, and tribal unity by binding the Blackfoot community together, undercut Monroe's parodic interpretation of his female namesake and his spirited attempts to return the Native children's bones to their natural place. Swimmer, at the end of the novel, may be setting off to begin yet another restoration project, this time purchasing and painting an 'old residential school ... near Medicine River' into the Canadian landscape (248). His wigs and outfits will remain part of that process of crossing the borders between sex/gender categories, and racial and national identities. However, the comic dimensions of Swimmer's restoration of the landscape and his artistic expressions of 'in-betweenness' are undercut by the tragedy of Lum's demise, as the young boy joins myriad other Indian children, whose bones now rest at the bottom of the river.

'Most people would rather laugh than cry'

In *Truth and Bright Water*, Monroe Swimmer enacts King's insistence that there are 'much more powerful' ways to articulate an oppositional perspective than simply lamenting one's oppression (Lutz 112). Swimmer takes what we have described as a central and ancient principle of comedy, the act of symbolic inversion, and reworks conventional roles in order to scrutinize their origin and purpose. He also teaches the young narrator how to use performance to subvert established conventions, and how to see and interpret different and often conflicting perspectives in a manner that acknowledges both the pleasure and the pain of Native survival and resistance. As Phelan argues in her discussion of the politics of performance, 'Taking the visual world in is a process of loss: learning to see is training careful blindness ... Just as surely as representational technologies – the camera, the canvas, the theatrical frame, language itself – order visual apprehension to accord with a (constructed) notion of the real so too do human eyes' (13). By challenging how the narrator looks at the world, and calling upon him to develop a sense of humour, Swimmer provides a model for reading King's novel: examine the margins, from the perspectives of those who typically are perceived as occupying those spaces; and make connections between various layers of story. The collaborative, communal possibilities of humour – exemplified by various members of the local population who mock what they perceive as non-Natives' lack of humour – displace the burden of 'difference' onto the centre, exposing how a single, stable notion of the 'real' has been constructed and perpetuated to silence Natives. Through a process of resignification or reiteration of dominant discourses, the Native characters in King's texts, from *Medicine River* to *Truth and Bright Water*, subvert and contest their reduction to the status of 'Other' in a variety of categories, including race, sex/gender, religion, sexual orientation, and nationality.

How one looks, what one sees, and whether one can recognize humour in a situation depend a great deal upon how one reads a text. Humour certainly may be a strategy for disarming those who favour dominant discourse; humour is also a tool for strengthening a community under siege, and creating an arena in which those who are traditionally on the outside become 'insiders' to the joke or the unfolding of a comic plot. With his ironically inflected brand of humour, King cultivates spaces of 'in-betweenness' that engender other thresholds of meaning and encourage new definitions of identity and community. He pushes characters and readers to imagine themselves and each other in different places by disrupting so-called normative subject positions. Favouring a comic vision of often tragic situations, King's texts use humour to take risks and to offer reading strategies that undermine conventional assumptions about Indians and their day-to-day lives. Through the employment of a 'trickster discourse,' King's narratives create a dialogue with readers that invites participation and fosters pleasure, while educating and encouraging imaginative reformulations of depictive worlds. As the narrator of *Truth and Bright Water* observes at the end of the novel, when he attends a local play shortly after Lum's funeral: 'There are more people at the theatre than were at the funeral, but that doesn't surprise me. Dying on stage can be funny, and most people would rather laugh than cry' (265). The young boy's own ironically doubled vision of this scene, in which the tragic and the comic are intimately interwoven, and his understanding of what makes humour – and the performance of humour – so compelling, aptly explain King's discursive strategies and his search for a balance between extremes, a means of survival that also ensures rejuvenation and reflects a central part of Native lives and identities.

CHAPTER SEVEN

Comic Intertextualities

In *Dreams of Fiery Stars: The Transformations of Native American Fiction*, Catherine Rainwater singles out Thomas King's *Green Grass, Running Water* as the text that 'best illustrates the maximum effects an author may achieve through a cross-culturally allusive work' (142). She argues that 'from the vast array of Western literary works available' King 'has fashioned an intertextual network of stories rich in subtextual messages about the relationship of European peoples to indigenous cultures throughout the world' (143). Through this process, King's work highlights the ways in which European settlers to the New World were – and their descendants continue to be – dependent upon a subordinated Other to create their identities and realities. Certainly, intertextuality is a powerful part of King's comic strategy, which, as we have argued, uses cultural reversals to throw traditional discursive constructions and generic formulations into question. But in the desire to pinpoint the myriad of King's allusions and to demonstrate how King enacts these comic inversions, scholars have overlooked another source of inspiration. King has developed an intertextual web of references to his *own* work and characters. These allusions provide insights into the complexity of his cross-border positioning, in all of its manifestations, and extend the comic conversation between his various texts in new directions by self-reflexively commenting on the development of his characters and his career, both as a writer and an academic. Such intertextual references also cultivate different kinds of insider/outsider relationships with readers and those who have seen/heard his work on television, radio, and in photography. Rather than knowing the Cherokee language or the history of Native North Americans, a knowledge of King's texts becomes an asset, creating an audience which, although it may remain excluded in some respects, can also take delight in King's deliberate linking of communities and characters across works. King even creates in-jokes for those academics who read across his creative and critical endeavours, weaving a web of intertextual references that highlight the playful aspects of this border-crossing dialogue. The narrator of *Green Grass, Running Water* repeatedly instructs Coyote to 'pay attention,' and that is exactly what King calls upon his audiences to do (83).

In *Green Grass, Running Water*, for example, Will Horse Capture, the protagonist of *Medicine River*, King's previous novel, makes a brief but significant appearance in his capacity as the local Native photographer. Will, in *Medicine River*, returns to his childhood tribal community from Toronto to attend his mother's funeral, but is convinced to set up shop in Medicine River by the persuasive rhetoric of Harlen Bigbear, who insists that, although there are lots of local photographers, there are no 'Indian photographers' (94). As Harlen explains: 'Real embarrassing for us to have to go to a white for something intimate like a picture' (94). While Harlen's concern over cultural sensitivity and the need for a photographer who is from within the community is compelling, Will's inclusion in *Green Grass* suggests that the shyness of the locals and their desire to support a Native photographer are not the only motives for setting up shop in his childhood town. The novel's narrator describes how Latisha, the owner of the very successful Dead Dog Café, goes to see Will 'over in Medicine River' to get assistance with her marketing plan for the restaurant, which is aimed at non-Native tourists' stereotypical notions of Indianness (92). As part of her efforts to profit from their naïvety and desire to keep such constructs alive, Latisha commissions Will to produce a series of photographs for the walls of the café that will sustain these clichés to profitable ends:

> She got ... [him] to make up a bunch of photographs like those you see in the hunting and fishing magazines where a couple of white guys are standing over an elephant or holding up a lion's head or stretching out a long stringer of fish or hoisting a brace of ducks in each hand. Only in these photographs, it was Indians and dogs. Latisha's favorite was a photograph of four Indians on their buffalo runners chasing down a herd of Great Danes. (92)

Fee and Flick have noted that, typically, the 'move from eschatology to scatology is part of Native subversive humour,' a shift that is epitomized by Norma's suggestion that Latisha use the 'racist epithet leveled at Indians ("dog-eater") and ... [turn] it on the tourists' (137). The reference to dog-eaters is, indeed, a loaded one, because historically the Sioux did resort to consuming dogs after the buffalo disappeared in order to stave off starvation (Fee and Flick 137).

But the comic dimensions of dog-eating in these photographs don't end there.[1] Will's photographs mock the narrow perceptions of non-Native tourists, who do not know the historical context that forced select tribes to eat dogs or die. Once the communities could no longer hunt buffalo on their horses, a situation created through over-exploitation of natural resources by the fur trade and the gradual decline of the buffalo, they were forced to find other sources of food.[2] Moreover, Will plays with the figure of the White, male hunter, who proudly displays his catch for the camera, a symbol of man's control over the natural world. In Latisha's favourite photograph, Indians on their buffalo runners replace the White hunters and pursue 'a herd of Great Danes' (92). Here, the opportunity to dominate nature is replaced by the thrill of the chase, and the enormous size of the buffalo is parodically invoked through the Great Danes, which are dwarfed by the Natives pursuing them on horseback. This visual inversion points up how absurd and yet powerful, as well as commercially successful, Eurocentric stereotypes of Natives remain; Will's photograph takes pleasure in playing with the assumption that Indians were, historically, unskilled hunters whose eating of dog-meat reflected their uncivilized ways. And, of course, Latisha recognizes the wider commercial potential of these photographs for her Café, making some of the 'better' ones into 'postcards that she sold along with the menus' and thus finding multiple ways to profit from the comic images (92).

Will's intertextual resurrection in *Green Grass, Running Water* can be read as serving several purposes. His presence affirms the ongoing relationships among the characters in King's fictional setting of the Native-populated border towns on the Prairies, giving life to these individuals beyond the limits of the text and suggesting that they continue to exist even after readers have finished the book. This is an important aspect of what King describes as 'associational' literature, which focuses on the community, gives non-Native readers 'limited and particular access to a Native world,' and demonstrates the existence of an 'active present marked by cultural tenacity and a viable future' ('Godzilla' 14). Will's appearance in *Green Grass* attests to this active present and viable future. Will, though initially uncertain about his identity and place in the Medicine River community, by this next novel, has become someone who feels comfortable using his skills comically to invert non-Native stereo-types and to create a series of 'inside' jokes that delight the local Native population. Will's pictures can also be read as an allusion to King's own photographic work, which (like Will's) is all about recognizing the con-tinued existence and viability of Native populations, in contrast to the famous photographs of Edward Curtis and others, who saw themselves as recording a dying breed of people. Notably, King first became inter-ested in photography seriously during the filming of the television movie of *Medicine River,* and, hence, Will's developing photographic style, which changes over the course of the novel *Medicine River,* mirrors King's own growing engagement with this medium. Through Will, King's photographic projects, or at least the ideas behind them, reach a different audience (those who read *Green Grass, Running Water*). This intertextual allusion, delivered via Will, enables King to cross the bor-ders that separate visual arts from the printed text and incorporate a critical commentary on how Native photographers have revised images for their own purposes.

Perhaps more overtly comic in its intertextuality is King's own appear-ance in the televised movie version of *Medicine River,* in which he plays the role of Lester, a hot-shot basketball player, who makes Will look bad on the courts. As the author of the television script, King is free to draw on his other previous work, but, in this case, King also takes on a small acting role that creates an entertaining intertextual allusion. In this case, King's behaviour on the court ironically recalls his confessional introduction to his 1990 critical essay, 'Godzilla vs. Post-Colonial,' in which he describes his desire to become a basketball star and his lack of natural ability:

> I grew up in Northern California, and I grew up fast. I don't mean that I was raised in a tough part of town where you had to fight to survive. I was raised in a small town in the foothills, quite pastoral in fact. I mean I grew up all at once. I already had my full height, while most of my friends were just beginning to grow.
>
> We had a basketball team at the high school and a basketball coach who considered himself somewhat of an authority on the subject of talent. He could spot it, he said. And he spotted me. He told me I had a talent for the game, and that I should come out for the team. With my size, he said, I would be a natural player. I was flattered.
>
> I wish I could tell you that I excelled at basketball, that I was an all-star,

that college coaches came to see me play. But the truth of the matter is, I wasn't even mediocre. Had I not been so very young and so very serious, I might have laughed at my attempts to run and bounce a ball at the same time. Certainly most everyone who saw me play did. (10)

While King uses this childhood memory to suggest the danger of making assumptions about any person or term, he seizes the opportunity in the televised movie to rewrite the basketball narrative for his own ends. King rectifies his teenage humiliation by taking on the role of an aging basketball star who poses a serious threat to Will and his mediocre teammates. Lester stands between the local team and the local championship, with its five thousand dollars in prize money, which is much needed in order to pay back loans that the Friendship Center council have taken out against a set of cameras, given to them by the government in error. And though Lester puts up a good fight, the local team, led by Will and Harlen, eventually defeat him.

Thomas King's appearance in front of the cameras, a cameo that pointedly – at least, for those who have read his essay – alludes to and revises this prior narrative, makes him both the 'butt of the joke' and enables the writer, photographer, and academic to border-cross yet again as an actor. With this, King offers another access point to his various texts, creating an insider relationship with the academic community even as he sustains a comic vision of the world that reaches a much larger audience through those who watch the film on television. The task of 'paying attention' not only pays off for those 'in the know,' who recognize King and are privy to his joke on some level, but his appearance in the televised film of his novel creates a dialogue between works, and highlights his ability to frame and reframe his narratives to suit a variety of different contexts. King himself takes on the role of trickster through his discourse, which, as we mentioned in chapter 1, is typically 'open-ended, unfolding, evolving, incomplete' and can be 'imagined in numerous verbal and visual narratives and a multiplicity of ... voices' (Ryan xiii). In doing so, King highlights the comic spirit of his works, and urges those who engage with his texts to join in this collective project through their recognition of and comic response to the various intertexts.

King's latest novel, *Truth and Bright Water*, also parodically refers to other texts from his oeuvre, continuing his tradition of strategically placed comic allusions to previous works. Bill Bursum, the owner of Bill Bursum's Home Entertainment Barn in Blossom, Lionel's boss and

Charlie's ex-boss, first appears in *Green Grass, Running Water*. He is a man who takes particular pleasure in watching old westerns, seems certain that his Native employees lack the ability fully to understand how to market his electronics business, and resents the way in which local Natives don't fit his vision of Indianness:

> Indians were the same way ... And you couldn't call them Indians. You had to remember their tribe, as if that made any difference, and when some smart college professor did come up with a really good name like Amerindian, the Indians didn't like it. Even Lionel and Charlie could get testy every so often, and they weren't really Indians anymore. (156)

Bursum's naïve racism, grounded in the clichéd stereotypes of Natives presented on film, leaves him vulnerable to the whims of Coyote and the four female Native mythic figures in *Green Grass, Running Water*, as when they alter his favourite John Wayne movie.

In *Truth and Bright Water*, however, Bursum's economic shrewdness is undermined and his inability to interact with the local Native community has apparently destroyed his business. When Tecumseh's father takes the young boy up to Canada in an empty truck to collect goods north of the border and bring them back to sell in the United States, they head for Blossom and the Home Entertainment Barn. But, as Tecumseh notes when he sees the store, 'There's a big red sign on a long, low building that says "Lionel's Home Entertainment Barn"' (87). Having just told Tecumseh that the problem with the world is 'Whites,' who have 'no sense of humour,' his father relays, with comic satisfaction, the story of the Barn: 'Indian guy owns this ... White guy went bankrupt a few years back and had to sell it. Now that's funny ... Not many times you see that happen' (86–7). Lionel's desire to make something of his life in *Green Grass, Running Water* and his uncertainty about what that might be is recalled and an answer is given. Lionel displaces Bursum, who could never conceive of Natives running his store, and demonstrates his skills as a businessperson by making the operation economically viable. Paradoxically, though, the artfully created 'Map' of North America that Bursum built using television sets remains part of the store's floor display, even with Lionel as its owner: 'One wall is nothing but televisions all stacked up on each other. If you look hard and use your imagination, it looks like a map of North America' (87). While Bursum constructs the display as an imperialistic vision of North America, in which distinctive tribal identities are erased and Canada is metaphorically consumed by the wonders of American capitalism, in Lionel's hands, the display may be read, in contrast, as an acknowledgment of many Native tribes' rejection of the forty-ninth parallel as their national border. The journey of Tecumseh and his father to reach the Entertainment Barn, a trip that includes a stop at the Canadian-U.S. border, during which the father plays 'the dumb Indian routine' to avoid a full-scale search, foregrounds the absurdity of such national divisions for this Native community (86). By retaining the Map but framing it differently, King's narrative comically inverts its significance and offers up an alterna(rra)tive that exposes Bursum's disconnection with the local population and the price he pays for such an attitude. Ultimately, the joke is on Bursum, who gets what he deserves in *Truth and Bright Water* precisely because he cannot laugh at himself.

King's works, therefore, present an opportunity for him to explore his own comic inversions, invoke a variety of intertexts, and laugh at his foibles, a strategy that creates inclusion rather than exclusion by sparing no one, including himself. This border-crossing stance at the level of genre and medium suggests the need to think more broadly about King's texts as a dialogue about Native identities and the centrality of a comic vision in his works. It is notable that much less attention has been given to King's photography, radio scripts, and acting career, perhaps because these endeavours challenge the boundaries that separate academic disciplines and artistic forms, and force scholars to engage in critical border crossings of their own. The diversity of his texts and his sustained interest in creating a comic strategy to deal with often tragic subjects raise important questions about how and why certain works are valued or ignored. As a Native and a Canadian writer, King challenges his readers to venture across a variety of borders themselves, at least figuratively, a journey that necessitates a sense of humour and a willingness to examine the 'in-between' spaces that are constituted and continually inverted by his various texts. Perhaps the best approach is to follow the narrator's instructions in *Green Grass, Running Water,* where Coyote is repeatedly told to 'pay attention.' Though it is a struggle for Coyote to heed this mantra, it offers great rewards, not only for the well-known trickster figure, but for anyone who enters King's worlds with the promise of yet another version of 'And here's how it happened' (360), and another opportunity to experience the comic richness of his texts.

Notes

Introduction: Whose Borders?

1 See Wyile for another approach to reading King's works cross-culturally.

2 We have used the term 'White' generally to refer to European-descent peoples and European-based cultures throughout the book in accordance with King's own choice of language. See the 'Introduction' to *The Native in Literature*, p. 13, his dissertation, and 'One Good Story, That One' for examples of how King employs the idea of 'Whiteness' in a pointedly political and playful manner to explore and reconfigure the presumed universality of non-Native, and particularly, European-descent perspectives.

3 Terminology is always a complex issue, and thus we have tried to be inclusive and respectful in our choice of terms used to describe Native populations. Certainly, as Strong-Boag and Gerson point out, 'usage varies among individual authors, scholars, and disciplines, and from one nation to another. What is acceptable in one time or place may well turn out to be deeply prejudicial in another' (8). The terms 'Native,' 'Aboriginal,' 'Native North American,' 'Indian,' and 'First Nations' are used interchangeably throughout this book. We have deliberately chosen to use both Canadian and American designations for these groups (e.g., 'First Nations' is prominent in Canada whereas 'American Indian' is frequently used in the United States) in order to acknowledge King's own border-crossing stance.

4 Drew Hayden Taylor's play, appropriately titled *alterNatives*, presents alternative Native perspectives that challenge formulaic depictions of the Indian. The play, first performed in 1999 and published in 2000, offers a comic portrait of the relationship between a White Jewish professor of Native literature, Colleen Birk, and an Ojibway writer, Angel Wallace. Notably, Colleen cites Thomas King's name several times during the play as a model for Angel, who wants to write science fiction. She argues that King is 'Native, a great writer,

and he has some things to say. I don't find it limiting for him' (104), a comment that suggests her own blindness to the stereotypes she has imposed on Angel and also, more broadly, mocks the scholarly community's interest in King's work.

5 The Canadian and American terms for tribal lands differ; Canadians describe these areas as 'reserves,' but Americans usually call them 'reservations' (McMillan 315). For the sake of clarity, we use the Canadian term throughout the book.

6 The field of border studies is a rapidly growing, interdisciplinary enterprise, primarily focused on the border between the United States and Mexico. See Anzaldúa, Rosaldo, Hicks, Calderón and Saldívar, Behar, Jay, and Michaelsen and Johnson, for a chronological overview of the development of border studies. In their introduction, Michaelsen and Johnson argue that the U.S.-Mexican border is 'the birthplace ... of border studies, and its methods of analysis' (1).

7 The terms 'border' and 'boundary' are typically used interchangeably in current critical discourse about nation and narration. In the *OED*, the noun 'border' is defined as a 'side, edge, brink or margin, limit or boundary,' and 'to border' is 'to keep within bounds'; here, boundary becomes synonymous with border. We, however, make a distinction between the two terms by using 'border' to refer primarily to the dividing line that separates one political entity from another (in this case, the forty-ninth parallel), and 'boundary' to describe the non-physical or metaphorical limits of the relationship between Canada, the United States, and various Native tribes. See New 4–7 for a more detailed discussion of differences between borders and boundaries. As New explains, 'boundaries seem to me to be metaphors more than fixed edges: *signs* of limits more than the limits themselves' (4). Although New insists that 'boundaries function as both descriptions of concrete agreements *and* as metaphors of relationship and organization' (5), in the discussion that follows, he uses 'borders' to refer to political and territorial lines, and 'boundaries' to discuss the metaphorical significance of these lines.

8 See Durland, Fisher, and Luna for discussions of 'Artifact Piece.'

9 See Corse 38, where she notes that 'the concept of "nation" in Canadian discourse is used to refer to (1) a pan-Canadian nation; (2) to the "nation" of English-Canada; (3) to the "nation" of French Canada.' Recent developments with Native land claim settlements in Canada further complicate what constitutes a nation. For example, the creation of an autonomous Inuit-led government in the Arctic territory of Nunavut, effective as of 1 April 1999, and the granting of self-government rights to the Nisaga'a in British Columbia (which gives the tribe law-making powers over adoption, citizenship, and

land management), also affect how the word 'nation' is defined in a Canadian context.

10 See Ziff and Rao, and Mihesuah, for extended discussions of the intellectual and pragmatic dimensions of cultural appropriation for Native North Americans.

1: Comic Contexts

1 See Lowe, 'Theories' 440 for a survey of definitions of the term 'ethnicity.'

2 See Fee and Flick 133–4 for a discussion of how the novel creates boundaries of knowledge that include some readers and exclude others. As Fee and Flick note, 'In order to really "get" the whole joke, one has to learn not only the facts, but also come to terms with a sense of humour that can only be described as subversive' (134). We take this concept of 'subversive' humour in a different direction by considering how Native North American authors effectively pair humour and irony in their texts, to undermine White, Western conventions and stereotypes of Natives.

3 See Chester for a detailed analysis of the orality of King's narrative.

4 See pages 3, 85, 189, and 271 of *Green Grass* for the four title pages with the Cherokee words for the four cardinal directions and the four sacred colours. Goldman argues that King's use of the sacred directions and colours suggests that the novel 'does not simply describe the Native ceremony, but is itself an evocation or map of the ritual' (37). Her interpretation of the text suggests that Native writers are creating their own counter-narrative to the geographical exploration and land claims of White, Western settlers, a counter-discursive manoeuvre that complements and extends in new directions our argument about King's use of 'code-switching.'

2: Comic Inversions

1 As Faludi has aptly demonstrated, the rhetoric of 'women's liberation' was used by its detractors throughout the 1980s and '90s to discredit the movement (e.g., 1980s and '90s 'backlash films' like *Fatal Attraction* and *Disclosure* employ the logic of feminism in order to reject it).

2 The impact of Christianity on Native communities in Canada and the United States has a long and vexed history, largely as a result of missionary efforts to eradicate tribal religious beliefs. Certainly, there are Native North Americans who have converted to Christianity, and are able to combine an awareness of the destructive historical legacy of Christianity, as imposed by non-Natives,

with their own religious convictions. However, King's writings tend strategically to critique the impact of various Christian churches and their Eurocentric belief systems, without giving much attention to Natives who are also practising Christians.

3 See Fee and Flick 135 for a discussion of how naming marks gender difference in *Green Grass*.

4 See Linton for an alternative reading of the relationship between inside and outside readers in King's novel. Linton argues that the breadth of the narrator's knowledge conversely narrows the characterization of the ideal reader, who must straddle 'two cultural realms': the Native and the Eurocentric (214). Our discussion of the insider/outsider status of readers differs from Linton's because we examine the levelling implications of humour in King's texts.

3: Genre Crossings

1 See Fee and Flick's 'Coyote Pedagogy: Knowing Where the Borders Are in Thomas King's *Green Grass, Running Water*' and Flick's 'Reading Notes for Thomas King's *Green Grass, Running Water*' for information on the many other historical figures who appear in King's narrative.

2 King describes this encounter with Mathews in an interview with Harmut Lutz, where he states: 'There was a guy at Victoria who got up after I gave a paper and wanted to know why I didn't picture Indians realistically as drunks, and down-and-outers, suicides, and whatnot. He has really bought the stereotype. Alcoholism and drugs and suicide are problems, but it doesn't mean that all Indians are like that. Hell most of us aren't' (111).

4: Comedy, Politics, and Audio and Visual Media

1 King's curriculum vitae lists his photographic publications and exhibitions, including the shows in Minneapolis and San Francisco, which one of the co-authors attended. Thanks to Helen Hoy for providing a faxed copy of King's CV to facilitate the writing of this chapter.

2 See Stackhouse A11 for a sample of listeners' reactions to *The Dead Dog Café Comedy Hour*.

5: Humouring Race and Nationality

1 See Lee for a discussion of Mormon beliefs and their arrival in Canada.

2 See *Picturesque Cardston* for descriptions of Ora Card's arrival in southern

Alberta, the creation of Cardston, and the eventual ceding of strips of land from the Blackfoot tribe.

3 See Fee and Flick 131–2 and New 29 for two other approaches to the subject of literal and figurative borders in King's texts.

4 See Ridington for a useful catalogue of King's allusions in *Truth and Bright Water.*

5 See Most for an insightful analysis of how the musical *Oklahoma!* became a vehicle of assimilation for Jewish people into mainstream American culture. Although marginalized ethnic and racial groups are represented in the musical through Ali Hakim, a Persian peddler who has immigrated to Oklahoma, and Jud, a 'bullet-colored' man who aggressively pursues the White heroine, Laurey (82), Natives are absent from the text.

6 See Foreman 302–3 for an account of Rebecca Neugin's memories of the Cherokee removal to Oklahoma in 1838. Foreman interviewed her in 1932, when Neugin was nearly one hundred years of age, and then incorporated her recollections into his own study of the removal. Neugin's memories have been reprinted in various places, including the *Journal of Cherokee Studies* (see Neugin).

7 See Silko's 'The Border Patrol State' for a poignant personal account of how Mexican Americans and Native Americans are treated by the U.S. Border Patrol, regardless of citizenship.

8 See also Saldívar-Hull 212–13 for a description of how the colonization of southern Texas and occupation by U.S. forces permanently altered the history of Chicano/a experience in the area.

9 King argues that, in *Truth and Bright Water,* 'as ... relationships between people in general and between races and between countries deteriorate ... this bridge symbolizes that. It won't hold the weight of the people trying to cross back and forth' (Andrews 173).

6: The Comic Dimensions of Gender, Race, and Nation

1 As Stacey explains, 'Hollywood stars produce cultural ideals of whiteness ... Indeed, in the 1950s this is especially the case, when Marilyn Monroe's blondeness, for example, was a key signifier of her glamour' (89).

2 See Dickason for a more detailed discussion of Bill C-31, passed into law in 1985, which granted Native women 'the right to retain their status upon marrying non-Indians and to pass it on to their children' (307).

3 See *Green Grass* 123.

4 However, Coyote is gendered male in King's second children's book, *Coyote Sings to the Moon.* A masculine version of Coyote also appears in two of King's poems, 'Coyote Learns to Whistle' and 'Coyote Sees the Prime Minister.'

5 See articles by Mihesuah, Riding In, Ferguson and Anyon, Jacknis, and Dongoske in a 1996 special issue of *American Indian Quarterly* for a detailed examination of the central issues concerning Native North American bone reclamation and repatriation.

7: Comic Intertextualities

1 See Fee and Flick 137 for an extensive discussion of Latisha's marketing of the Dead Dog Café.
2 See Dickason 213, 214, 257, 266, 269, 271, and 276.

Works Cited

Abrams, M.H. *A Glossary of Literary Terms*. 6th ed. Fort Worth: Harcourt Brace, 1993.

Allen, Paula Gunn. *The Sacred Hoop: Recovering the Feminine in American Indian Traditions*. Boston: Beacon, 1986.

Anderson, Benedict. *Imagined Communities: Reflections on the Origin and Spread of Nationalism*. London: Verso, 1983.

Andrews, Jennifer. 'Border Trickery and Dog Bones: A Conversation with Thomas King.' *Studies in Canadian Literature* 24.2 (1999): 161–85.

– 'Reading Thomas King's *Green Grass, Running Water*: Border-Crossing Humour.' *English Studies in Canada*. Forthcoming.

Angus, Ian. *A Border Within: National Identity, Plurality, and Wilderness*. Montreal and Kingston: McGill-Queen's UP, 1997.

Anzaldúa, Gloria. *Borderlands / La Frontera: The New Mestiza*. San Francisco: Aunt Lute Books, 1987.

Atwood, Margaret. 'A Double-Bladed Knife: Subversive Laughter in Two Stories by Thomas King.' *Canadian Literature* 124/5 (1990): 243–50.

Babcock, Barbara A. 'Arrange Me into Disorder: Fragments and Reflections on Ritual Clowning.' In *Rite, Drama, Festival, Spectacle: Rehearsals Toward a Theory of Cultural Performance*. Ed. John J. MacAloon. Philadelphia: ISHI, 1984. 102–28.

– 'Introduction.' In *The Reversible World: Symbolic Inversion in Art and Society*. Ed. Barbara A. Babcock. Ithaca: Cornell UP, 1972.

Babcock, Barbara, and Jay Cox. 'The Native American Trickster.' In *Handbook of Native American Literature*. Ed. Andrew Wiget. New York: Garland, 1996. 99–105.

Babcock-Abrahams, Barbara. '"A Tolerated Margin of Mess": The Trickster and His Tales Reconsidered.' *Journal of the Folklore Institute* 11.3 (1975): 147–86.

Barrie, J.M. *Peter Pan; or, The Boy Who Would Not Grow Up.* London: Hodder and Stoughton, 1928.

Basso, Keith. *Portraits of 'the Whiteman': Linguistic Play and Cultural Symbols among the Western Apache.* London: Cambridge UP, 1979.

Beddoes, Julie. 'White Press, Talking Indian: "Thomas King" as Signifier in the Construction of an Imaginary Indian.' Paper presented to the ACSUS Conference, Seattle, November 1995.

Behar, Ruth. *Translated Woman: Crossing the Border with Esperanza's Story.* Boston: Beacon, 1993.

Bengough, J.W. *A Caricature History of Canadian Politics: Events from the Union of 1841, As Illustrated by Cartoons from the 'Grip,' and Various Other Sources.* Vol. 1. Toronto: The Grip, 1886.

Bennett, David. 'Introduction.' In *Multicultural States: Rethinking Difference and Identity.* Ed. David Bennett. London: Routledge, 1998. 1–25.

Bennett, David, and Homi K. Bhabha. 'Liberalism and Minority Culture: Reflections on "Culture's in Between."' In *Multicultural States: Rethinking Difference and Identity.* Ed. David Bennett. London: Routledge, 1998. 37–47.

Berger, John. *About Looking.* New York: Pantheon, 1980.

Bergson, Henri. 'Laughter.' In *Comedy.* Ed. Homi K. Wylie Sypher. Baltimore: Johns Hopkins UP, 1980. 61–190.

Bhabha, Homi K. 'Introduction: Narrating the Nation.' In *Nation and Narration.* Ed. Homi K. Bhabha. London: Routledge, 1990. 1–7.

– *The Location of Culture.* London: Routledge, 1994.

Blaise, Clark. *The Border As Fiction.* Orono, ME: Borderlands, 1990.

Brennan, Timothy. 'The National Longing for Form.' In *Nation and Narration.* Ed. Homi K. Bhabha. London: Routledge, 1990. 44–70.

Brunvand, Jan Harold. 'A Classification for Shaggy Dog Stories.' *Journal of American Folklore* 76 (1963): 42–68.

Butler, Judith. *Bodies That Matter: On the Discursive Limits of Sex.* New York: Routledge, 1993.

– *Gender Trouble: Feminism and the Subversion of Identity.* New York: Routledge, 1990.

Byars, Jackie. 'Gazes/Voices/Power: Expanding Psychoanalysis for Feminist Film and Television Theory.' In *Female Spectators: Looking at Film and Television.* Ed. Deidre E. Pribram. London: Verso, 1988. 110–31.

Calderón, Hector, and Jose David Saldívar, eds. *Criticism in the Borderlands: Studies in Chicano Literature, Culture and Ideology.* Durham: Duke UP, 1991.

Castronovo, Russ. 'Compromised Narratives along the Border: The Mason-Dixon Line, Resistance, and Hegemony.' In *Border Theory: The Limits of Cultural Politics.* Ed. Scott Michaelsen and David E. Johnson. Minneapolis: U of Minnesota P, 1997. 195–220.

Cawelti, John. *Adventure, Mystery, and Romance: Formula Stories As Art and Popular Culture.* Chicago: U of Chicago P, 1976.

– 'The Study of Literary Formulas.' In *Detective Fiction: A Collection of Critical Essays.* Ed. Robin Winks. Englewood Cliffs, NJ: Prentice-Hall, 1980. 121–43.

Chester, Blanca. '*Green Grass, Running Water.* Theorizing the World of the Novel.' *Canadian Literature* 161/2 (1999): 44–61.

Coltelli, Laura. 'Paula Gunn Allen.' In *Winged Words: American Indian Writers Speak.* Lincoln: U of Nebraska P, 1990. 10–39.

Corse, Sarah. *Nationalism and Literature: The Politics of Culture in Canada and the United States.* Cambridge: Cambridge UP, 1997.

de Certeau, Michel. *Heterologies: Discourses of the Other.* Trans. Brian Massumi. Minneapolis: U of Minnesota P, 1986.

– *The Practice of Everyday Life.* Trans. Steven Rendall. Berkeley: U of California P, 1984.

de Lauretis, Teresa. *The Practice of Love: Lesbian Sexuality and Perverse Desire.* Bloomington: Indiana UP, 1994.

Dead Dog Café Comedy Hour. Thomas King, Producer. CBC Radio. 1995–2000.

Deloria, Vine, Jr. *Custer Died for Your Sins: An Indian Manifesto.* New York: Macmillan, 1969.

'Diamonds Are a Girl's Best Friend.' *Globe and Mail,* 17 April 1992, p. C6.

Dickason, Olive Patricia. *Canada's First Nations: A History of Founding Peoples from Earliest Times.* 2nd ed. Toronto: Oxford UP, 1997.

Donovan, Kathleen M. *Feminist Readings of Native American Literature: Coming to Voice.* Tucson: U of Arizona P, 1998.

Douglas, Mary. 'The Social Control of Cognition: Some Factors in Joke Perception.' *Man* 3 (1968): 361–76.

Durland, Steven. 'Call Me in '93: An Interview with James Luna.' *High Performance* 14.4 (1991): 34–9.

Eco, Umberto. 'Innovation and Repetition: Between Modern and Postmodern Aesthetics.' *Daedalus* 114 (1985): 159–88.

Ellis, John. *Visible Fictions: Cinema, Television, Video.* London: Routledge and Kegan Paul, 1982.

Erikson, Erik H. 'Play and Actuality.' In *Play and Development.* Ed. Maria W. Piers. New York: Norton, 1972. 127–67.

Faith, Karlene. *Madonna, Bawdy and Soul.* Toronto: U of Toronto P, 1997.

Faludi, Susan. *Backlash: The Undeclared War against American Women.* New York: Crown, 1991.

Fanon, Franz. *Black Skins, White Masks.* Trans. Charles Lam Markmann. New York: Gove Weidenfeld, 1967.

Fee, Margery. 'Romantic Nationalism and the Image of Native People in Contemporary English-Canadian Literature.' In *The Native in Literature*. Ed. Thomas King, Cheryl Calver, and Helen Hoy. Oakville, ON: ECW, 1987. 15–33.

Fee, Margery, and Jane Flick. 'Coyote Pedagogy: Knowing Where the Borders Are in Thomas King's *Green Grass, Running Water*.' *Canadian Literature* 161/2 (1999): 131–9.

Fischer, Michael M.J. 'Ethnicity and Post-Modern Arts of Memory.' In *Writing Culture: The Poetics and Politics of Ethnography*. Ed. James Clifford and George E. Marcus. Berkeley: U of California P, 1986. 194–233.

Fisher, Jean. 'In Search of the "Inauthentic": Disturbing Signs in Contemporary Native American Art.' *Art Journal* 51.3 (1992): 44–50.

Fleras, Augie, and Jean Leonard Elliott. *The 'Nations Within': Aboriginal – State Relations in Canada, the United States, and New Zealand*. Toronto: Oxford UP, 1992.

Flick, Jane. 'Reading Notes for Thomas King's *Green Grass, Running Water*.' *Canadian Literature* 161/2 (1999): 140–72.

Foreman, Grant. *Indian Removal: The Emigration of the Five Civilized Tribes of Indians*. 1932. Norman: U of Oklahoma P, 1956.

Foucault, Michel. *The History of Sexuality: An Introduction*. Volume 1. Trans. Robert Hurley. New York: Random House, 1978.

Francis, Daniel. *The Imaginary Indian: The Image of the Indian in Canadian Culture*. Vancouver: Arsenal Pulp, 1992.

Freud, Sigmund. 'Humour.' In *Art and Literature*. Trans. James Strachey. New York: Penguin, 1985. 425–33.

– *Jokes and Their Relation to the Unconscious*. Trans. James Strachey. New York: W.W. Norton, 1960.

Frow, John. 'Economies of Value.' In *Multicultural States: Rethinking Difference and Identity*. Ed. David Bennett. London: Routledge, 1998. 53–68.

Frye, Northrop. *Anatomy of Criticism: Four Essays*. Princeton: Princeton UP, 1957.

Gledhill, Christine. 'Pleasurable Negotiations.' In *Female Spectators: Looking at Film and Television*. Ed. Deidre E. Pribram. London: Verso, 1988. 64–89.

Goldie, Terry. *Fear and Temptation: The Image of the Indigene in Canadian, Australian, and New Zealand Literatures*. Kingston and Montreal: McGill-Queen's UP, 1989.

Goldman, Marlene. 'Mapping and Dreaming: Native Resistance in *Green Grass, Running Water*.' *Canadian Literature* 161/2 (1999): 18–41.

Guibernau, Monserrat. *Nationalisms: The Nation-State and Nationalism in the Twentieth Century*. Cambridge: Polity, 1996.

Harrod, Howard L. *Renewing the World: Plains Indian Religion and Morality*. Tucson: U of Arizona, 1987.

Hicks, D. Emily. *Border-Writing: The Multi-Dimensional Text.* Minneapolis: U of Minnesota P, 1991.

Hulan, Renée. 'Introduction.' In *Native North America: Critical and Cultural Perspectives.* Toronto: ECW P, 1999. 9–19.

Hutcheon, Linda. *Irony's Edge: The Theory and Politics of Irony.* London: Routledge, 1995.

− *The Politics of Postmodernism.* London: Routledge, 1989.

Jacobs, Sue-Ellen, Wesley Thomas, and Sabine Lang. 'Introduction.' In *Two-Spirit People: Native American Gender Identity, Sexuality, and Spirituality.* Urbana: U of Illinois P, 1997.

Jay, Paul. 'The Myth of "America" and the Politics of Location: Modernity, Border Studies, and the Literature of the Americas.' *Arizona Quarterly* 54.2 (1998): 165–92.

Katakis, Michael. 'The Illusion of the Image.' In *Excavating Voices: Listening to Photographs of Native Americans.* Philadelphia: U of Pennsylvania Museum of Archeology and Anthropology, 1998. 1–5.

Keeshig-Tobias, Lenore. 'Stop Stealing Native Stories.' *Globe and Mail*, 26 Jan. 1990, p. A7.

King, Thomas. 'Artist's Statement: The Medicine River Photographic Expedition: Shooting the Lone Ranger.' Six 20" x 24" silver prints and accompanying text. October 1997 to summer of 1998. Weisman Museum, Minneapolis, Minnesota. Ansel Adams Center for Photography, San Francisco, California.

− *A Coyote Columbus Story.* Toronto: Groundwood Books, 1992.

− 'Coyote Learns to Whistle.' *Canadian Literature* 124/5 (1990): 250–1.

− 'Coyote Sees the Prime Minister.' *Canadian Literature* 124/5 (1990): 252.

− *Coyote Sings to the Moon.* Toronto: Key Porter, 1998.

− 'Definitely a Laughing Matter.' Interview with Malcolm Jones, Jr. *Newsweek*, 12 April 1993, p. 60.

− 'Godzilla vs. Post-Colonial.' *World Literature Written in English* 30.2 (1990): 10–16.

− *Green Grass, Running Water.* Toronto: HarperCollins, 1993.

− 'Inventing the Indian: White Images, Native Oral Literature, and Contemporary Native Writers.' Ph.D. diss., University of Utah, 1986.

− *Medicine River.* Markham, ON: Viking, 1990.

− 'New Voices / New Visions.' Ten 11" x 14" silver prints. October 1998 to January 1999.

− *One Good Story, That One.* Toronto: HarperCollins, 1993.

− 'Peter Gzowski Interviews Thomas King on *Green Grass, Running Water.*' *Canadian Literature* 161/2 (1999): 65–76.

– 'Shooting the Lone Ranger.' *Hungry Mind Review* 34 (1995): 36–7.

– *Truth and Bright Water.* Toronto: HarperCollins, 1999.

– *Truth and Bright Water.* MS version.

King, Thomas, ed. *All My Relations: An Anthology of Contemporary Canadian Native Fiction.* Toronto: McClelland and Stewart, 1990.

King, Thomas, Cheryl Calver, and Helen Hoy, eds. *The Native in Literature: Canadian and Comparative Perspectives.* Oakville: ECW, 1987.

King, Thomas, and Greg Staats. 'Native Writers of Canada: A Photographic Portrait of Twelve Contemporary Authors.' *Books in Canada* 23.5 (1994): 12–18.

Koestler, Arthur. *The Act of Creation.* London: Hutchinson, 1964.

Kroetsch, Robert. 'Reading across the Border.' In *Studies on Canadian Literature: Introductory and Critical Essays.* Ed. Arnold E. Davidson. New York: Modern Languages Association of America, 1990. 338–43.

Krupat, Arnold. *The Voice in the Margin: Native American Literature and the Canon.* Berkeley: U of California P, 1989.

Lamont-Stewart, Linda. 'Androgyny As Resistance to Authoritarianism in Two Postmodern Canadian Novels.' *Mosaic* 30.3 (1997): 115–30.

Lang, Sabine. 'Various Kinds of Two-Spirit People: Gender Variance and Homosexuality in Native American Communities.' In *Two-Spirit People.* Ed. Sue-Ellen Jacobs et al. Urbana: U of Illinois P, 1997. 100–18.

Lee, Lawrence B. 'The Mormons Come to Canada, 1887–1902.' *Pacific Northwest Quarterly* 59 (1968): 11–22.

Li, Peter S. 'Race and Ethnicity.' In *Race and Ethnic Relations in Canada.* Toronto: Oxford UP, 1990. 3–17.

Lincoln, Kenneth. *Indi'n Humor: Bicultural Play in Native America.* New York: Oxford UP, 1993.

Linton, Patricia. '"And Here's How It Happened": Trickster Discourse in Thomas King's *Green Grass, Running Water.*' *Modern Fiction Studies* 45.1 (1999): 212–34.

Lipsitz, George. *Time Passages: Collective Memory and American Popular Culture.* Minneapolis: U of Minnesota P, 1990.

Lorenz, Konrad. *On Aggression.* Trans. Marjorie Kerr Wilson. New York: Harcourt, Brace, 1963.

Lowe, John. 'Coyote's Jokebook: Humor in Native American Literature and Culture.' In *Dictionary of Native American Literature.* Ed. Andrew Wiget. New York: Garland, 1994. 193–205.

– 'Theories of Ethnic Humor: How to Enter Laughing.' *American Quarterly* 38.3 (1986): 439–60.

Luna, James. 'Allow Me to Introduce Myself.' *Canadian Theatre Review* 68 (1991): 46–7.

Lutz, Hartmut. 'Interview with Thomas King.' *Contemporary Challenges: Conversations with Canadian Native Authors.* Saskatoon: Fifth House, 1991. 107–16.

Matchie, Thomas, and Brett Larson. 'Coyote Fixes the World: The Power of Myth in Thomas King's *Green Grass, Running Water.*' *North Dakota Quarterly* 63.2 (1996): 153–68.

McCormack, Eric. 'Coyote Goes Slapstick.' *Books in Canada* 22.3 (1993): 40–1.

McMillan, Alan D. *Native Peoples and Cultures of Canada: An Anthropological Overview.* 2nd ed. Toronto: Douglas and McIntyre, 1995.

Medicine River. Screenplay by Thomas King. CBC Television, 1994.

Michaelsen, Scott, and David E. Johnson. 'Border Secrets: An Introduction.' In *Border Theory: The Limits of Cultural Politics.* Ed. Scott Michaelsen and David E. Johnson. Minneapolis: U of Minnesota P, 1997. 1–39.

Milhesuah, Devon, ed. *Natives and Academics: Researching and Writing about American Indians.* Lincoln: U of Nebraska P, 1998.

– 'Repatriation of American Indian Skeletal Remains and Sacred Cultural Objects.' Special issue of *American Indian Quarterly* 20.2 (1996).

Miller, Jonathan. 'Jokes and Joking: A Serious Laughing Matter.' In *Laughing Matters: A Serious Look at Humour.* Ed. John Durant and Jonathan Miller. Essex: Longman, 1988. 5–16.

Miller, Nancy K. 'The Text's Heroine: A Feminist Critic and Her Fictions.' *Diacritics* 12.2 (1982). 53–74.

Mitchell, Lee Clark, and Alfred L. Bush. *The Photograph and the American Indian.* Princeton: Princeton UP, 1994.

Mosse, George L. *Nationalism and Sexuality: Respectability and Abnormal Sexuality in Modern Europe.* New York: Howard Fertig, 1985.

Most, Andrea. '"We Know We Belong to the Land": The Theatricality of Assimilation in Rodger's and Hammerstein's *Oklahoma!*' *PMLA* 113.1 (1998): 77–89.

Nelson, T.G.A. *Comedy: An Introduction to Comedy in Literature, Drama, and Cinema.* Oxford: Oxford UP, 1990.

Neugin, Rebecca. 'Memories of the Trail.' *Journal of Cherokee Studies* 3 (1978): 176.

New, William. *Borderlands: How We Talk about Canada.* Vancouver: UBC P, 1998.

Palmer, Jerry. *Taking Humour Seriously.* London: Routledge, 1994.

Parker, Andrew, et al. 'Introduction.' In *Nationalisms and Sexualities.* New York: Routledge, 1992. 1–18.

Phelan, Peggy. *Unmarked: The Politics of Performance.* London: Routledge, 1993.

Picturesque Cardston and Environments: A Story of Colonization and Progress in Southern Alberta. Cardston, AB: N.W. MacLeod, 1900.

Purdie, Susan. *Comedy: The Mastery of Discourse.* Toronto: U of Toronto P, 1993.

Rabinowitz, Peter. '"How did you know he licked his lips?" Second Person Knowledge and First Person Power in *The Maltese Falcon.*' Unpublished ms., 1992.

Radway, Janice. *Reading the Romance: Women, Patriarchy, and Popular Literature.* 1984. Chapel Hill: U of North Carolina P, 1991.

Rainwater, Catherine. *Dreams of Fiery Stars: The Transformations of Native American Fiction.* Philadelphia: U of Pennsylvania P, 1999.

Ramsey, Jarold. *Reading the Fire: Essays in the Traditional Indian Literatures of the Far West.* Lincoln: U of Nebraska P, 1983.

Ridington, Robin. 'Happy Trails to You: Contexted Discourse and Indian Removals in Thomas King's *Truth and Bright Water.*' *Canadian Literature* 167 (2000): 89–107.

Rodway, Allan. 'Terms for Comedy.' *Renaissance and Modern Studies* 6 (1962): 102–25.

Rooke, Constance. 'Interview with Tom King.' *World Literature Written in English* 30.2 (1990): 62–76.

Rosaldo, Renato. *Culture and Truth: The Remaking of Social Analyses.* 2nd ed. Boston: Beacon, 1993.

Ross, Oakland. 'King Hones Sharp-edged Writing into Fine Tales.' *Globe and Mail,* 30 Oct. 1993, p. C27.

Ross, Val. 'Book Learning.' *Globe and Mail,* 18 April, 1992, p. C14.

Ryan, Allan J. *The Trickster Shift: Humour and Irony in Contemporary Native Art.* Vancouver and Toronto: UBC P, 1999.

Said, Edward W. *Culture and Imperialism..* New York: Knopf, 1994.

Saldívar-Hull, Sonia. 'Feminism on the Border: From Gender Politics to Geopolitics.' In *Criticism in the Borderlands: Studies in Chicano Literature, Culture, and Ideology.* Ed. Hector Calderon and Jose David Saldívar. Durham: Duke UP, 1991. 203–20.

Schatz, Thomas. *Hollywood Genres.* New York: McGraw-Hill, 1981.

Sedgwick, Eve Kosofsky. 'Nationalisms and Sexualities in the Age of Wilde.' In *Nationalisms and Sexualities.* Ed. Andrew Parker et al. New York: Routledge, 1992. 235–45.

Silko, Leslie Marmon. *Almanac of the Dead.* New York: Simon and Schuster, 1991.

Sontag, Susan. *On Photography.* New York: Doubleday, 1977.

Stacey, Jackie. *Star Gazing: Hollywood Cinema and Female Spectatorship.* London: Routledge, 1994.

Stackhouse, John. 'Comic Heroes or "Red Niggers"?' *Globe and Mail,* 9 Nov. 2001, pp. A10–A11.

Stallybrass, Peter, and Allon White. *The Politics and Poetics of Transgression*. London: Methuen, 1986.

Stratton, John, and Ien Ang. 'Multicultural Imagined Communities: Cultural Difference and National Identity in the USA and Australia.' In *Multicultural States: Rethinking Difference and Identity*. Ed. David Bennett. London: Routledge, 1998. 135–62.

Strickland, Rennard. *Tonto's Revenge: Reflections on American Indian Culture and Policy*. Albuquerque: U of New Mexico P, 1997.

Strong-Boag, Veronica, and Carole Gerson. *Paddling Her Own Canoe: The Times and Texts of E. Pauline Johnson (Tekahionwake)*. Toronto: U of Toronto P, 2000.

Sullivan, Lawrence. 'Multiple Levels of Religious Meaning in Culture: A New Look at the Winnebago Sacred Texts.' *Canadian Journal of Native Studies* 2 .2 (1982): 221–47.

Sypher, Wylie. 'Appendix: The Meanings of Comedy.' In *Comedy*. Ed. Wylie Sypher. Baltimore: Johns Hopkins UP, 1980. 193–260.

Tagg, John. *The Burden of Representation: Essays on Photographies and Histories*. Amherst: U of Massachusetts P, 1988.

Taylor, Drew Hayden. *alterNatives*. Burnaby: Talonbooks, 2000.

Thornton, Russell. 'The Demography of the Trail of Tears Period: A New Estimate of Cherokee Population Losses.' In *Cherokee Removal: Before and After*. Ed. William L. Anderson. Athens: U of Georgia P, 1991. 75–95.

Todorov, Tzvetan. *The Poetics of Prose*. Trans. Richard Howard. Ithaca: Cornell UP, 1977.

Vizenor, Gerald. 'Follow the Track Routes: An Interview with Gerald Vizenor.' In *Survival This Way: Interviews with American Indian Poets*. Ed. Joseph Bruchac. Tucson: Sun Tracks and U of Arizona P, 1987. 287–310.

– 'Fugitive Poses.' In *Excavating Voices: Listening to Photographs of Native Americans*. Ed. Michael Katakis. Philadelphia: U of Pennsylvania Museum of Archeology and Anthropology, 1998. 7–15.

– 'Trickster Discourse: Comic Holotropes and Language Games.' In *Narrative Chance: Postmodern Discourse on Native American Literatures*. Albuquerque: U of New Mexico P, 1989. 187–211.

Walker, Cheryl. *Indian Nation: Native American Literature and Nineteenth-Century Nationalisms*. Durham: Duke UP, 1997.

Walton, Priscilla. '"Telling Our Own Stories": Politics and the Fiction of Thomas King.' *World Literature Written in English* 30.2 (1990): 77–84.

Weaver, Jace. *That the People Might Live: Native American Literatures and Native American Community*. New York: Oxford UP, 1997.

Williams, Walter L. *The Spirit and the Flesh: Sexual Diversity in American Indian Culture.* Boston: Beacon, 1986.

Wyile, Herb. '"Trust Tonto": Thomas King's Subversive Fictions and the Politics of Cultural Literacy.' *Canadian Literature* 161/2 (1999): 105–24.

Yuval-Davis, Nira. *Gender and Nation.* London: Sage, 1997.

Ziff, Bruce H., and Pratima V. Rao, eds. *Borrowed Power: Essays on Cultural Appropriation.* New Brunswick: Rutgers UP, 1997.

Index

Abrams, M.H., 31
Allen, Paula Gunn, 37–8
Anderson, Benedict, 125, 157, 159
Anzaldúa, Gloria, 148–9, 150

Babcock, Barbara, 35, 36
Babcock, Barbara, and Jay Cox, 176
Babcock-Abrahams, Barbara, 176
Bakhtin, Mikhail, 34
Barrie, J.M., 79–80,
Beddoes, Julie, 13–14
Berger, John, 102
Bergson, Henri, 35
Bhabha, Homi, 15, 17, 177
Blaise, Clark, 150
border studies, 27, 141, 148–51,
    153–4
borders, 13–18, 27, 122–5, 130,
    141–2, 148–51, 153–4
Brennan, Timothy, 16–17
Butler, Judith, 66–7, 68, 70
Byars, Jackie, 118

Castronovo, Russ, 150–1
Cawelti, John, 15, 29
Chester, Blanca, 45
Coltelli, Laura, 37

comedy, 29–31, 39–40, 41–4, 46–8,
    154–5, 163, 195–6
Curtis, Edward, 100, 104, 106

de Certeau, Michel, 18, 27
de Lauretis, Teresa, 63–4
Deloria, Vine, 29–30, 40
Douglas, Mary, 32

Eco, Umberto, 75–6

Fanon, Frantz, 137
Fee, Margery, 135–6
Fee, Margery, and Jane Flick, 67, 89,
    198–9
Fischer, Michael, 42
Foucault, Michel, 49–50
Francis, Daniel, 14, 21, 41, 136
Freud, Sigmund, 38–9
Frye, Northrop, 31

Gledhill, Christine, 118–19
Globe and Mail, 3, 77–9
Goldie, Terry, 135

Hicks, D. Emily, 149, 150
Hulan, Renée, 141

Hutcheon, Linda, 41, 98

Keeshig-Tobias, Leonore, 27
King, Thomas: life, 3–7; 12–13; photography 10; 99–109; Works: *All My Relations*, 7–8; 'Borders,' 14–15, 122–5, 126, 141, 151; *A Coyote Columbus Story*, 10, 77–85, 177; *Coyote Sings to the Moon*, 10, 85–7; *Dead Dog Café Comedy Hour*, 3, 10, 13, 97, 112–16; dissertation, 5–6; 'Godzilla vs. Post-Colonial,' 7, 18, 42, 44, 199, 200; *Green Grass, Running Water*, 3, 10, 28, 33–4, 45–6, 47, 51–4, 61–2, 67–74, 88–93, 96, 110–11, 127–30, 133–4, 136–41, 151, 163–83, 199–200, 203; 'How Corporal Colin Sterling Saved Blossom,' 18–26; 'Joe the Painter and the Deer Island Massacre,' 130–2; *Medicine River*, 3, 6, 10, 36–7, 43–4, 53, 62–6, 96, 98, 111, 198–200; *Medicine River* (film), 119–21, 200; *The Native in Literature*, 6–7, 93; 'The One about Coyote Going West,' 10, 177; *One Good Story, That One*, 10, 99; 'One Good Story, That One,' 55–60; 'A Seat in the Garden,' 93–4; *Truth and Bright Water*, 9–10, 45, 89, 141–8, 152–6, 160–3, 183–96, 202–3
Kinsella, W.P., 93
Kroetsch, Robert, 16
Krupat, Arnold, 98, 110

Lamont-Stewart, Linda, 178
Lang, Sabine, 179
Lincoln, Kenneth, 30, 43
Lipsitz, George, 26–7, 49, 95

Lowe, John, 33, 40–1, 44–5
Luna, James, 21
Lutz, Hartmut, 30, 194

Matchie, Thomas, and Brett Larson, 54
Mathews, Robin, 93
McCormack, Eric, 154
Michaelson, Scott, and David E. Johnson, 148
Miller, Nancy K., 71
Mitchell, Lee Clark, 96
Monroe, Marilyn, 160–2, 193

New, William, 14–15
Niro, Shelley, 160–1

Oklahoma!, 145–7
orality, 110–12

Purdie, Susan, 46–8

Radway, Janice, 76
Rainwater, Catherine, 197
reverse discourse, 70, 73–4
Robinson, Harry, 45
Rodway, Allan, 42
Rooke, Constance, 14, 125–6, 136, 154
Ross, Oakland, 154
Ryan, Allan, 161

Said, Edward, 25, 87
scatology, 33–7
Schatz, Thomas, 117
Sedgwick, Eve Kosofsky, 157
Silko, Leslie, 11–12, 37–8, 149
Sontag, Susan, 97
Strickland, Rennard, 96,

television, 116–19
Trail of Tears, 89, 145–6
trickster, 33, 35, 54–5, 60–1, 80–1,
    173–8, 195–6, 201
two-spirit people, 179–80

Vizenor, Gerald, 33, 37–8, 104

Walker, Cheryl, 126
Weaver, Jace, 8, 10, 12
Williams, Walter, 180

Yuval-Davis, Nira, 172